Cecily Neville

Cecily Neville

Mother of Richard III

John Ashdown-Hill

AN IMPRINT OF PEN & SWORD BOOKS LTD.
YORKSHIRE – PHILADELPHIA

First published in Great Britain in 2018 by
PEN & SWORD HISTORY
An imprint of
Pen & Sword Books Ltd
Yorkshire - Philadelphia

ISBN 9781526706324

A CIP catalogue record for this book is available from the British Library

Typeset in India by Geniies IT & Services Private Limited
Printed and bound in India by Replika Press Pvt. Ltd.

Pen & Sword Books Ltd incorporates the Imprints of Aviation, Atlas, Family History, Fiction, Maritime, Military, Discovery, Politics, History, Archaeology, Select, Wharncliffe Local History, Wharncliffe True Crime, Military Classics, Wharncliffe Transport, Leo Cooper, The Praetorian Press, Remember When, Seaforth Publishing and Frontline Publishing.

For a complete list of Pen & Sword titles please contact

PEN & SWORD BOOKS LTD
47 Church Street, Barnsley, South Yorkshire, S70 2AS, England
E-mail: enquiries@pen-and-sword.co.uk
Website: www.pen-and-sword.co.uk

Or
PEN AND SWORD BOOKS
1950 Lawrence Rd, Havertown, PA 19083, USA
E-mail: Uspen-and-sword@casematepublishers.com
Website: www.penandswordbooks.com

There are many ways of regarding, for instance, a historical fact. Take an example: many books have been written on your Mary Queen of Scots, representing her as a martyr, as an unprincipled and wanton woman, as a rather simple-minded saint, as a murderess and an intriguer, or again as a victim of circumstances and fate! One can take one's choice.

Agatha Christie, *Five Little Pigs*, London 1943 (2013), p. 118.

Πάνω στην άμμο την ξανθή
γράψαμε τ' όνομά της.
Ωραία που φύσηξε ο μπάτης
και σβήστηκε η γραφή.
Γιώργος Σεφέρης· *Άρνηση*

(On the golden sand
we wrote her name.
The lovely breeze blew
and wiped out the writing.
Giorgos Seferis: *Denial* – trans. J.A-H)

Dedicated in honour of Our Lady of Walsingham, whose Norfolk shrine was patronised by Cecily and her husband.

Contents

Introduction

Confronting the problems

There are a number of problems in presenting the subject of this book. Two key issues concern her name and her appearance. Those will be dealt with here, in this introduction, before the story of her life commences. Other controversial issues include her moral reputation, her political loyalties, the significance of her Beaufort relationship on her mother's side, where she was on specific dates, what she thought, what she did, and who were the people whom she patronised and what was *their* political loyalty. Even the birthdates of herself, her siblings, her husband and many of her children – though the alleged dates are often glibly published as stated facts – are uncertain. Each of those much more complex issues will be explored as far as possible in the subsequent chapters of this study.

The main problem is the lack of surviving documentary evidence relating directly to the Duchess of York. Intriguingly, a recent book that claims to be about her bears in its introduction the author's statement to the effect that she considered 'the time was right to *recreate* Cecily's story'.[1] As we shall see, the Patent Rolls of the young cousin of the Duchess, King Henry VI, mention her name on only two occasions. Although we know that she sent letters, not much of her correspondence survives. And those letters the text of which does survive are sometimes not personal in terms of their content, but deal with matters of business. It is therefore very hard to get at the sender's feelings.

For the first fifteen or so years of her life she was controlled by her parents – probably particularly by her mother. Precisely how she fitted into her family is unclear. So too is the question of how she related to her siblings. But an attempt will be offered in Chapter 1 to suggest the sequence of her siblings' births. From this will emerge the identity of the sisters to whom she was probably most closely related in terms of her age.

Subsequently, for about thirty years the Duchess of York was a wife and mother. Where she was – and when – as a wife, and what precisely she was doing, are facts which often remain unknown, even though previously published accounts tend to claim that she frequently lived – and gave birth – at Fotheringhay Castle. In reality her location and her actions presumably depended upon the whereabouts and actions of her husband. Certainly her husband's love-making had a highly significant outcome for her, in the form of her repeated pregnancies and childbirths. Roughly contemporary sources relating to those do exist. And while the three surviving sources present contradictions and inconsistencies, all three of them will be studied in great detail in Chapter 3. At that point, possible conclusions will be offered. While those conclusions will not be 100% proven, they will be based as firmly as possible upon the available evidence, and upon logic.

Unfortunately, earlier accounts of the Duchess have sometimes included interpretations of her movements and behaviour which are based on little or no genuine contemporary evidence. Curiously, the same earlier accounts have sometimes omitted other facts that must have been true, even though no written record of them may have survived. As a result, hypotheses have sometimes been put forward as though they were facts, while certain real facts – such as the obvious point that she could not possibly have married her husband without a papal dispensation – have simply been ignored and left out. In this present study, however, every effort will be made, both to cite – and interpret – surviving authentic sources that offer documentary evidence as to her whereabouts, her conduct, and her entourage, while at the same time applying background logic.

One particular feature of the present study is that details will be revealed here of the men and women who comprised the household of the Duchess of York; of those who formed her clientele; of those who received her patronage; and of the people who were in her mind when she was making her will. This is because such details may well be significant. For example, the leaving of a final bequest to a person who had served one of her children, with clear mention of that individual's name (even though mention of the child in question is omitted) presumably shows that, for the Duchess of York, what had been done for the child in question was still important more than forty years later. What thus emerges is the fact that the Duchess apparently remembered, when she was making her will, what services certain living people had performed for members of her immediate family who had not survived. And this suggests what thoughts may have been in her mind as her own death approached.

Nevertheless, the fact remains that the Duchess avoided making any mention of the specific connections of her beneficiaries, in terms of service to herself or members of her family, when she was listing her legatees and their individual bequests in her will. That point must also be revealing. It presumably means that she wished to ensure that her underlying aims and intentions should pass unnoticed when her will was being proved. Obviously those men who were responsible for granting probate would not have searched back through the

Patent Rolls or other sources (as the present author has done) to seek out the names and connections of the men and women to whom the Duchess wished to leave bequests. Thus they would have done nothing to determine why the Duchess was remembering her beneficiaries.

In connection with this point, one specific piece of intriguing evidence will be presented later, which clearly shows that when planning her bequests the Duchess was quite determined to reward services to the royal house of York. The evidence in question also reveals that she was very well aware of the worrying fact that in the 1490s the government of the reigning monarch might well be opposed to some of the things she wanted to do. At the same time the evidence in question clearly demonstrates her own cleverness. It shows that she herself was quite capable of devising a secret and roundabout way of achieving the bequest she wished to make, in spite of the fact that it might have caused difficulties had she openly included mention of it in her will.

All these points will be explored later, in the main chapters of the book. First, however, evidence regarding the name of the Duchess of York will be examined, together with the claims which have been advanced since the nineteenth century in respect of her alleged portrayal.

1. What was her real name?

Various medieval and later written forms exist of the first name of the Duchess of York. The modern accounts generally employ the spelling 'Cecily'. But in surviving contemporary documents one can find 'Cicelie', 'Cicely', 'Cicili', 'Cicilia', 'Cecil', 'Cecilia' and 'Cecille'. In the medieval English text of her will, the lady in question refers to herself as 'Cecille'. That spelling might superficially appear to invite a modern pronunciation which would comprise only two syllables. However, it is equally possible that the final 'e' was meant to be heard, producing a three-syllabled version of the name, similar in sound to the modern English 'Cecily'.

Superficially, her surviving seal also appears to back the pronunciation 'Cecily'. This is because the inscription bears the spelling 'Cecilie' (see plate 25). But of course the inscription on the seal is not in English. It is in Latin. Thus the spelling 'Cecilie' is the Latin genitive form of the name 'Cecilia'. In the standard modern version of Classical Latin that would be pronounced 'Kekilia'. However, that kind of pronunciation is merely the allegation of eighteenth- and nineteenth-century English-speaking academics. It may not really be how Latin was pronounced in the Classical period, and it certainly may not correspond with Latin pronunciation in the Middle Ages. The traditional Church Latin pronunciation would produce the sound 'Chechilia'.

In other words, we have varying evidence from different sources of the precise form of her Christian name which was in daily use by the subject of this book and her contemporaries during her lifetime. Fortunately, however, a letter which the Duchess sent to the mayor of Folkestone in 1463 (see below)[2] appears to have borne her personal signature. This was in the form 'Ceycily'. It seems likely on the basis of this evidence that the Duchess herself used a form of her first name which would have corresponded closely in sound (if not necessarily in spelling) to the modern 'Cecily'. Thus, except when quoting different forms from original documents, this account retains that generally accepted standard modern spelling.

There are also variant spellings of her maiden surname, including 'Nevil', 'Nevile', 'Nevill', 'Nevell' and 'Neville'. But all of these would presumably sound much the same. The last of them is the standard version nowadays, so that will also be employed in this account – once again, without any implication that the subject of this book is known to have used that format.

2. What did she look like?

It is frequently claimed that 'Cecily, Duchess of York, had once been a famous beauty of her age'.[3] However, not a single contemporary source exists which so describes her. On the internet and elsewhere one can find images reputed to represent Cecily Neville and her husband, Richard, Duke of York. These are usually nineteenth-century engravings, based on two mistakenly identified fragments of stained glass from the church at Penrith. For images of the engravings, see below.

Photographs of the original fragments of medieval glass are reproduced in plates 2 and 3. One typical example of erroneous use of the engraving which is claimed to be the image of Cecily Neville can be found on a webpage of the University of Leicester.[4]

The two surviving medieval face fragments – one male and one female – were rescued in the nineteenth century and reused in new windows of the church at Penrith. As releaded in the nineteenth-century windows, the images are labelled in the glass as Richard, Duke of York, and his wife, Cecily Neville. However, the modern guide leaflet of Penrith Church states clearly that this is a nineteenth-century error. The images in question actually represent, not the Duke and Duchess of York, but the Duchess's parents, the Earl and

Copy of an early 19th century drawing erroneously claimed to be of Cecily Neville, and based on a medieval stained glass window fragment at Penrith.

Countess of Westmorland. The evidence upon which this identification is based is as follows:

> One of the present writers went to the College of Arms in September 1948 and was able to inspect the MS. of Dugdale's Visitation of Cumberland made in 1665 [*MS. C. 39*]. There, at folio 2, he found a page of drawings of glass and monuments in Penrith Church, done by Gregory King, Dugdale's secretary. The Chapter of the College

Copy of a 19th century engraving of the image erroneously claimed to be of Richard, Duke of York, and based on a medieval stained glass window fragment at Penrith.

kindly allowed us to have this page photographed and to reproduce it here (fig. 1).

At the top of the page are drawings of four figures which were in the glass of the east window of the chancel in 1665. The two right hand pictures—those of St. George and of a member of the Nevill family—have vanished completely, and we suggest that of the other two figures only the heads, a pair of supplicating arms [*These are now in front of the man, but he was in armour and they cannot be his. They obviously belong to the lady.*], and the legend *Mater Dei miserere mei* survives, and that they are those which in Jefferson's time were in the north window of

Fig. 1. The woman wearing the royal arms and the man wearing the Neville cross, depicted in the former east window of the church at Penrith. Orginally drawn by Dugdale's secretary in 1665. Redawn by the present author from the 1665 version as published in 1951.

the chancel and are now in a window of the south aisle of the nave of the church. In figs. 2 and 3 we give photographs of the heads as they appear today [*see plates 2 and 3*], and we submit that they are the only remaining features of the four figures which Gregory King saw and sketched in 1665.

Fig. I shows that the lady has the Royal arms embroidered on her under-garment or kirtle and those of Nevill on her cape or mantle. It was the custom for married women to be represented wearing their own arms on the kirtle, and the husband's arms on the mantle. The lady in the sketch was therefore a member of the Royal family who married a Nevill. The fact that the arms of old France occur as a quartering in the Royal arms shows that the glass cannot have been later than the beginning of the 15th century. It was then that our sovereigns who persisted in quartering the Royal arms of France altered the old coat of semy of *fleurs de lis* to three only—a change which had been made in France in 1370.

We have not far to look for the lady of royal birth who married a Nevill before 1400. On November 29 1396 Ralph Lord de Nevill (later first Earl of Westmorland) and Joan his wife, daughter of the King's uncle John (of Gaunt) Duke of Lancaster, were granted the manors and towns of Penrith and Soureby, with the hamlets of Langwathby, Scouteby and Carleton. [*Cal. Pat. R 1396-1399. 39*]. According to G.E.C.[*Complete Peerage V., pedigree between pp. 320 and 321*], Ralph Nevill's first wife died on June 9 1396, so that the date of his marriage to Joan Beaufort, widow of Sir Robert de Ferrers, must lie between then and November 1396.

We submit that the lady in Gregory King's sketch who wears the Royal arms [*Mr H. Stanford London, F.S.A., points out that the Royal Arms as worn by Joan Beaufort were surrounded (differenced) by a bordure gobony silver and azure. This has been omitted in the drawing, probably owing to the difficulty of showing it on such a small scale.*] on her kirtle and her Nevill husband's arms on her cape represents Joan Beaufort, and the man kneeling next to her, with the undifferenced arms of Nevill on his surcoat or jupon, is intended to represent Ralph Nevill, first Earl of Westmorland.

The military costume he is wearing suggests the time of Richard II, for in the reign of Henry IV the jupon— a leather or woollen covering to a man's body armour—was abandoned. In the Visitation sketch all three men wear the jupon. Two of them are bareheaded, and are bearded in the fashion of the time. St. George has a helmet of a distinctly Lancastrian type—i.e. without the camail which was a kind of chain mail muffler to protect a man's neck, and was laced on to the pointed bascinet, which was not so securely fastened to the body armour as was the Lancastrian helmet.

It is possible that Gregory King omitted to sketch St. George's headgear when he visited Penrith and later drew the sort of helmet he imagined the saint ought to be wearing.

As we have said, Penrith was given to Ralph Nevill and Joan his wife in 1396, and it may well be that the church was re-built by them, in conjunction with William Strickland, later Bishop of Carlisle, who founded a chantry in the church at this time.[5]

Since the Penrith stained glass windows, which have so often been said to represent the Duchess of York and her husband, actually represent Cecily's parents, that means that they do, in fact, remain relevant to Cecily's story. It is therefore appropriate to include them among the illustrations of the present study. But here they are not mislabelled as alleged portraits of Cecily and her husband. They are correctly identified as surviving images of the Earl and Countess of Westmorland.

Images of the Duke and Duchess of York which are more likely to be authentic are also offered here. Contemporary fifteenth-century representations of both Richard and Cecily have been chosen, which are taken from manuscript miniatures. The identity of the figures in both of the chosen images is beyond any shadow of doubt (see plates 13 and 14). But of course that fact does not guarantee the absolute accuracy of their 'portraits'.

Chapter 1

Cecily's Family Background

Cecily Neville is generally said to have been born on 3 May 1415 at Raby Castle. For example, one recent account states that:

> Cecily Neville was born on 3 May 1415. … As she lay in her cradle at Raby Castle that summer, alternatively rocked and suckled by her nursemaids, a fleet of wooden ships filled with soldiers crossed the Channel and landed on the coast of Normandy.[1]

However, the author cites no source, either for the alleged date or for the alleged location.

Even the most serious modern published accounts of Cecily's life generally fail to offer any contemporary source for her alleged birth date. For example, in his portrayal of her, written for the *ODNB*, Christopher Harper-Bill certainly assumes that Cecily was born on 3 May 1415, but he cites no source for that claim.[2]

The only source I have been able to find for the date in question is the version of William Worcester's *Annales* published by Stevenson. This reads :

> 1415. … *Hoc anno nata est Caecilia, uxor Ricardi, ducis Eboraci, filia comitis Westmerlandiae, iij die Maii.*[3]

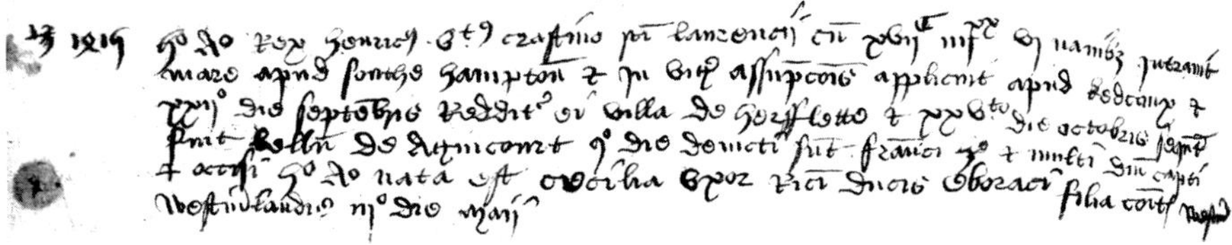

William Worcester's record of the birth of Cecily Neville. The final sentence of the record for 1415 dates Cecily's birth as 3 May. College of Arms Arundel MS 48, f. 124v. Reproduced by permission of the Kings, Heralds and Pursuivants of Arms.

Raby Castle, Durham.

Unfortunately, as will emerge in Chapter 3, this particular version of Worcester's *Annales* can be shown to contain apparent errors in respect of some of its later asserted dates – and places – relating to the births of Cecily's children. It must therefore remain questionable whether its alleged birthdate of Cecily herself is correct, given that no other surviving fifteenth-century evidence has been found.

Fortunately, in spite of accepting her suggested birth date of 3 May 1415, Harper-Bill did not assert in his *ODNB* account that Cecily had been born at Raby Castle.[4] Presumably, therefore, he was aware of the fact that the story in question was concocted in the late eighteenth century. At that time the nickname 'Rose of Raby' was apparently invented for Cecily by the historical novelist, Agnes Musgrave – just as the label 'Wars of the Roses' was apparently invented by Sir Walter Scott thirty-four years later, in 1829.[5]

Musgrave employed the phrase 'Rose of Raby' as a subtitle for her four volume novel about the Duchess of York. However, her book consisted entirely of fantasy (see below: Appendix 4). In the novel she presented Cecily herself as asserting that 'my infantine years were principally spent at the Castle of Brancepeth and Raby'.[6] It is entirely possible that the little girl did reside at each of those northern castles at certain points during her childhood. However, it is by no means certain that they were her only residences during her infancy. Nor is there any evidence available to prove that she was born at Raby Castle.

It is normally said that Cecily was the last of the twenty-two known children of Ralph Neville, first Earl of Westmorland. The statement that she was the youngest of Ralph's offspring may well be correct. Cecily's mother, Joan Beaufort, was the Earl's second wife. Thus, eight of her father's known children were only the little girl's half-brothers and half–sisters. Apparently the relationship between Cecily's mother, Joan, and her step-children may not always have been a good one. Ralph's grandson (and his heir in terms of his title), Ralph Neville, second Earl of Westmorland, apparently believed that an earlier will drafted by his grandfather had favoured the children of his first marriage, because in his inheritance disputes with Joan Beaufort and her children 'he sought unsuccessfully to have its contents made public'.[7] The situation was not an entirely unusual one. Later in the fifteenth century a similar situation occurred in the family of John Talbot, first Earl of Shrewsbury.[8] More recently something similar occurred three generations back in the maternal line of the present author! In addition, the eldest of Cecily's half-siblings were some thirty years older than she was, so it is somewhat doubtful how well she would have known them (but see below, Chapter 9).

Her father was probably in his early fifties when Cecily was born. Subsequently he died a few months after what is claimed to have been her tenth birthday.

Through Ralph, Cecily was descended from the Anglo-Norman Neville, Percy, Clifford and Clare families. She was also descended from the Norman-Welsh / Anglo-Irish Fitzgerald family. Through the Fitzgeralds Cecily was of royal Welsh descent.

Ralph Neville held substantial inherited lands in Durham and North Yorkshire. He did not, however, inherit any major title. The earldom of

de Clares, Earls of Gloucester | Anglo-Irish Fitzgeralds

Thomas **de Clare**, Lord of Thomond m. Juliana **Fitzgerald**

Robert 1st Baron de **Clifford** m. Maud de Clare

Henry 2nd Baron **Percy** of Alnwick m. Idoine de Clifford

John, 3rd Baron **Neville** de Raby m. Maud Percy

Ralph Neville, 1st Earl of Westmorland
*c.*1364-1425

The Ancestry of Cecily's Father

Westmorland, which he acquired on 29 September 1397, was created for him by King Richard II, whose cause Ralph had supported against that king's manipulative uncle, Thomas of Woodstock, Duke of Gloucester.

Ralph's acquisition of his earldom occurred more than a year after the demise of his first wife, Lady Margaret Stafford. Margaret had died on 9 June 1396. She therefore never enjoyed the title of countess. However, her successor, Ralph's second wife, had already been joined to her husband when he received his earldom. Thus he became the first Earl of Westmorland and she became the first Countess.

The second of Ralph's two wives was some fifteen years younger than her husband. The precise date of Ralph's second marriage is not on record, but it probably took place in the autumn of 1396. 'It had taken place by 29 November, and was unlikely to have occurred before the bull of legitimation, which was issued on 1 September, had been received in England.'[9] When the couple married, Ralph was in his early thirties. His second wife was about half his age – in her mid teens.

As we have seen, the girl in question was Joan Beaufort. For Joan, as for Ralph Neville, their partnership constituted her second marriage. She had first been married at the age of twelve to Robert Ferrers, Baron Boteler of Wem. In spite of her young age, Joan had produced two daughters for Robert prior to his decease. Intriguingly, on his mother's side, Robert Ferrers was the second cousin of Ralph Boleter, later Baron Sudeley. Thus, one curious result of her first husband's Boteler family relationship, and of Joan Beaufort's partnership with him, was that she thereby acquired quite a close connection by marriage with Eleanor Talbot, Lady Boteler , who later played a significant role in the lives of two of Joan's royal grandsons (see below).

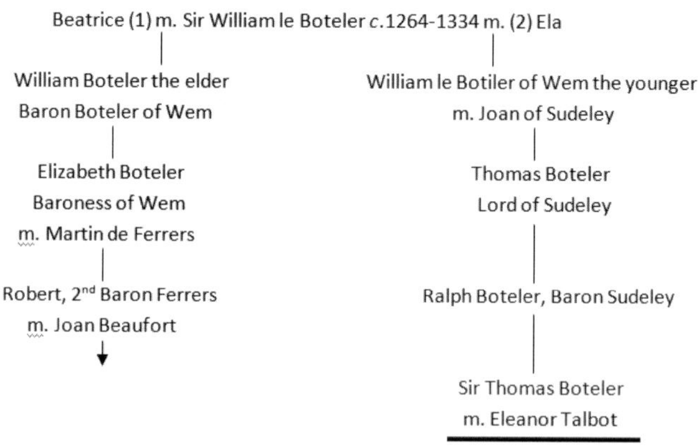

The Boteler Family (simplified)

Incidentally, Cecily Neville also had a connection with Eleanor's father, John Talbot, first Earl of Shrewsbury, on her own father's side. A younger brother of Ralph Neville, first Earl of Westmorland, was Thomas Neville, Baron Furnival. Maud Neville, Cecily's first cousin, and Thomas' daughter by his first wife, became the first wife of John Talbot – who was also her step-brother, because her father took as his second wife John's mother, Ankarette Lestrange.

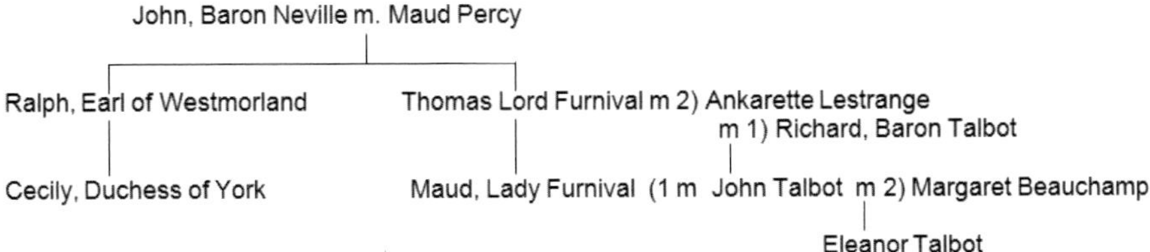

Cecily's connection with John Talbot, later first Earl of Shrewsbury.

Joan Beaufort was the daughter of John of Gaunt, Duke of Lancaster, by his third wife, Catherine de Roët. However, her parents had not been married when Joan was born, so that technically she and her siblings, the Beauforts, were initially royal bastards. Indeed, it was only a few months prior to Joan's own second marriage to Ralph Neville that her parents finally became a legally united couple.[10] A papal bull legitimising the couple's children was then issued (see above). The marriage of her parents also led to Joan and her elder brothers being recognised as legitimate by their cousin, King Richard II.

Joan was of mixed European descent. On her mother's side her family (probably both parents) came from the Low Countries. As for her father, his royal ancestors included the Norman and Angevin royal houses of England, the royal houses of France and of Castile, and the ruling family of Hainault – once again in the Low Countries.

In spite of the fact that he was raised to the earldom of Westmorland by King Richard II, Ralph Neville later abandoned that king. He had long been one of the retainers of Richard's uncle, John of Gaunt, Duke of Lancaster. And of course his second marriage united him more closely to John of Gaunt, who thus became his father-in-law. As a result, in 1399 Ralph supported the rebellion of John of Gaunt's son and heir, King Richard II's cousin, the Lancastrian

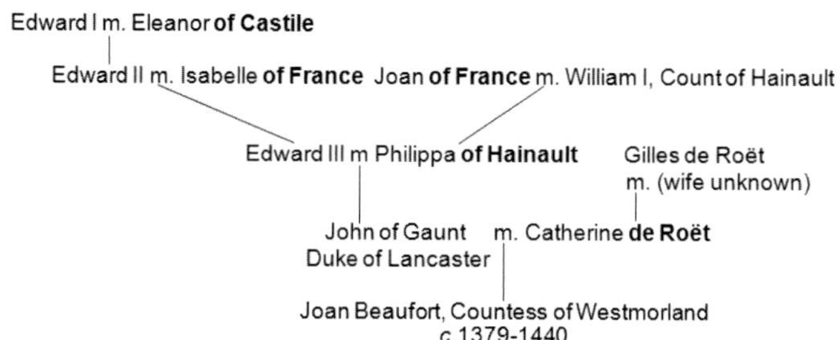

The Ancestry of Cecily's Mother

usurper, Henry, Earl of Derby (Henry IV). Henry was the much older half-brother of Ralph's second wife, Joan, to whom in her childhood (at a time when she was still a bastard) Henry had given presents.[11] Ralph's support for Henry brought Ralph the title and role of Marshal of the realm (though he gave up that post in 1412).

Following the deposition of her cousin, King Richard II, Ralph's second wife, Joan Beaufort, found herself suddenly much closer to the centre of power:

> She remained on good terms with her half-brother Henry who had now become king. Members of Henry IV's household believed she had influence with him: in 1407, for example, she wrote to Henry on behalf of one of his esquires, Christopher Standith, who had served him in Wales but was destitute after being dismissed from his father's service because he and his wife had married each other 'purely for love'. She asked Henry to give his wife, Margaret, a place in the queen's household, and the letter is signed in what is probably her own handwriting: 'Voster tres humble et obaisant servnt si vous plest J de W'.[12]

Opposition from some quarters sprang up in response to Henry IV's seizure of the crown. However, the Earl of Westmorland supported Henry's claim. This was partly thanks to the fact that his local rivals in the north of England – the Percy family – were taking the other side. The outcome for Ralph was positive. In July 1403, after the Battle of Shrewsbury, the Lancastrian king asked his brother-in-law, the Earl of Westmorland to prevent his local rival, the Earl of Northumberland, from marching south. Henry IV may not have wanted to make the Neville family more powerful in the north of England than the

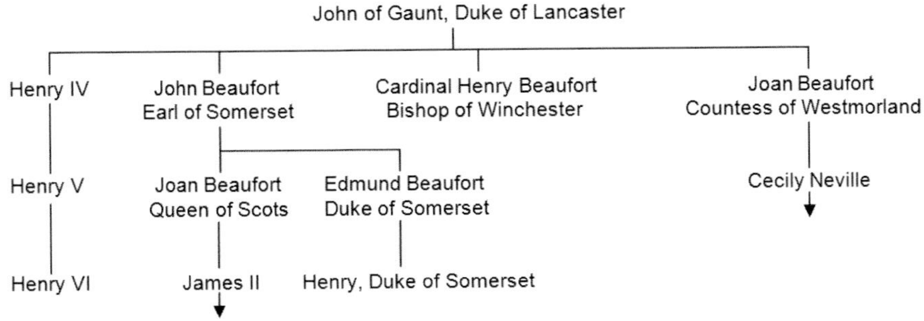

Lancastrian Relatives of Cecily Neville (simplified)

Percys, for the king subsequently tried to reconcile himself with the Earl of Northumberland. But a year later a second rebellion against Henry IV broke out. Once again, Ralph Neville played a key role in defending the king. From then on the Earl of Westmorland found himself in the role of guardian of the north for the new royal house of Lancaster.

In 1413 Henry IV died and was succeeded by his eldest son, King Henry V. Ralph played no role in the new king's French war. Instead he remained at home, guarding the north and also making plans for the inheritance of his estates and the future of his children. Curiously, since his second marriage Ralph had been trying to disinherit his children by his first wife, and to ensure that as much as possible of his inheritance should pass to his children by Joan.[13]

One of the earlier children of Ralph's second marriage was the couple's daughter, Eleanor, who was born in 1398. A marriage had been arranged for her with a grandson of Edmund of Langley, Duke of York. But her young husband died in 1414, before any children were begotten, and possibly before their marriage had even been consummated (see below). So a second marriage was then arranged for Eleanor – this time with the young Henry Percy, Earl of Northumberland. That was an attempt by her father to make peace with his former rivals in the north of England.

Across the Channel in France, the young king, Henry V, died in 1422. In his will he left a gold cup to his uncle and aunt, the Earl and Countess of Westmorland. The Earl also found himself appointed to the council of regency for the new baby king, Henry VI. However, Ralph's tenure of that role proved to be of short duration, for he died on 21 October 1425.

Ralph left behind him a number of living children. The following list of twenty-two individuals was published in 1844 by Caroline Halsted:

ENUMERATION OF THE TITLES BY WHICH THE BROTHERS OF CECILY DUCHESS OF YORK WERE ENNOBLED, TOGETHER WITH THE NAMES OF THE ANCIENT FAMILIES WITH WHICH HER SISTERS WERE ALLIED.[14]

1. John, who died during the lifetime of his father, leaving a son, who afterwards succeeded his grandfather as Earl of Westmoreland.
2. Ralph, married to Mary, co-heir to Sir Robert Ferrars.
3. Maud, married to Peter Lord Manley.
4. Alice, married first Sir Thomas Gray of Heton; secondly, Sir Gilbert de Lancaster.
5. Philippa, married to Thomas Lord Dacres of Gillesland.
6. Margaret, married to Richard Lord Scrope of Bolton.
7. Anne, married to Sir Gilbert de Umfraville, knight.
8. Margery, Abbess of Barking.
9. Elizabeth, a nun, of the Order of St. Clare at the Minories, London.
10. Richard Neville, Earl of Salisbury.
11. William Lord Faulconberg.
12. George Lord Latimer.
13. Edward Lord Abergavenny.
14. Robert Bishop of Durham.
15. Cuthbert Neville, }
16. Henry Neville, } who died without issue.
17. Thomas Neville, }
18. Catherine, wife of John Mowbray, second Duke of Norfolk, and afterwards married to Sir John Woodville, son of Richard Earl Rivers.
19. Eleanor, wife first of Richard Lord Spencer, and secondly of Henry Percy, Earl of Northumberland.
20. Anne, wife first of Humphrey Duke of Buckingham, and afterwards of Walter Blount Lord Mountjoy.
21. Jane, a nun.
22. Cecily, married to Richard Plantagenet, Duke of York.

However Halsted did not specify which of the children had which mother. Also her list appears to contain a few errors. For example her claim that a daughter called Margery Neville became the Abbess of Barking appears to be false.

Possibly she was misled by the fact that Margaret Swynford (a half-sister of Joan Beaufort, Countess of Westmorland) was the Abbess of Barking from 1419 until her death in1433.

In more recent years, lists of Ralph Neville's offspring containing some corrections, and a note of which children had which mother, have appeared on the internet.[15] As presented here the updated lists also contain some additional information about the children.

Children of Ralph Neville, Earl of Westmorland, by Margaret Stafford

1. John (died before May 1420 –his father was therefore succeeded by John's son) married Elizabeth Holland.
2. Ralph
   married his step-sister Mary Ferrers (see below).
3. Maud (or Matilda) (possibly died young)
   married Peter Lord Mauley (who died in 1415 leaving no issue).
4. Alice (still living in August 1453) married
   i) (before 1408) Sir Thomas Grey of Heton (executed 1415)[16]
   ii) Sir Gilbert de Lancaster.
5. Philippa (born 1386, died after 1453)
   married Thomas, Baron Dacre of Gilsland.
6. Elizabeth, a nun.
7. Anne
   married before 3 Feb 1412/3 Sir Gilbert de Umfraville, knight (1390-1421).
   (Apparently this couple had no children. Perhaps Anne died young – before about 1427.)
8. Margaret (d. 1463)
   married i) Richard, Baron Scrope of Bolton (d.1420)
   ii) William Cressener.

(It is possible that by his first wife Ralph also had another daughter called Anastasia, who died in infancy.)

Children of Ralph Neville, Earl of Westmorland, by Joan Beaufort

9. Richard Neville, Earl of Salisbury.
10. Henry Neville.
11. Thomas Neville.

12. Cuthbert Neville.
13. Robert Bishop of Salisbury; Bishop of Durham.
14. William, Earl of Kent.
15. John Neville.
16. George, Baron Latimer.
17. Edward, Baron Bergavenny.
18. Joan Neville, a nun.
19. Catherine
    married i) John Mowbray, second Duke of Norfolk
    iv) Sir John Woodville, son of Richard Earl Rivers.
20. Eleanor
    married i) Richard Lord Spencer[17] (d. 1414)
    ii) (circa 1416?) Henry Percy, Earl of Northumberland.
21. Anne
    married i) Humphrey, Duke of Buckingham
    ii) Walter Blount Lord Mountjoy,
22. Cecily
    married Richard Plantagenet, Duke of York.

In addition, of course, Cecily Neville also had two elder half sisters fathered by her mother's first husband, Robert Ferrers, 5th Baron Boteler of Wem. They were:

1. Elizabeth Ferrers, Baroness Boteler of Wem, *c.*1393–1434.
2. Mary Ferrers *c.*1394–1458
   married her step brother, Ralph Neville (see above).

Sadly, however, the updated internet lists of the children of Ralph Neville appear not to sequence his children in the order of their birth. Yet that is a significant factor in attempting to understand the family background within which Cecily Neville grew up. If possible we should therefore try to clarify the sequence in which the children were born.

As far as Ralph's children by his second wife are concerned, it seems that the couple's first child must have been one of their daughters. The claim has generally been made that their eldest daughter was Catherine Neville, Duchess of Norfolk. Certainly a very high-ranking marriage was celebrated for that daughter in January 1411/2, so it seems probable that she was indeed the eldest daughter. Her date of birth has often been guestimated as *c.*1400, but that appears to be incorrect. As we have already seen, Catherine's younger sister,

Eleanor, who first married Baron Berghersh, but who, in 1414, acquired a higher ranking husband (the Earl of Northumberland), was born in 1398. Therefore it appears that Catherine, Duchess of Norfolk, must have been born in 1397.

The first son of Ralph's second marriage, Richard Neville, later Earl of Salisbury, was apparently the third child of that union, for he came into the world in 1400. After Ralph's birth there is some confusion. Birth dates have been proposed for some of the children – but not for all of them. But it seems that the last two children of Ralph's second marriage were his last two daughters, Anne (born in 1414) and Cecily (born in 1415).

With the doubtful dates and the questionable positions in the birth sequence marked with question marks and italicisation, it therefore appears that the children of Ralph Neville and Joan Beaufort should perhaps be listed as follows:

1. b.1397 – Catherine, Duchess of Norfolk
2. b.1398 – Eleanor, Lady Spencer; Countess of Northumberland
3. b.1400 – Richard Neville, Earl of Salisbury
?4. b. c.1402 – Henry Neville
5. b.1404 – Robert, Bishop of Salisbury (later Bishop of Durham)
6. b. *c.*1405 – William, Earl of Kent
? 7 b. c.1406 John Neville
8. b. *c.*1407 – George, Baron Latimer
? 9 b. c.1409 – Thomas Neville
? 10 b. c.1410 – Cuthbert Neville
11. b. before 1414 (? *c.*1412) – Edward, Baron Bergavenny
?12 b. c.1413 – Joan Neville, a nun
13. b.1414 – Anne, Duchess of Buckingham; Lady Mountjoy
14. b.1415 – Cecily, Duchess of York

This presents an overview of the immediate family of Cecily Neville in terms of her siblings. The four boys in this list who bear no titles all died young, so that in effect Cecily apparently had four full blood sisters and five full blood brothers. Her sisters apparently comprised two duchesses, one countess, and one nun. Her brothers seem to have been two earls, two barons, and one bishop. Of course, she also had two half sisters on her mother's side, and reportedly she had two half-brothers and six half-sisters on her father's side.

It is intriguing to compare the above lists of children with the images of Cecily's family as depicted in the Neville Book of Hours (see plates 7 and 8). The first image (plate 7) apparently represents Cecily's father kneeling in prayer, together with his sons by both his wives and some of his daughters by his first wife. Nine sons and three daughters are shown kneeling behind their father. Since one of the sons is clearly a bishop, the image must have been painted after 1427, when Robert Neville was created Bishop of Salisbury. Probably it was painted in the 1430s, but it is very difficult to date it precisely. Thus, although he himself is shown in the picture, the Earl of Westmorland must have been dead when the picture was painted, because he passed away in 1425. Presumably that explains why his wife (widow), Joan Beaufort, is depicted in widow's weeds in the second picture (plate 8).

As for the Neville children, nine sons and nine daughters (comprising a total of eighteen children) are depicted in the two pictures. Yet according to the above lists, Ralph Neville had reportedly fathered a total of eleven sons and eleven daughters by his two wives. Thus two sons must be missing from the first picture. That is curious because it seems that *five* sons had predeceased their father. So why should only two of them have been left out?

As for the Neville daughters, nine is probably the correct number in respect of the manuscript illustrations, given that two of the eleven girls became nuns and are therefore left out of the pictures. In theory, the daughters who are illustrated should all be identifiable from the relevant coats of arms shown beneath the two pictures. In principle, each coat of arms relating to a daughter should presumably represent her in terms of the marriage partnership within which she was living at the time when the images were painted. Yet the actual situation is more complex.

Of the six daughters born to the Earl's first wife, only three are depicted in the first picture. Of those three, Philippa Neville (Baroness Dacre) is clearly

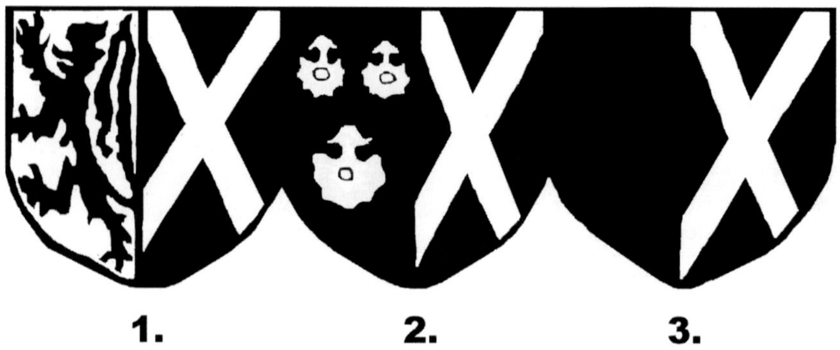

Arms of the Neville daughters redrawn from Picture 1 in the Neville Book of Hours. The arms are those of: 1. Unidentified; 2. Philippa, Baroness Dacre; 3. ?either Margaret, Mrs Cressener, or Anne, wife of Sir Gilbert de Umfraville.

identifiable in respect of her married coat of arms. The central shield of the three Neville women's coats of arms shown beneath the first picture represents Philippa's Neville cross impaled by a shield gules, three escallops argent – the arms of her husband, Thomas, 6th Baron Dacre of Gilsland.

Possibly the third coat of female arms represents Margaret Neville (Mrs Cressener). It shows the Neville cross impaled by a blank red shield which could be interpreted as bearing no male arms. It might therefore be argued that it represents the fact that Margaret's second husband, William Cressener of Suffolk, apparently had no coat of arms. On the other hand it could possibly represent Anne Neville, wife of Sir Gilbert de Umfraville. The arms attributed to earlier members of the Umfraville family seem to have been gules, an orle (narrow border) ermine.[18] However, in this instance the male arms are simply depicted as gules, with no orle ermine.

The other daughter represented in the first picture might perhaps be Alice Neville, wife of Sir Gilbert de Lancaster. However the first female coat of arms which is depicted cannot be interpreted for certain. The male arms shown impaling its Neville cross do not correspond with those which are now generally attributed to the Lancaster family. Nor do they correspond with the arms assigned by modern sources to Lord Mauley,[19] husband of Maud, or Matilda Neville.

As for the second picture, which shows Joan Beaufort with a group of Neville daughters, a total of six girls accompany her. Joan reportedly bore Ralph only five daughters, one of whom became a nun and therefore never married. Yet six coats of arms of married daughters figure beneath the second picture. Therefore two of the daughters present must be children not of Joan Beaufort but of her predecessor, Margaret Stafford.

Arms of the Neville daughters redrawn from Picture 2 in the Neville Book of Hours. The arms are those of: 1. Cecily, Duchess of York; 2. Catherine, Duchess of Norfolk; 3. Eleanor, Countess of Northumberland; 4. Anne Duchess of Buckingham; 5. ?Alice, Lady Grey of Heton; 6. ?Margaret, Lady Scrope of Bolton.

The coats of arms of Joan's own recorded daughters, Cecily, Catherine, Eleanor and Anne Neville, can easily be recognised. They are the second, third, fourth and fifth shields from the left, the first shield on the left being that of Joan Beaufort herself as Countess of Westmorland.

As for the sixth coat of arms, it is possible that it represents Alice Neville (a daughter not of Joan Beaufort but of Margaret Stafford) and that the barry argent and azure arms of the husband impaling the Neville cross represent Alice's first husband, Sir Thomas Grey.[20] That would seem somewhat strange, however, because he had died in 1415 and she had remarried. Moreover, conflicting evidence exists in respect of the arms used by the medieval Grey family of Heaton. Some sources claim that their arms were gules, a lion rampant and bordure indented, argent.[21]

On the seventh shield, the husband's arms impaling its Neville cross might perhaps represent those of Lord Scrope of Bolton, who was the first husband of Margaret Neville.[22] His arms were azure, a bend or. But, as in the case of Alice's first husband, he had died long before the picture was painted, and (like Alice) Margaret had then remarried. An additional problem is the fact that the husband's arms in the picture of the seventh shield are now damaged. Thus it is not absolutely certain that what was originally represented was azure, a bend or.

It is therefore evident that there is a great deal of confusion about the pictures in terms of the Earl of Westmorland's daughters by his first wife. It may be the case that whoever commissioned the Book of Hours – and supplied the required information to the artists – had little up-to-date accurate information about some of the girls born of the first marriage.

As for the birth sequence of the Neville children, one interesting point which appears to have emerged from that is the fact that Cecily's closest sibling in terms of age and sex was probably her slightly older sister, Anne (later Duchess of Buckingham). This suggests that those two girls may have been very closely connected during their childhood. It is therefore a curious fact that Cecily is said later to have effectively become a prisoner of Anne (see below, Chapter 7). Although their husbands were then on opposite sides politically, it seems more probable that, on the occasion in question, Anne Neville would have done her best to look after and protect her younger sister and former childhood companion. For the political allegiances of Cecily's siblings, see below, Appendix 5.

Chapter 2

Cecily's Childhood and Marriage

As if the family of Cecily Neville in terms of siblings was not already large enough, in 1422 the guardianship and marriage of Richard, Duke of York, a young, orphaned cousin of the child king, Henry VI, were sold to Ralph Neville, Earl of Westmorland, husband of the child king's great aunt. The boy Richard is usually said to have been born on 21 or 22 September 1411. If this is roughly correct then the closest to him in terms of age of Cecily Neville's brothers may have been Edward Neville, later Baron Bergavenny, who was probably slightly younger than the little Duke of York, and George, later Baron Latimer, who would have been slightly older. Depending on how long they lived, Thomas and Cuthbert Neville may also possibily have still been around when young Richard joined the Neville household, but probably they had both died soon after birth.

As in the case of Cecily herself, in most modern publications no precise contemporary source for the alleged date(s) of birth of the Duke of York is cited. However, Johnson records Richard's birthdate as 22 September, based upon the following information in his footnote:

> *Complete Peerage*, xii/2, citing BL Cotton MS Vespasian E VII fo. 58v (new foliation), gives 21 September (feast of St. Matthew) but the source says 'feast of St. Maurice' (i.e. 22 Sept.).[1]

Later evidence dating from the year 1432 shows that there then appears to have been some doubt as to the precise date when Richard reached the age of twenty-one years (see below). Nevertheless it was apparently then accepted that he had indeed been born on some date in the year 1411. The year of his birth seems also to be roughly confirmed by other documents such as an inquisition *post mortem* dated 30 October 1415, which states, in respect of inheritance received from Edmund of Langley, 1st Duke of York, that 'Richard son of Richard, brother of Edward, is his heir, aged 3 years and more'.[2] However, this implies that Richard had a later date of birth than *September* 1411. If he had been born in September he would have been *four* years old on 30 October 1415. The picture is further confused by another inquisition *post mortem* (no. 391), which is also dated 30

October 1415, because that states that 'Richard his heir is aged 4 years and more'.[3] Confusingly some of the inquisitions *post mortem* also raise questions about Richard's name! Two of them confusingly refer to him as 'Henry'.[4]

His mother had apparently died shortly after his birth. Subsequently, his father was executed in 1415 for his role in the Southampton plot. As a result, young Richard became a royal ward. Initially he was placed in the custody of Sir Robert Waterson. However, Richard was recognised as the heir of his uncle, Edward, Duke of York, when the latter was killed at the Battle of Agincourt, not long after the execution of his father.

At the age of about eleven the young Richard must suddenly have found himself surrounded by Neville children – including the youngest daughter of the Earl and Countess of Westmorland, little Cecily Neville, who was then aged about seven. How those two children got on with one another at that time, we have no way of knowing. But young Richard is more likely to have actually spent his time – and been educated – with those of Cecily's brothers who were closest to him in terms of age, namely George and Edward Neville. Because the York heritage was potentially a very promising acquisition, the Earl of Westmorland proposed to keep it in his family by arranging a marriage for Richard with one of his daughters. Since her closest sister, Anne, was probably already betrothed to Humphrey, Earl of Stafford (later Duke of Buckingham) in 1422, little Cecily may have been the only Neville daughter who was still available.

As reported by the early nineteenth-century author, Caroline Halsted, 'Immense Possessions [were] Inherited by the House of York.'[5] Halsted focused chiefly on 'the castles of Fotheringay in Northamptonshire and Berkhampstead in Hertfordshire'. These, she asserted, 'were the patrimonial inheritance of the family of York; all the dukes'.

It is certainly the case that on 8 October 1376 King Edward III had granted the reversion of the castles and manors of Fotheringhay (Northants.) and Ansty (Herts.) to his fifth son Edmund of Langley, Earl of Cambridge.[6] The two castles were then held by Marie de St. Pol, dowager Countess of Pembroke, and Edward III decreed that when the Countess of Pembroke died they should initially remain in the hands of four of his servants for life. Only when all four servants had also died were they to pass to his son, Edmund. The Countess of Pembroke died five months later, on 16 or 17 March 1376/7. But two months after her death, on 25 May 1377, her four heirs for life surrendered the properties in question, and their rights to them, to the king. It was at that point that Edward III handed the castles and manors over to his son, Edmund, and the latter's wife, Isabel of Castile.[7]

Edmund, who was later created the first Duke of York in 1385, by his nephew, King Richard II,[8] is then said to have spent a good deal of his time at Fotheringhay Castle. Reportedly he:

> ...rebuilt the castle and the keep in the form of a fetterlock, the device of the house of York. His son Edward, the second duke, who chiefly resided at Fotheringay, founded and endowed its magnificent collegiate church, for which he was obliged to mortgage great part of his estate, and in the choir of which he was buried, having been brought to England for that purpose after the battle of Agincourt, where he lost his life. From him Fotheringay Castle descended to his nephew and heir, the third duke, father of Richard III., who was born in this favourite abode of his ancestors.[9]

However, Halsted's assertion that young Richard was born at Fotheringhay Castle when that belonged to his uncle seems improbable. Other property of Richard, Duke of York, included Ludlow Castle in Shropshire and Wigmore Castle, both of which were inherited from his mother's family, the Mortimers. His Mortimer inheritance also included Clare Castle in Suffolk, and the Irish Castle of Trim.

In addition to these, Richard also inherited a few other castles, and numerous manors. Halsted's account claims that, in addition, 'the castle of Berkhampstead ... came to the house of York from the first duke of that title,

Clare Castle, Suffolk.

King Richard II having bestowed it upon his uncle, Edmund de Langley, the said duke'.[10] However, that claim appears to be an error. Although Berkhamsted Castle was undoubtedly held by Richard II, who inherited it from his father, the Black Prince, and who granted the use of it to two other named individuals,[11] there is no evidence that he ever gave the castle to his uncle Edmund. Much later, however, the castle was held by Cecily Neville, as we shall see in due course.

The young Duke of York was potentially a very wealthy and high-ranking individual, and it was thanks to his royal connections and his promising inheritance that, at some stage – probably in 1424 – Richard found himself betrothed to his guardian's youngest daughter, Cecily Neville. The marriage itself appears to have been formalised five years later (see below).

> Westmorland died on 21 October 1425, and was buried in the choir of his collegiate church at Staindrop. … Westmorland's final will, made at Raby on 18 October 1424, was niggardly in its legacies to his children with his first wife. Their daughters Matilda, Philippa, Alice, and Margaret received bequests of gold and silver plate, but their grandson Ralph, heir to the title, is not mentioned, and their second son, Ralph, was left the barony of Bywell and Styford, Northumberland, in tail male together with 'a flock of sheep, twenty-four cows, one bull' and some gold and silver plate (register of wills of John Kempe, fol. 495).[12]

In 1426, following the death of her husband in the previous autumn, Joan, Countess of Westmorland put forward a petition for an increased income for her late husband's ward, Richard, Duke of York, whose care she had inherited in her capacity as her late husband's executrix.[13] On 26 May 1426 the government of the child-king, Henry VI, granted at Leicester an additional annuity of 100 marks for the maintenance of Richard, Duke of York.[14] This was in addition to an earlier royal grant of 200 marks a year.[15] The document reads as follows:

> For the Duke of York, who has been knighted.[16]
>
> The King, to all those to whom, &c., greetings.
>
> It has been shown to us that our dear relative, Joan, Countess of Westmorland, as executrix of the testament of her dear Lord and husband, Ralph, the late Earl of Westmorland, now deceased, has custody, and control of our beloved kinsman, Richard, Duke of York, by the virtue of our grant made to the same late earl.

For whose support of which duke, at the advice of our council, we granted to the same late earl 200 marks for annual receipt during the minority of this duke.

With these two hundred marks the aforesaid duke cannot honourably be sustained as befits his status, because he has become a knight, and he is growing in honour, age and inheritance, confronting greater expenses and costs for the great burden imposed, as our kinswoman says.

After considering the above, by the advice and consent of our council, beyond the aforesaid two hundred marks, we have granted our aforesaid kinswoman one hundred marks to be received annually for the support of the duke, during the minority of the said duke, from the demesnes, lands and tenements which belonged to the late Edmund, Earl of March, now in our hands on account of the minority of the present duke, in the counties of Dorset and Suffolk, from the hands of the farmers or occupants thereof; to wit, one half of the above-mentioned sum from the hands of the aforesaid farmers, lordships, lands, and tenements within the county of Dorset, and the other half of that sum from the hands of the aforesaid farmers, lordships, lands, and tenements within the county of Suffolk.

Of which &c, witness the King at Leicester, the twenty-sixth day of May.

By writ of Privy Seal.[17]

It was at Leicester, in 1426, that the young Duke of York (then aged about fifteen) was knighted, together with thirty-four others, including his four-year-old cousin the king. The knighting ceremony was carried out by Henry VI's senior surviving male relative, John of Lancaster, Duke of Bedford, who was then the heir presumptive to the English throne. Evidently Richard's guardian, Joan Beaufort, must have taken him with her to Leicester. Of course, there is no way of knowing whether she also took his fiancé, her youngest daughter Cecily. However, Richard's visit there was significant in another way, because it appears to have marked the start of his subsequent close friendly relationship with his cousin (King Henry VI's younger living uncle) Humphrey of Lancaster, Duke of Gloucester, who was then in his mid thirties.

That had a significant outcome. Subsequently, in April 1428, Richard (probably aged about sixteen and a half) was formally removed from the guardianship of the dowager Countess of Westmorland in order that he – together with three other young noblemen who had been knighted with him at Leicester – should become resident at the royal court, where they and their attendants would wear the king's livery.[18] Since Henry VI himself was then still only approaching his seventh birthday, this decision was obviously not made by him. Presumably it was taken by his uncle, the Duke of Gloucester, who was then the Lord Protector of the realm of England.

Interestingly, Humphrey had originally expected to become virtual regent of the English kingdom following the death of his eldest brother, Henry V.

> In a codicil to his will Henry had bestowed on him the *tutelam et defensionem nostri filii carissimi principales* ('principal tutelage and protection of our dearest son'; Strong and Strong, 99). Initially the council may have accepted this, but when Gloucester interpreted *tutela* as conferring under Roman law the governance of the kingdom accountable solely to the child monarch, he faced determined opposition from both Bedford and the council, and had to accept merely a pre-eminence in council with the title of protector and defender.[19]

One of Humphrey's leading opponents on the royal council had been his uncle, Cardinal Beaufort (the Countess of Westmorland's brother). From that point onwards 'politics of the minority in England became dominated by rivalry in government between Humphrey and his Beaufort uncle'.[20]

In 1427 one of the consequences of that contest had been a decision made at the Parliament in Leicester,[21] which opposed the desired second marriage of Humphrey's sister-in-law, Catherine of France (mother of Henry VI) with Humphrey's cousin, Edmund Beaufort, Count of Mortain (later Duke of Somerset).[22] Since Humphrey had opposed the wishes of Cardinal Beaufort and the Cardinal's nephew, Edmund Beaufort, in that respect, it is equally possible that Humphrey's removal of his young cousin, Richard, Duke of York, from the guardianship of his Beaufort aunt, Joan, Countess of Westmorland, also formed part of his opposition to his Beaufort relatives. Of course, it would be very interesting to know how Richard himself felt about the change in his situation which now resulted from his removal from the guardianship of Joan Beaufort. Unfortunately no explicit evidence of that survives. However, Richard definitely seems to have become a close friend of Humphrey Duke of Gloucester. He also became an opponent of the Beauforts. It is also intriguing that no evidence exists to indicate that, after his actual marriage to Cecily Neville, he maintained any kind of friendly relationship with his mother-in-law (and former guardian).

Another interesting possibility at this stage in Richard's growing-up is the thought that he may also have felt somewhat intrigued by the marital policy of his cousin Humphrey. The Duke of Gloucester had previously been married to Jacqueline of Bavaria, godmother of the young Henry VI. That had not been an arranged marriage. However, in the end it appears not to have been very successful. As a result (inspired, perhaps, by the precedent set by his grandfather, John of Gaunt), in 1425 Humphrey had taken Eleanor Cobham, one of his wife's attendants, as his mistress. Subsequently, on 9 January 1427/8, his marriage to Jacqueline was suddenly declared invalid by Pope Martin V. Instead of contesting that decision, Humphrey had then married Eleanor.

> Though condemned as a *mésalliance*, the union proved a success. Eleanor was beautiful, intelligent, and ambitious and Humphrey was cultivated, pleasure-loving, and famous. Together they developed a manor at Greenwich into a pleasure garden, La Plesaunce, encircled by a wall with walks bordering the Thames, a tower, and a conduit. Here they gathered poets, musicians, scholars, physicians, and their friends to form a miniature court. ... [In due course] Eleanor was accorded full recognition of her position ... [and] at court she exercised some influence over the young king.[23]

One intriguing outcome of Humphrey's actions in respect of his marriage was the fact that young Richard, Duke of York, now found himself associated with a royal cousin who had chosen his own wives. That could possibly have set Richard asking himself private questions about his own arranged union with young Cecily Neville.

Richard's young companions in his new situation in the royal household were Thomas, Lord Roos, James Butler, son and heir of the Earl of Ormond, and John de Vere, Earl of Oxford. Interestingly, Thomas, Lord Roos, aged twenty-one, was married to Lady Eleanor Beauchamp, the second daughter of the king's tutor, Richard Beauchamp, Earl of Warwick.

By 1428, Thomas and Eleanor had already become the parents of a son and heir. But in 1430 Lord Roos would die, after which Eleanor Beauchamp married as her second husband Edmund Beaufort, Duke of Somerset! Moreover, shortly after her second marriage, Eleanor Beauchamp also became the maternal aunt of her namesake, Eleanor Talbot, whose secret relationship with Richard's son, Edward IV will figure in Cecily Neville's story later (see below).

In terms of his age, James Butler was much closer to the little king than the other three. In 1428 James was only about eight years old. As for John de Vere,

Eleanor Beauchamp, Lady Roos (Duchess of Somerset), as originally depicted in the Lady Chapel window of St Mary's Church in Warwick (F. Sandford, A Genealogical History of the Kings and Queen of England, London 1707, p. 332).

he was nineteen, and he too already had a wife – namely Elizabeth Howard. The fact that two of his new companions were already married may have encouraged the slightly younger Richard to ponder about his own future in that direction. But of course, that does not prove that his bride – young Cecily – was now at the royal court. Moreover, given his removal from the guardianship of her mother, it appears that at this point Richard was by no means close to Cecily and her family in terms of the practical elements of his daily life. Resident now at court, from this point onwards he began to be given government roles. On 20 January 1429/30, for example, he was appointed to take on the role of Constable of England in respect of a forthcoming duel.[24]

Although he and Cecily may have been betrothed as early as 1424, their actual marriage was probably formalised in the autumn of 1429.[25] Presumably the ceremony was organised for them by the dowager Countess of Westmorland. In September of that year Richard may have had his eighteenth birthday. At that time, however, Cecily would probably only have reached the age of about

The marriage of a young couple in the fifteenth-century.

fourteen. As a result, at the time when the marriage of the young couple was celebrated it is highly unlikely to have been consummated.

In connection with the probable marriage date, it may be significant that on 25 November 1429, although Richard, during his minority, was already receiving an annual income totalling 300 marks, he was granted a further 200 marks a year by his eight-year-old cousin, King Henry VI.[26] Maybe that increase was intended to take account of the fact that Richard now had a young wife to support.

At this period, consummation of a marriage was not normally permitted while one of the partners was regarded as a minor. Consummation was deferred until both partners had reached what was seen as a suitable age. The precise age required for consummation has been disputed. However, evidence does exist which implies that the bride generally seems to have been expected to attain sixteen years of age before sexual activity on the part of her husband should begin, even though the groom may have been some years older.[27] And although a claim has been put forward that Cecily's eldest sister, Catherine, Duchess of Norfolk, bore her first child at the age of fifteen,[28] the evidence presented earlier in this present study in respect of Catherine Neville's own birthdate indicates that actually, when she gave birth to her son, the future third Duke of Norfolk, Catherine would probably have been about eighteen.

As for Cecily Neville, she would probably not have had her sixteenth birthday until 1431. Meanwhile, the Duke of Gloucester had removed Richard from the care of Cecily's mother, Joan Beaufort, and was himself developing a friendship with the young Duke of York. That new friendship implies that underlying opposition to the Beaufort family may now have been evolving on the part of Richard. It is therefore conceivable that, however he had previously felt about his marriage to Cecily, at this moment in his life he had some questions in his mind in respect of his bride – a daughter of Joan Beaufort. Possibly that may have been one of the factors which accounts for the apparent delay which took place in the generation of any York children.

Because of their consanguinity – which made them second cousins, Cecily and Richard could not possibly have married without the grant of a papal dispensation. The normal way of calculating the consanguinity which requires a papal dispensation was, and is, to count the number of generations between the couple planning to marry and their closest common ancestor. In the case of Cecily and Richard, their closest common ancestors were King Edward III and his wife, Philippa of Hainault. That royal couple comprised the great grandparents of both Cecily and Richard, who were therefore related in the third degree.

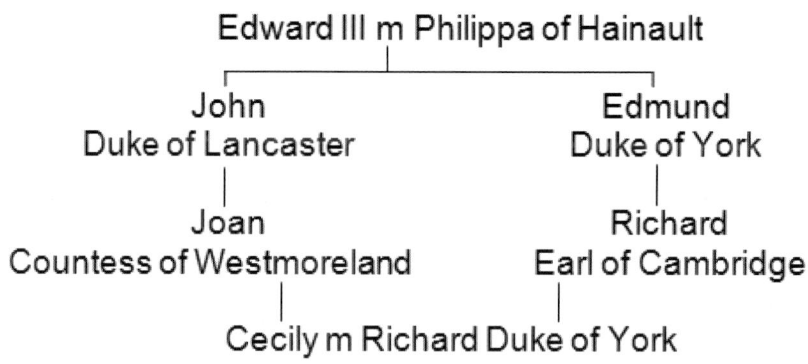

Cecily's need for a Papal Dispensation

It is not known precisely where their marriage was celebrated. A suggestion has been put forward that the ceremony probably took place 'either in London or County Durham' and St Stephen's Chapel at the Palace of Westminster has been proposed as the most likely location.[29] However, the available evidence – or the lack thereof – seems to contradict that claim. The fact is that a dispensation must have been granted by Pope Martin V for the young couple to marry.

Given that no evidence exists of where the wedding took place, it is difficult to ascertain within which English diocese the essential papal dispensation would have been received. But so far, no trace of such a document has been found. Certainly the published records relating to the London episcopate of William Grey (who was Bishop of London from 1425 to 1431) and his immediate predecessor, John Kempe (Bishop of London from 1421 to 1425),[30] contain no record of a papal dispensation issued in respect of the York marriage, though other papal dispensations are sometimes mentioned in the London episcopal records. There is also no record of such a dispensation in the Calendar of Papal Registers covering the reign of Pope Martin V.[31] This seems strange, because although Richard's parents had married in secret early in 1408, they were also related to one another within the forbidden degrees. Thus that young couple had found themselves forced to obtain a belated papal dispensation in May 1408. In their case the relevant record can be found in the Calendar of Papal Registers.[32] It therefore seems improbable that the marriage of Richard and Cecily could possibly have taken place in London.

Pope Martin (whose previous name was Otto, or Oddone, Colona) was elected sovereign pontiff at the Council of Constance, in November 1417. At

The coronation of Pope Martin V.

the time of his election, Cecily would probably have been only about two and a half years old. Even Richard had then probably barely passed his sixth birthday. However, Martin's papal election ended the Western Schism, and his reign as the sovereign pontiff continued until 1431. Thus his pontificate clearly covered the period both of Cecily's betrothal and of her marriage to Richard.

In spite of the fact that no trace of the necessary papal dispensation has yet been found, permitting Richard and Cecily to marry, clear evidence does survive of other papal authorisations in respect of the young couple. In 1429 the Duke of York sought two permits from Pope Martin V. These comprised permission for the use of a portable altar, and permission to make a choice of confessor. The two resultant Papal indults were accordingly issued to 'Richard, duke of York, and Cecily his wife, noblewoman'.[33] The first of these, in particular, was obviously a permit which would have been required in the context of some kind of travel which was to be undertaken both by the young Duke of York and by his bride. It is therefore significant that the young Duke was probably then preparing for his (and his wife's) participation in the coronations of his young cousin, the king. The second of those coronations would obviously require travelling, as it was to be celebrated in France.

Henry VI's English coronation was held at Westminster Abbey in November 1429. The Duke of York attended, and it is possible that his young bride was also present. Five months later, in April 1430, the young king and his entourage crossed the Channel to his other kingdom. There Henry remained for almost two years, only returning to England in February 1431/2. His French coronation was celebrated at the Cathedral of Notre Dame in Paris in December 1431. Henry's cousins, the Duke and Duchess of York, were presumably both in France with him. The evidence of the two papal indults requested and received by the Duke of York, suggests that Richard must have been planning for his young bride to accompany him on his trip to France, in spite of the fact that, at that point, she had probably still not reached the age required for the consummation of their marriage (see above).

Henry's French coronation was organised for him by his uncle, John of Lancaster, Duke of Bedford, who was then serving as the young king's Lieutenant in France. One element of his preparations was the trial and burning at the stake in Rouen of Joan of Arc. Joan was martyred on Wednesday 30 May 1431 – the eve of the Feast of Corpus Christi.

A possibly significant part of the French celebrations from Cecily's point of view would have been when Henry VI entered the *Palais de la Cité*, on the island in the centre of the River Seine. He first went to the *Sainte Chapelle* to venerate all the religious relics housed there. Then he proceeded to a dinner at which all

John of Lancaster, Duke of Bedford.

the ladies of his royal entourage, led by Anne of Burgundy, Duchess of Bedford, were waiting to receive him. Presumably we should therefore picture the young Cecily, Duchess of York amongst those royal ladies in the *Palais de la Cité* in Paris. After the dinner King Henry went on to greet his maternal grandmother, the dowager Queen Isabeau of France.[34]

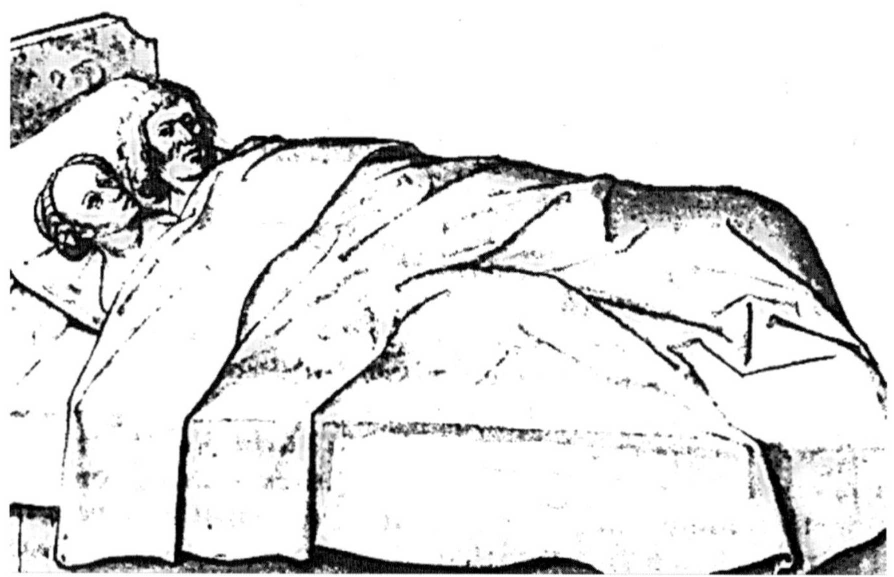

A fifteenth-century lady in bed with her husband. Redrawn from a contemporary illustration in The Fables of Bidpai.

It was probably in about 1431 that the marriage of Richard and Cecily could finally have been consummated. It is said that during the medieval period people of both sexes normally went to bed in the nude.[35] The above illustration appears to confirm that, although 'there are contemporary illustrations showing the contrary, at least for particular occasions such as 'lying-in'.[36] (See below) Of course, when a woman was lying in, her main object for being in bed was not sleeping. However, it seems that for sleeping no such thing as medieval nightclothes existed.

If initial sexual activity of the young couple did indeed take place in 1431 or thereabouts, it appears not to have led to an immediate pregnancy for Cecily. On 12 May 1432 Richard, Duke of York, was granted livery of his estates.[37] However, it appears that he was then still officially a minor, because on 24 May 1432 the young king granted a living in Herefordshire to a priest 'by reason of the minority of Richard, duke of York'.[38] On 15 October 1432 permission was given to Richard to receive income from his Irish estates, even though he was not resident in Ireland.[39]

The production of Yorkist heirs may then have been further delayed by government jobs – and the consequent travelling – which were assigned to Richard. In November 1432, in February 1432/3, in May, August and September 1433, and in March 1433/4, he received commissions of the peace in respect of a number of counties.[40] In 1433 he was made a Knight of the Garter. In September 1435 the Duke of Bedford died – and was buried – at Rouen. Humphrey, Duke of Gloucester, now became the heir presumptive to the English throne, and he again claimed regency powers in England during the minority of his nephew, the king. But once again he was opposed by members of the royal council. Also about two years later (in December 1437) the young King Henry VI came of age, so that regency powers were then no longer available.

Another result of the death of the Duke of Bedford was the fact that, on 8 May 1436, the Duke of York found himself appointed as Bedford's successor in the post of Lieutenant of France. It is possible that, in addition to his attendance at Henry VI's Paris coronation, Richard had already been in France on at least one other occasion before Bedford's death, for in May 1435 a muster of his men was sent there, together with the musters of the Earl of Salisbury and the Earl of Suffolk.[41] However, in April, May, July and November 1435, Richard received more commissions of the peace in respect of various English counties,[42] which suggests that he was then in England. Certainly provision was made for his transport to France in March–April 1436.[43] On 7 May a further muster of his men was also shipped there,[44] and York then served in France for some months.

One of the most effective military commanders of the English forces in Normandy was then John, Lord Talbot and Furnival. As was shown in Chapter 1, John Talbot was a cousin by marriage of Richard's young wife, Cecily. But Talbot was older than Cecily and Richard, having been born in about 1387. Also his marital relationship with Cecily had, in one sense, come to an end in 1422, when his first wife, Maud Neville had died. Since then Talbot had remarried. His second wife was Lady Margaret Beauchamp, the eldest daughter of Richard Beauchamp, Earl of Warwick, and the elder sister of Eleanor Beauchamp.

With the help of the young Duke of York, Talbot saved Rouen from a French attack.

> When Rouen itself was threatened, Talbot counter-attacked, routing the French at Ry, 10 miles east of the city, and securing Caudebec downstream. While he could do nothing to save Paris in April 1436, a surprise attack on Gisors took further pressure off Normandy. In June the garrison was finally relieved by the duke of York with reinforcements from England.[45]

But though Rouen had been saved, Paris had been abandoned. It had been recaptured by King Charles VII.

Pope Eugene IV.

One document survives which proves Richard's presence in France at this time. On 24 October 1436 Pope Eugene IV (a nephew of Pope Martin V, whom he had succeeded as the sovereign pontiff in March 1430/1) sent a message from Bologna, to Richard at Rouen:

> To the duke of York.[46] The pope has translated Lewis, elect of Rouen, chancellor of France, to the said church [of Rouen], knowing him to have been and to be faithful and acceptable to the king, and believing that it will please the duke, to whom the pope commends the said elect and his church.[47]

Probably this time Richard had travelled to France alone, unaccompanied by Cecily. But it may have been that by this time he had established a working relationship with his young bride. In the spring of 1437 he requested permission to return to England, and in November 1437 he did return home. One of the motives behind his request to leave his post in France might possibly have been his desire to be with his young wife, together with his hope that he and Cecily could now begin to produce a family.

Obviously the marriage of the Duke and Duchess of York had been arranged by Cecily's parents when Richard and Cecily were both minors, and the possibility has been explored that, in his late teens, Richard may briefly have felt somewhat dubious about young Cecily because of her Beaufort connections. Subsequently, however, the young couple certainly seem to have genuinely come to love one another. There are no records of the Duke ever having any mistresses, so it definitely seems that he loved, and was content with his wife, to whom he behaved with consistent fidelity. The couple also spent a great deal of time together, and their relationship included regular pregnancies for Cecily, leading to the birth of a number of children.

It was about a year after her husband's return to her from France, probably in November 1438 (see below), that Cecily conceived the couple's first known child, Anne, who was born in England in August 1439. As a poem written some years later at Clare Priory in Suffolk expressed it,

> *Post annos steriles multos sit primula proles*
> *Anna decora satis*[48]

> After many fruitless years the first child is
> The very lovely Anne

Anne was the only child of the Duke and Duchess of York who had any chance of enjoying the existence of a living grandparent. When the little girl came into the world her mother's mother, Joan Beaufort (from whom Anne and her descendents inherited mitochondrial DNA – see below, Chapter 16), was still alive.

In May 1440, in England, Cecily conceived the couple's second known child. Some six weeks later, on 2 July 1440, the Duke of York was reappointed Lieutenant of France. However, he did not depart from England immediately. Thus he and his wife were still resident in their homeland in February 1440/1, when Cecily gave birth to their second child. This time it was a son, who was apparently given the name of Henry in honour of his cousin, the young king. Like his elder sister, Anne, the little boy was reportedly born at Hatfield in Hertfordshire (see below). But it seems that his life was short. Probably he died very soon after coming into the world.

Before losing Henry, Cecily had also lost her own mother. The dowager Countess of Westmorland, died at Howden in Yorkshire on Sunday 13 November 1440. According to her own wish Joan Beaufort was buried, neither with her first husband, nor with her second husband, but at Lincoln Cathedral, next to her mother, the Duchess of Lancaster. It seems unlikely that Cecily was present at her mother's interment. Not only was she some six months pregnant at the time, but also at this period it was not considered essential for all relatives to attend burials. It was much more important to ensure that the soul of a dead person was prayed for.

The death of Joan Beaufort, Countess of Westmorland, occurred at about the same time as the political eclipse of her once powerful brother, Cardinal Henry Beaufort, thanks to evidence presented before Parliament by Humphrey, Duke of Gloucester. Earlier, the Cardinal had been hoping to award the lieutenancy of France to his nephew, John Beaufort, Earl of Somerset, but, as we have seen, that post had now been assigned to Humphrey's candidate, Richard, Duke of York. However, Humphrey did not now find himself holding exclusive power in England.

One of the strongest individuals in the royal council was now William de la Pole, Earl of Suffolk, whose wife, Alice Chaucer, was:

> the daughter of the king's butler, Thomas Chaucer. A close relative of Cardinal Henry Beaufort, and his ally on Henry VI's minority council, Chaucer was a valuable connection. It seems likely that he embraced Suffolk as a son: the earl was soon using men from Chaucer's estates in the Thames valley as his agents, and it was surely with the butler's agreement that the earl became constable and steward of Queen Catherine's honour of Wallingford in June 1434. By the time Chaucer died, at the end of that year, Suffolk had largely stepped into his shoes.[49]

Thus, the contest for real power in England was ongoing.

A record survives of Letters Patent issued on 7 May 1441, 'by which Richard, Duke of York, Earl of March, etc., lieutenant and governor of France, grants to his beloved councillor, Sir John Fastolf, an annuity of £20'.[50] This record is preserved in England, and the grant was presumably issued in that country, because it was not until June 1441 that the Duke of York is said to have returned to Normandy. This time he was accompanied by his wife, and probably also by their little daughter, Anne. The Duke and Duchess of York then seem basically to have remained in Normandy until September 1445.

Richard and Cecily must both, by now, have become well aware of the fact that competition was ongoing for the tenure of real power in the kingdom of England. However, it was only shortly after their departure to France that Richard's friend, Humphrey, Duke of Gloucester, suddenly found himself effectively ruined politically. This was achieved by bringing an accusation of treasonable necromancy against his chosen beloved wife, Eleanor Cobham (see below, Chapter 5).

Chapter 3

Cecily's List of Children

In terms of children – and therefore of marital intimacy – the union of Cecily Neville and Richard, Duke of York, appears to have been a very close one. The evidence for this is shown in the table relating to dates of birth and conception presented at the end of this chapter. This shows that between 1438 and 1455 regular marital sex between Cecily and her husband must have been the norm. Indeed, their sexual intimacy could well have started earlier, and may also have continued beyond 1455. It is possible that there were earlier pregnancies than that of 1438–39; pregnancies which failed to produce living children and which are therefore not on record. Also, shortly after 1455 (when Cecily had passed the age of 40) she may well have entered her menopause. That would account for the lack of further pregnancies, without in any way implying that the marital relationship had ended.

It is also interesting to note that the marital fidelity of Richard and Cecily appears to have been inherited by several of the children they brought into the world. Their middle daughter, Elizabeth of York, Duchess of Suffolk, produced many children with her husband, just as her mother and father had done. Their middle son, George, Duke of Clarence and his wife, Isabel Neville, also had a faithful and fruitful marriage, though their number of children was limited by the early death of the Duchess of Clarence. Like his father, the Duke of York, the Duke of Clarence also appears to have had no mistresses, and no illegitimate offspring.

As for the other two married sons of the York couple, superficially their marital history may, at first sight, appear to have been different. But the general impression on that point is probably another example of mythology which has been accepted as genuine history. Richard III produced only one son by his wife, Anne Neville. But that was probably due to a problem which Anne had. Richard III also fathered two acknowledged bastards. However they both seem to have been fathered in his teens, well before his marriage to Anne. As for Edward IV, he is generally thought to have been an epitome of infidelity. But the genuine historical evidence clearly reveals that from 1464 until 1480 he had a consistent and regular relationship with Elizabeth Widville which was regarded as marriage.[1] Apart from the illegitimate children produced for him by Elizabeth Widville, Edward, like his younger brother, Richard, also had one or two other illegitimate offspring. However, the claims that he had mistresses and numerous other bastard children are based on absolutely no genuine contemporary evidence.[2]

The other two York daughters had rather different marital relationships than that of their parents. The eldest daughter, Anne of York, Duchess of Exeter, had two marriages and produced two daughters, but her first marriage proved difficult. As for her second marriage, that was of relatively short duration, due to Anne's death. The youngest surviving daughter of Cecily and Richard was Margaret of York. She was married to the Duke of Burgundy, but the marriage proved fruitless. Indeed, it may never really have been consummated. It appears that, despite his three arranged marriages, Charles the Bold was probably more attracted to members of his own sex.[3]

In his *ODNB* entry for Cecily, Harper-Bill accepts that the Duchess of York produced a total of twelve children, of whom only six survived to adulthood.[4] However, it will shortly be seen that the first part of this assertion can actually be questioned in two ways, because, while the list of children of the Duke and Duchess of York is normally thought to be quite well known, in reality some of the facts are not quite so straightforward as is usually depicted. As in all the cases of questionable historical assertions, the only way forward is to attempt to check the original source material. Unfortunately Harper-Bill also accepts a version of William Worcester's *Annals* (see below) which asserts that Anne of York (Duchess of Exeter) was born at Fotheringhay – though he does acknowledge that Margaret of York (Duchess of Burgundy) may have been born elsewhere. Once again, the birth places which are commonly alleged for some of Cecily's children need to be checked.

The claim that Cecily gave birth to at least twelve children (though not all of her babies remained alive) is based upon the most complete surviving list of children of the Duke and Duchess of York. This is the list which is offered in a poem written by one of the Austin friars at Clare in Suffolk, and entitled 'The Dialogue at the Grave of Dame Joan of Acre'. The English text of the two relevant verses reads as follows:

> Sir aftir the tyme of longe bareynesse,
> God first sent Anne, which signyfieth grace,
> In token that al her hertis hevynesse
> He as for bareynesse wold fro hem chace.
> Harry, Edward, and Edmonde, eche in his place
> Succedid; and after tweyn daughters cam
> Elizabeth and Margarete, and afterward William.

John aftir William nexte borne was,
Which bothe be passid to goddis grace:
George was next, and after Thomas
Borne was, which sone aftir did pace
By the path of dethe to the hevenly place
Richard liveth yet: but last of alle
Was Ursula, to him whom God list calle.[5]

This is thought to have been written in the late 1450s. The York children named in the poem comprise:

1. Anne
2. Harry
3. Edward
4. Edmonde
5. Elizabeth
6. Margarete
7. William
8. John
9. George
10. Thomas
11. Richard
12. Ursula ('the last of alle')

The poem also appears to suggest that Cecily had proved barren for a number of years. However, that does not necessarily mean that she had never been pregnant. It may simply be that before the birth of her daughter, Anne, she had failed to carry a foetus for the full term. In other words she may possibly have experienced earlier pregnancies than those of 1438–1439.

Thus, it is not absolutely certain that the list of children provided in the Clare poem is either accurate or complete. For example, another problem relates to child number 10 – a boy named as Thomas. This child of the Duke and Duchess of York is not cited by any other surviving fifteenth-century source. It is therefore not confirmed that he really existed. However, it also makes it conceivable that some children who were either born dead or who proved to be short-lived have been omitted from *all* the surviving sources. It has already been hypothesised that Cecily might possibly have had one or two pregnancies prior to the birth of Anne. As will become clear later, if there are any other gaps during which unrecorded gestation events could potentially have occurred, these are most likely to have crept in towards the end of the list as given in the poem. At that stage, based only upon the lists of York children which survive, longer periods of time seem sometimes to have elapsed between Cecily's recorded childbirths. However, in the longest gap, between the last two children named by the Clare poem, clear evidence exists, in the form of a letter written by Cecily herself (see below, Chapter 6), which proves that in 1453 she experienced a disasterous pregnancy which produced no living child.

Although the Clare poem lists twelve children, and in a few instances records their early deaths, it provides no information regarding when or where the children were born. However, two other surviving fifteenth-century sources do claim to offer such information. These other two lists are both to be found in the *Annals* of William Worcester. The first of them – referred to hereinafter as Worcester *Annals* List 1 – is simply a list of 'the following generation of the most illustrious prince Richard, Duke of York &c by the most serene princess, his wife, Cecily'.[6] The second – Worcester *Annals* List 2 – forms part of a much longer list of events, which begins in 1324,[7] and ends in 1491,[8] and which also includes the alleged birth date of Cecily Neville herself (see above: Chapter 1). Under the appropriate year dates within this second record, covering almost two centuries, births of children of the Duke and Duchess of York are again recorded.

Unfortunately, though, the information contained in Worcester *Annals* List 1 and Worcester *Annals* List 2 conflicts in various ways. Worcester *Annals* List 1, which appears superficially to be the earlier of the two lists, is definitely incomplete. In it, for example, the eldest son, named as Harry in the Clare poem, is omitted. Also, the list terminates with George (later Duke of Clarence). This seems to suggest that it may have been written early in 1450, shortly after George's birth (but before the appearance of any further children). Yet it also includes mention of the death of Edmund (Earl of Rutland) at the battle of Wakefield in 1460. That suggests that the list must have been put together at a later date. An alternative explanation could possibly be that the Wakefield information was simply an update, subsequently added to the original list of children which had been put together in about 1450. However, the existing medieval manuscript source for List 1 displays no change in the handwriting or the colour of the ink.

Worcester *Annals* List 1 can be found in the *Annals* of William Worcester as published in T. Hearne, *Liber Niger Scaccarii nec non Wilhelmi Worcestrii Annales Rerum Anglicarum*, vol. 2, London 1774, pp. 525–526. Worcester *Annals* List 1 offers the following information about the children of the Duke and Duchess of York:

1. Anne b. Hatfield,[9] 9 August 1439, 17.00 hours.
3. Edward (IV) (2nd son)[10] b. Rouen, 27 April 1442, 14.45 hours.
4. Edmund b. Rouen, 17 May 1443, 7 pm. Killed Wakefield.[11]
5. Elizabeth b. Rouen, 21 September 1444, 14.00 hours.[12]
6. Margaret b. Waltham Abbey, 3 May 1446.
7. William b. Fotheringhay Castle, 7 July 1447.
8. John b. Neyte,[13] Westminster, 7 November 1448.
9. George b. Dublin Castle, 12 noon, 21 October 1449.

No days of the week are mentioned in this version of the list.

William Worcester's first record of the birth of Edward IV, dating it as 27 April 1442. College of Arms Arundel MS 48, f. 85v. Reproduced by permission of the Kings, Heralds and Pursuivants of Arms.

Worcester *Annals* List 2 includes updated information in respect of York family childbirths which postdated that of George, Duke of Clarence. List 2 was clearly put together after 1455, since it includes the birth of Ursula. Presumably it dates from the 1490s (see above). Sadly, however, Worcester *Annals* List 2 – which attempts to name some of the days of the week upon which births took place – definitely contains inaccuracies. It also cites hours for the birth in certain cases, which conflict with the times given in Worcester *Annals* List 1, and it appears to contain errors in respect of several of the birth locations. Curiously, it also omits any record of the tenth child (Thomas), despite the fact that he was named in the poem (see above).

Worcester *Annals* List 2 has been published in J. Stevenson, ed., *Letters and Papers Illustrative of the Wars of the English in France during the Reign of Henry the Sixth, vol, 2, part 2*, London 1864. Where it refers to days of the week which are definitely incorrect, and where it names what appears to be an incorrect date (particularly the month) or an incorrect location, these are noted with underlining and the word [*sic*].

1. Anne (Exeter) b. Fotheringhay [*sic*], between 5 and 6 am on Tuesday [*sic*] 10 August 1439.[14]
2. Henry (Harry) b. Hatfield, 5 am, Friday 10 February 1441,[15] d. before 1445.[16]

3. Edward (IV) b. Rouen, 2 am, Monday [*sic*] 28 [*sic*] April [?*sic*] 1442, conceived at Hatfield.[17]
4. Edmund b. Rouen, 7 pm, Monday [*sic*] 17 May 1443.[18]
5. Elizabeth b. Rouen, 2 am, Tuesday [*sic*] 22 April [*sic*] 1444.[19]
6. Margaret b. Fotheringhay [*sic*], Tuesday 3 May 1446.[20]
7. William b. Fotheringhay, 7 July 1447.[21]
8. John b. Neyte,[22] Westminster, 7 November 1448.[23]
9. George (Clarence) b. Ireland, 12 noon, Tuesday 21 October 1449.[24]
10. *Thomas b. 1450/1451 is omitted from this list.*[25]
11. Richard (III) (Glos.) b. Fotheringhay, Monday 2 October 1452.[26]
12. Ursula b. 20 July (Feast of St Margaret) 1455.[27]

It is interesting to note that the details given for the birth of George, Duke of Clarence, correspond very closely to those in the earlier list, and contain no obvious errors. They therefore seem to comprise one of the most believable sets of data.

In respect of the other children, where the dates and places cited in this list have not been queried, they may be correct. Unfortunately though, the fact that there are obvious errors in some cases leaves all the information open to possible questions. None of it can be considered perfect. The fact that in at least one case (Elizabeth) the wrong birth month is stated means that elsewhere, when the day, the number, and the month which are offered in the list are inconsistent, and do not match in respect of the stated year, one cannot simply assume that the error is in terms of *the day of the week*. It is equally possible that the wrong *month* has been cited.

This is, of course, particularly relevant in the case of Edward IV. In Worcester *Annals* List 2 his birth date is alleged to have been Monday 28 April 1442. This is different from the date offered in Worcester *Annals* List 1 (see above). Also it is clearly a ridiculous claim, because in actuality 28 April 1442 fell, not on a Monday, but on a Saturday. However, it cannot simply be assumed that *the day of the week* has been wrongly recorded. Maybe – as in the case of his younger sister, Elizabeth – Edward's birth month has been wrongly recorded. One alternative possible correction could therefore be phrased to read that Edward was born on Monday 28 *May* 1442! Obviously another possibility is that the day, the number, and the month are all wrongly recorded in Worcester *Annals* List 2. That second Worcester list of the York children also includes the statement that Edward was conceived at Hatfield. That is a later note added in a different hand. However, the note could conceivably be a more accurate statement than the alleged birth date to which it has been added, in a list which obviously contradicts Worcester

Annals List 1, not only in respect of Edward's date of birth, but also in respect of the dates and places of birth of some of the other children.

If the added note is accurate, and Edward was conceived at Hatfield, that suggests that he would have been born several weeks earlier than in the third week of April 1442 – perhaps in February or March 1441/2. This is because his parents could both have been at Hatfield in May 1441, but they are known to have left England in June of that year (see below, Chapter 4). The problem is that William Worcester's Annals comprise the only surviving fifteenth-century source which claims to reveal Edward IV's birth date. Since Worcester supplies conflicting information, some elements of which are clearly erroneous, it is now absolutely impossible to pretend that we know precisely when Edward was born.

As we have seen, if Edward was born in February / March 1441/2 his conception would have occurred in May or early June 1441. Alternatively, if he was born toward the end of May 1442, he would probably have been conceived towards the end of August 1441. On the earlier of those possible conception dates the Duke and Duchess of York could have been together at Hatfield in England. On the later date they would have been together at Rouen in France. All this is highly significant in the context of the later (and modern) allegation that Edward was a bastard (see below, Chapter 11). What has now emerged is the clear fact that it is impossible to say where the Duke of York was when Edward was conceived, because the boy's date of conception cannot be specified. Thus the claims in this respect which have been put forward as solid facts by some recent writers are, in reality, nothing more than speculations.

The following table summarises Cecily Neville's life as a mother by offering possible conception dates for all the known children. It also notes the probable time gaps between Cecily Neville's recorded pregnancies.

POSSIBLE CONCEPTION DATES AND THE GAPS BETWEEN THEM

	Conception	birth	gap
1. Anne (Exeter)	Nov 1438	Aug 1439	
			9 months
2. *Henry (Harry)*	May 1440	Feb 1441	
			3/4 months
3. Edward (IV)	May / June 1441	Feb / March 1442	
			5/6 months
4. Edmund (Rutland)	Aug 1442	May 1443	
			7 months
5. Elizabeth (Suffolk)	Dec 1443	Sep 1444	
			11 months
6. Margaret (Burgundy)	Aug 1445	May 1446	
			5 months
7. *William*	Oct 1446	Jul 1447	
			7 months
8. *John*	Feb 1447/8	Nov 1448	
			2 months
9. George (Clarence)	Jan 1448/9	Oct 1449	
			c. 9 months?
10. *Thomas**	*c.* July 1450?	*c.* April 1451?	
			c. 9 months?
11. Richard (III) (Glos.)	Jan 1451/2	Oct 1452	
			5/6 months?
12. *preterm*☼	*c.* March 1453?	*c.* August 1453	
			14 months?
13. *Ursula*	Oct 1454	Jul 1455	

* No version of Worcester's list includes Thomas, and his date of birth is unknown.
☼ See below, chapter 5: Cecily's letter to Margaret of Anjou.

Chapter 4

Wife and Mother in France

As we have seen, during the 1430s while the Duke of York was serving in France, it is possible that he left his wife in England. Later, however, she seems to have accompanied him more or less everywhere on a regular basis – except when the situation was dangerous and he was escaping to safety.

On the basis of the information received regarding the birth of her children (see above, Chapter 3), it appears that in August 1439 Cecily was probably at Hatfield in Hertfordshire, staying at the manor of the Bishop of Ely. There she reportedly gave birth to her eldest daughter, Anne. And she was probably once again at Hatfield in February 1441, giving birth there to her eldest son, Henry (Harry).

At that time the Bishop of Ely was Cardinal Louis of Luxembourg, Archbishop of Rouen and Bishop of Frascati. He was a leading mainland European supporter of the Lancastrian claim to the French throne. In 1433 one of his nieces, Jacquette of Luxembourg, had married Henry VI's senior living uncle, John of Lancaster, Duke of Bedford. The Duke was then the Lieutenant of France for his nephew, the young king. Bedford held the French post until his death in 1435. After Bedford's death in France, Cardinal Louis's niece, Jacquette, secretly remarried. As a result she then became the mother of Elizabeth Widville, whose significant role in Cecily's story will emerge later.

Incidentally, the Duchess of Bedford (later Countess Rivers) is often referred to in modern English texts under an anglicised three-syllabled version of her first name, as 'Jacquetta'. However, contemporary evidence shows clearly that, even in England, she herself retained the original two-syllabled French version of her name. For example, in a petition to Edward IV she referred to herself as 'your humble and true liegewoman Jaquet duchesse of Bedford, late the wyf of your true and faithfull knyght and liegeman Richard late erle of Ryvers'.[1]

It was the weakening of the position of the English – and of King Henry VI – in France which led to Jacquette's uncle, the Cardinal Archbishop of Rouen, being granted a third episcopal see, in England. On 27 September 1437 he was created Bishop of Ely. That was the fifth most valuable episcopal see in England. It was thus both a reward for Cardinal Louis, and a safeguard, in case he should lose control of his French archbishopric. However, in the event, the

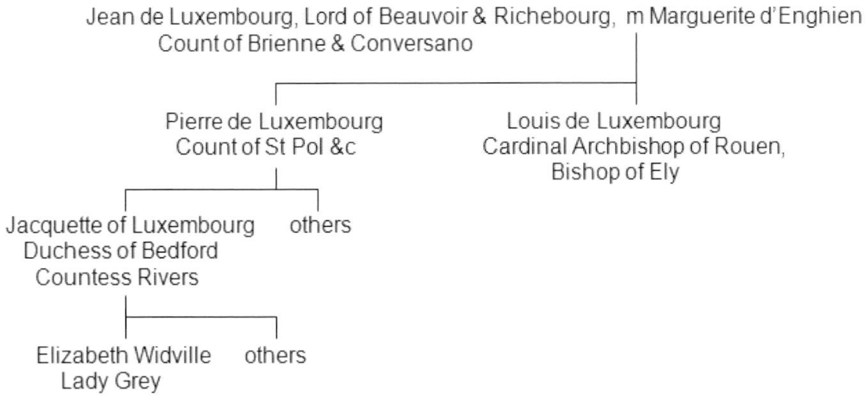

The House of Luxembourg (simplified)

cardinal died in 1443, six years before Charles VII of France recaptured Rouen. Thus Cardinal Louis of Luxembourg never actually set foot in the see of Ely – or indeed, in England. As a result, the Bishop of Ely's manor at Hatfield in Hertfordshire was never used as a residence by him.

One outcome of this was the fact that the episcopal manor house remained vacant. It was therefore available for loan to the Duke and Duchess of York, during the two years from the summer of 1439 until the summer of 1441. The Duke of York was then actively involved in English government. But at that time he possessed no residence in London. From 1439 until 1441 it seems that he therefore used Hatfield Manor House as his *pied-à-terre*.

Interestingly, that house had also previously been used for a time as the residence of Henry VI's mother, Catherine of France. And she too is said to have given birth there to one of her children – her third son, Jasper (later Earl of Pembroke). However, that had been earlier in the 1430s,[2] before the bishopric of Ely passed to Cardinal Louis of Luxembourg. At that time the Bishop of Ely had been a Welshman, called Philip Morgan. Given his Welsh origins, Bishop Morgan may possibly have had a connection of some kind with Queen Catherine's final partner, Owen Tudor, who is claimed by some historians (though on the basis of no solid evidence) to have been secretly married to Catherine, and who was later acknowledged by Jasper as his father.[3] Bishop Philip Morgan had died at Hatfield on 25 October 1435. As for Queen Catherine, she died at Bermondsey Abbey on 3 January 1436/7.

Later, when the young Duke of York had returned from his post in France – but prior to his inheritance of Baynard's Castle from his cousin and friend, Humphrey of Lancaster, Duke of Gloucester – he was allowed to use Waltham Abbey in Essex as his residence near the capital when he needed to be performing government work in London (see below: Chapter 5). In terms of roads, the two locations were approximately equidistant from London. Waltham Abbey was about fifteen miles away, while the episcopal manor house at Hatfield required a journey of about twenty miles.

It must have been well known in fifteenth-century England that from 1439 until 1441 the Duke and Duchess of York used Hatfield as their near-London residence. It is therefore not surprising that, according to one surviving source, Cecily's second son, Edward (IV) was reported to have been 'conceived in the chamber next to the chapel in the Palace of Hatfield'.[4] As we have seen, that phrase is a later addition to William Worcester's *Annals*, so it can not be accepted as definitely true. However, it indicates that Cecily and her husband were both known to have still been in England – and staying at the Hatfield manor house – in the late spring / early summer of 1441.

Michael Jones has argued that 'this location is impossible, for York and Cecily had left for France by mid-June 1441'.[5] However, Jones's conclusion is merely based upon the groundless assumption that he has certain knowledge of Edward IV's birth date. As the information in Chapter 3 has now clearly revealed, such a claim is absolutely impossible.

Other modern versions of the story seem to suggest that Edward was not only born, but may also have been conceived, in France. For example, Mary Clive states that :

> In May 1441 the Duke of York arrived in Rouen, the capital of Normandy, at the head of an expeditionary force. His wife, Cecily, accompanied him, and in the following spring, on 28 April 1442, she gave birth to a son in the castle of Rouen. This was the future Edward IV.[6]

But as we saw earlier (see above, Chapter 2) the Duke of York definitely appears to have been in England in May 1441. He and his wife are only reported to have left for France in June of that year. Thus, given the fact that the birth date of their second son, Edward (IV) has now been shown to be completely uncertain, there is no justification for any assertion that the boy could not possibly have been conceived at Hatfield.

In June 1441, when the Duke and Duchess of York sailed across the Channel to France, Richard was presumably approaching his thirtieth birthday. As for Cecily, probably she had recently attained the age of twenty-six. As part of his assertion that he has found evidence supporting the claim that Edward IV was illegitimate, Michael Jones has also put forward amazing claims regarding the appearance of Cecily and Richard in the 1440s. First, he says 'while York had provided Cecily with wealth, rank, power and prestige, *he was short and small of face*'.[7] However, he cites not one single source for his statement in respect of the Duke of York's appearance. In respect of Cecily, Jones then goes on to say: 'if the eye of *this notorious beauty* was to wander it might come to rest on the only attribute York lacked. A *tall and manly* archer could just fit the bill.'[8]

Unfortunately for Jones and his groundless contention, a poem written in about May 1460, when the Duke of York was still alive, clearly describes him as 'manly and myȝtfulle', and 'of gret substaunce'.[9] That obviously implies that he had a strapping figure and that – like both his ancestor King Edward I ('Longshanks') and his son, the future King Edward IV – he was of above average height and build. In other words *York himself* could probably have been appropriately described as 'tall and manly'.[10] In respect of his colouring and his facial appearance, that is best shown in a manuscript illustration of about this time (see plate 14). It seems that the Duke of York had fair hair, and a profile which quite closely resembled that of his youngest son, the future King Richard III – with a prominent, slightly hooked Roman nose, and a prominent chin.

As for his wife, Cecily, in spite of Jones's assertion, once again there is no contemporary source material which puts forward a claim that she was a 'notorious beauty'.[11] She may well have been attractive, but there is no solid evidence in that respect. In fact, the only clear description we have of her states that she was 'a woman of *small stature* but of moche honour and high parentage'.[12] This is not quite a contemporary description, for it was written by Edward Hall, who was born in about 1498. Obviously Hall cannot possibly have seen Cecily with his own eyes, because she had died in 1495. However, he may have spoken to people who had known her, and the point he makes about her 'small stature' certainly does not sound like a piece of political rewriting of history.

What is more, contemporary evidence definitely exists which shows that Cecily's elder full-blood brother, William Neville, Lord Fauconberg (later Earl of Kent), was described in 1460 as 'little Fauconberg'.[13] It is possible, therefore, that smallness of stature was a family feature which was shared by some of the children of Ralph, Earl of Westmorland, and his second wife. If so, young Cecily may have resembled her elder brother, William, in that respect.

In terms of her colouring, Cecily may possibly have been a brunette. Although the hair of decent women was not normally on public display in the fifteenth century, the surviving manuscript miniatures showing her father and brothers seem to suggest that the majority of Cecily's Neville siblings had brown hair. Also, that was a characteristic which was inherited by Cecily's son, the future Edward IV. In addition, it seems possible that Edward inherited from his mother's family his rather small, straight nose and a chin which was less prominent than that of his father.[14] For Cecily's facial appearance, see plate 13. Although it is not certain that this image of Cecily, from the Neville Book of Hours, is absolutely accurate, she and all her sisters are portrayed there with similar features.

It is not precisely clear how many members of their family can have travelled to France with the Duke and Duchess of York. When Richard and Cecily set off they were presumably accompanied by their little daughter, Anne. But unfortunately it is not clear whether their son, Henry, was then still alive. It seems that he must have been a sickly child. Indeed, he may well have died very soon after his birth. Certainly he died before 1445, because in that year letters written by the Duke of York refer specifically to his second son, Edward, as his heir. We have no way of knowing whether Henry died before Edward was born, or afterwards. If Henry was taken to France, and died there, presumably he would have been buried at Rouen Cathedral – though one dubious source claims that he (together with other siblings who died young) was buried at Fotheringhay.[15] Whenever he died and wherever he was buried, Henry's known ill-health and his short life-span could perhaps have been motives which caused Richard, Duke of York to arrange to have his second son baptised as a matter of urgency, very soon after the latter's birth (see below).

Since Edward IV's precise date of birth is unclear, and since it has been shown to be quite possible that he was conceived at Hatfield, he might possibly have been born at Rouen in *March* 1441/2. But when his mother travelled to France in June 1441 she would probably not yet have been aware that she was again pregnant, and no sign of the pregnancy would yet have been visible. Thus the Duke and Duchess of York would probably not have known that they were also transporting their unborn third child with them to France.

In 1442, 1443 and 1444 Cecily was clearly resident for most of the time at the Castle of Rouen in France, where she gave birth to three of her children: Edward, Edmund and Elizabeth (see above, Chapter 3). It is virtually certain that all three of these children were born somewhere within the Castle of Rouen, which was then the headquarters of English government in Normandy. Only one tower of Rouen Castle survives today, and that was definitely not part of the apartments within which the York family would have resided in the 1440s. In fact it was the prison tower within which Joan of Arc had been confined about ten years earlier while she was being tried for sorcery.

Rouen Castle.

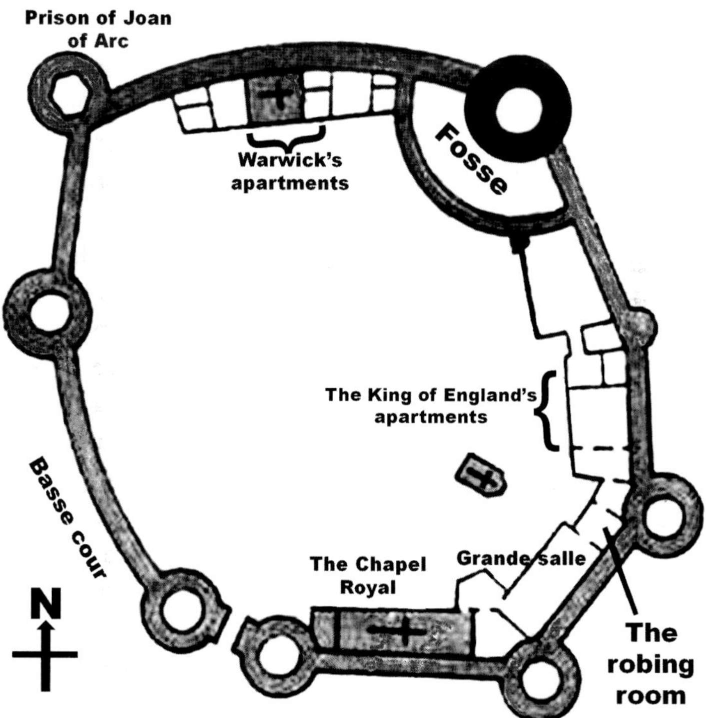

Plan of Rouen Castle.

Since the royal quarters of the castle would have been in use by their father, and since the normal practice of the period would have required their mother to be shut away before, during and after their births it may be that the area assigned to Cecily was the apartment which had earlier been used by Richard Beauchamp, Earl of Warwick. That Earl had died in the castle at Rouen on 30 April 1439, almost three years before the Duchess of York would have required rooms for her lying-in.

In terms of the English medieval calendar the New Year began not on 1 January, but on 'Lady Day' (25 March). Thus, in terms of that calendar, it was perhaps either at the very end of 1441 or early in 1442 when the time may have been drawing near for Cecily to give birth for the first time to one of her children in France. As the birth date approached, Cecily must have withdrawn into the special chambers at the Castle of Rouen which had been assigned to her for this purpose. Most of the chamber windows will have then been covered up. Only one of them would have been left accessible. The keyholes of the doors would also have been blocked. All this would have been done about three weeks prior to the expected birth of the coming child. Cecily would then have been shut away from the rest of the world. Only her women servants would have had access to her during the final days of her pregnancy.

On a date which has now been shown to be a mystery, Cecily would have entered into labour. In due course, with the aid of midwives, she would then have given birth to her second son. After his birth the little boy would have been handed over to his nurse. It seems that she was a local woman from Normandy, named Anne de Caux. Under no circumstances would Cecily herself ever have breast-fed this little boy – or any of her other children – because doing that could have delayed her ability to conceive another possible heir for her husband.

Evidence of the fact that Anne de Caux was Edward's nurse has been preserved for us in later records. Edward IV granted her an annual pension of £20 in 1474, as a reward for her services to him.[16] Subsequently, payment of that pension was re-endorsed by Richard III.[17] It seems that Anne must have accompanied the York family back to England in October 1445.

The suggestion that Anne's surname shows that she was a Norman woman was recently put forward by the present writer.[18] Although a place named *Caux* exists in southern France (Gascogne), which has widely been assumed to be the source for the surname *de Caux* (or *Decaux*), there is also a *Pays de Caux* north of Rouen, around the ports of Le Havre and Dieppe. The Norman coastal region seems much more likely to have been the home of Anne de Caux, and the source from which she derived her surname.

A medieval royal childbirth (redrawn from a medieval manuscript).

Following the birth of her second son, Cecily had to remain in the seclusion of her birth chambers for some weeks. Initially, she would have been lying down, but little by little she would have begun to sit up, get up and walk around. Finally she would have regained access to the rest of Rouen Castle. At that stage she had to undergo the religious purification which was then required after childbirth. This was achieved by means of the ceremony of 'churching'. This was a short church service which was meant both to purify the mother and to give thanks for the childbirth. Accompanied by her women, Cecily would have walked to a church or chapel, carrying in her hand a lighted candle. There, priests would have received her and sprinkled her with holy water.

However, this church visit of Cecily's would have been long preceded by a church visit on the part of her new-born son. Belief at this period focused

Churching.

very much on the idea that until a child was baptised his or her soul would be in peril. For this reason baptism normally took place at the earliest possible moment. Since mothers were then always still lying-in, it was never normal for them to attend the baptism of their own children. Even fathers, who might have been available, were neither required – nor generally expected – to attend. Instead a child was taken to its baptism by the people who had been asked to be its godparents.

There were always three godparents at a baptism. If the child was a girl, two of them were godmothers and one was a godfather. But if the child was a boy there were two godfathers and one godmother. For his first son born in Rouen the Duke of York chose Elizabeth Boteler, Lady Say, as the godmother. She was one of the sisters of Ralph Boteler, Lord Sudeley, who was later, in a curious way, to prove a significant figure in the life-story of his sister's royal Yorkist godson. Elizabeth Boteler had acquired the title of Lady Say from her first husband – Sir William Heron, Lord Say. Her first marriage proved childless, and was of relatively short duration. However, Elizabeth had later become a mother. Her offspring were fathered by her second husband, John Norbury, and by her third husband, Sir John Montgomery. The latter was still living, and in the service of the Duke of York, when Richard asked Elizabeth to become godmother to his new-born son.

Lady Say's godmotherly role at the baptism of this baby boy is on record because a gift was made to her in February 1464 by her godson. By that time he had become King of England, and he ordered his chief butler that 'ye deliver … a butt of tyre unto our right dear and entirely beloved godmother, Dame Elizabeth, Lady Say'.[19]

One of Edward's two godfathers was Thomas, Lord Scales. Together with Cecily's cousin by marriage, John Talbot (now created first Earl of Shrewsbury) and Cecily's elder brother, William Neville, Lord Fauconberg, Scales was one of the leading English generals in France. He later passed away before his godson acquired the English crown. But a document exists which refers to Lord Scales in July 1460 as 'godfather of the said Earl of March'.[20] The second godfather is said to have been the baby boy's maternal uncle, Richard, Earl of Salisbury – though no specific source is known for that claim.

As for the baby boy, he was baptised with the name of Edward, which was a link to his great uncle, the second Duke of York, and to his great great grandfather, King Edward III. Obviously he was baptised somewhere in Rouen. But the location has been a huge subject of controversy, which has been linked by more recent historians to the contention that the baby was a bastard.

It seems clear that Edward's younger brother, Edmund (born 1443), and his younger sister, Elizabeth (born 1444), were both baptised at Rouen Cathedral. But in the case of Edward solid evidence proving that he too was baptised there seems to be lacking. Cora Scofield wrote that 'according to a note left by antiquarian John Stow, the christening took place in the cathedral of Rouen.'[21] However, she cites no source for that statement. Her conclusion may have been based upon the work of Edward IV's earlier biographer, Laurence Stratford, who tells us that 'a note in MS in the British Museum speaks of his being christened in the Cathedral Church of Rouen.' However Stratford also notes that 'the Chapter Book of Rouen Cathedral has no entry of any such event, while permission for the reception and baptism at the Cathedral of his younger brother Edmund is recorded on May 18, 1443, as also that of his sister Elizabeth on September 22nd, 1444.'[22]

Stratford goes on to suggest that Edward may have been baptised in the chapel at Rouen Castle in *October* 1442, when the Duke of York was given permission by the cathedral to borrow certain liturgical ware from the cathedral. However, that claim seems ridiculous. Edward must have been born by June 1442, because two months later his mother was once again pregnant (carrying her third son, the future Edmund).[23] In the fifteenth century no baptism would ever have been delayed for more than four months after a child's birth. At that time baptism was seen as the way of safeguarding the soul of a child who, if (s)he died unbaptised would be consigned to 'limbo'.

In the end, as Scofield concluded, the surviving evidence in respect of where Edward (IV) was (or was not) baptised 'is of too negative a character to be of much value'.[24] Scofield's case seems to be a good one. Like the precise date of Edward's birth (and conception), his place of baptism remains unconfirmed.

It seems that Edward's younger brother, Edmund, was subsequently baptised at Rouen Cathedral on the day immediately following his birth in 1443. As for their younger sister, Elizabeth, her christening also took place at the cathedral, and the service was celebrated within ten days of the baby girl's birth in 1444.[25]

Some historians have assumed that the lack of evidence in the case of Edward proves that he was definitely not baptised at the cathedral – and that this can be taken as proof that he was illegitimate. Their argument is that only illegitimacy could explain why the little boy's baptism might have been considered insignificant by the Duke of York. However, the surviving letters written by the Duke of York in 1445, in which he names Edward as his son and heir and seeks to arrange a royal marriage for him, definitely prove that in the 1440s Edward was accepted by Cecily's husband as his own legitimate son.

Unfortunately one thing which is very obvious is the fact that the arguments put forward in respect of Edward's place of baptism and what that might show clearly indicate that some recent historians have little understanding of fifteenth-century (and modern) Christianity. Thus they do not perceive what baptism meant (and means) in its religious context. Instead, they simply seem to see baptism as a social event, allowing the family to celebrate the arrival of an offspring. But, as we have already seen, at medieval baptisms family members were not required to be present, and they may well normally have been absent. Indeed, in the case of mothers, absence was virtually certain.

For Christians, baptism is not primarily a social event. It is a ritual of great religious significance. In the medieval period, if a child seemed weak or sickly when (s)he was born, (s)he had to be baptised as rapidly as possible for the sake of his or her soul's salvation. Neither then nor in the present day is it necessary for a baptism to be carried out in a church. A child can be baptised anywhere. Nor is it necessary for the ritual of baptism to be carried out by a priest. Any Christian can perform the rite.

As we have seen, when Edward was born the Duke and Duchess of York had probably already lost their first son, Henry. What therefore emerges from the surviving evidence (or lack thereof) in respect of the baptism of their second son is the possibility that, when Edward was born, there may have been some anxiety about his state of health. For that reason the decision may have been taken to baptise the new-born child as rapidly as possible, in the nearest convenient location. Perhaps the next two York babies – Edmund and Elizabeth – seemed healthier and more vigorous when they came into the world. For that reason decisions may have been taken to baptise them more publicly.

On 19 November 1443, after his third son, Edmund had been born, but at a time when his wife had not yet conceived their second daughter, Richard's authority in Normandy was formally recognised by Pope Eugene IV. The pope then wrote once again to the Duke of York:

> Exhorting him to favour Martin, bishop of Avranches, Peter Francisci, canon of Evreux, and Ralph Herbert, clerk, of the diocese of Bayeux, whom the pope has appointed to be vicars-general of Peter, bishop of Evreux, in those places of the diocese of Evreux which are and which shall be subject to the temporal dominion of Henry, king of England.[26]

Evreux lies just to the south of Rouen, where the Duke and Duchess of York and their three living children were then resident.

It was presumably at the Castle of Rouen that Anne of York and her two younger brothers, Edward, and Edmund, were now growing up, under the care of Anne de Caux and other French women. Although their parents and some other people – including John Talbot, Earl of Shrewsbury – may have addressed the children in English, presumably Anne de Caux, and the other women caring for them, regularly communicated with their charges in French. Thus the children must have become bilingual.

Later evidence in the case of Edward (IV) clearly shows that he had an excellent command of the French language. Philippe de Commynes reported that Edward spoke 'quite good French',[27] and he had certainly met the king

Seal of Richard, Duke of York and governor of France (17th century engraving).

personally on several occasions in a diplomatic context. In 1475 Commynes also saw a letter which had been sent by Edward IV to King Louis XI of France. The letter was written in French of a quality so impressive that Commynes felt that 'no Englishman could have had a hand in composing it!'[28]

As the York children grew a little older, their parents must also have started planning for their futures. In 1447, after the family had returned from France to England, the eldest daughter, Anne, was married to her cousin, Henry Holland, Duke of Exeter. In the English context that was a high-ranking marriage for Anne, and in all probability plans for her marriage had been negotiated by her parents while Anne and her family were in France.

As for the male children, although Edward and Edmund were still very small, in 1445 their father began formally negotiating a French royal marriage for

Edward. The little boy's planned bride was to be one of the daughters of King Charles VII. Some of the relevant correspondence survives, and it shows clearly that King Charles was in favour of the plan. However, some disagreement then ensued over which of the French king's daughters would have been the most suitable consort for Edward. Probably it was as a result of that disagreement that no French royal marriage for young Edward ever actually took place.

The context of the French royal marriage negotiations for her son, Edward, may have produced one intriguing – but influential – meeting for Cecily, Duchess of York. As her husband explained to Charles VII, in a letter which he wrote to the French king at Rouen on 18 April 1445, Richard's reply to Charles's earlier correspondence in respect of the plans for Edward's marriage had been somewhat delayed.

> Your said letters by me received, I was immediately inclined to send my ambassadors to your highness, for the business; a thing which I could not do and accomplish so speedily as I could well have wished, in consequence of the arrival, on this side, of my lady the queen [*Margaret of Anjou*], whom, after that she was brought to and had arrived at the town of Pontoise, I have accompanied, as reason was, until she had embarked on the sea to go into England to the king, your nephew, and my sovereign lord. [29]

Margaret of Anjou, whose paternal aunt was Marie of Anjou, the cousin and queen consort of Charles VII, had been chosen as the consort of King Henry VI. Margaret was 'a good-looking and well-developed girl',[30] described as dark,[31] and she was about fifteen years old when the Duke of York received her at Rouen. Her reception by him probably took place in March 1444/5, because in February Margaret had attended the marriage of her elder sister, Yolande, in Nancy, prior to beginning her own journey to Rouen via Paris.[32]

It seems that Margaret may have suffered from some health problems during her journey to England, on which she was accompanied by John Talbot, Earl of Shrewsbury, together maybe with his second wife, Margaret Beauchamp, and possibly also some of his children. At Rouen 'she was not well enough to attend the splendid welcoming pageant, and her place in the procession was taken by the duchess of Suffolk.'[33] Nevertheless, presumably the young royal bride must have been seen and attended in person, not only by the Duke of York (as he states clearly in his letter), but also by his wife. It seems that Cecily must also have taken part in the formal reception pageant which was held. After all, the Duchess of Suffolk, who was playing the leading role in that pageant, was

Cecily Neville's friend (during the period 1445-1455), Margaret of Anjou, Queen of England, at prayer. Redrawn after a miniature of 1475, in the London Skinners' Fraternity of the Assumption Guild Book.

Cecily's second cousin, Alice Chaucer. For details of their blood relationship see below, Chapter 8.

At the time of the meeting in Rouen, Cecily would have been about twice Margaret's age, while her husband, Richard, would have been about thirty-four years old. As for Cecily's second cousin, the Duchess of Suffolk, she would have been about forty. When the reception of Margaret took place at Rouen, for Cecily it was about six months after the birth of her most recent child, her second daughter, Elizabeth. Superficially, it might therefore appear potentially significant that the York baby in question was subsequently married to her slightly older relative, John de la Pole (later second Duke of Suffolk). In other words, Elizabeth of York's eventual husband was Alice Chaucer's son! However, his own parents initially planned to marry young John to another cousin – Lady Margaret Beaufort, daughter of the Earl of Somerset. It was only after his father had been disgraced and killed (2 May 1450) that the original marriage project was formally annulled (February 1452/3), in order that Margaret Beaufort could be married to the king's half-brother, Edmund, Earl of Richmond. After that, at some point, a new plan was made to marry John to Elizabeth (see below, Chapter 6).

As for the young Margaret of Anjou, following her marriage to Henry VI, she is recorded as having maintained very close relationships with the Duke and Duchess of Suffolk. Probably she felt that they virtually held the role of her surrogate parents in England. In particular, 'relations between the queen and the duchess of Suffolk seem to have been close. Alice was the regular recipient of gifts of jewels and other favours from the queen until 1450.'[34]

Yet, intriguingly, for almost ten years after Margaret became Queen of England, there also seems to have been a close relationship between her and Cecily Neville:

> It should not be assumed that the queen had always regarded York as a dynastic threat. He and the duchess are recorded as regular recipients of gifts in the queen's jewel accounts between 1445 and 1453. An undated letter written by Cecily, duchess of York, to Margaret some time during her pregnancy indicates that the duchess saw the queen as a possible mediator between her husband and the king.[35]

The Duke of York's letter to Margaret's uncle, Charles VII appears to confirm that initially he and his wife experienced no problem in dealing with Margaret. Thus it seems that the meeting between Richard, Cecily and Margaret which took place at Rouen in March 1444/5 must have gone well. Sadly, however, as will emerge later, considerable difficulties subsequently arose between them.

Chapter 5

Wife and Mother in Ireland

The Duke of York had done his best to avoid direct conflict in France with King Charles VII. However, Cardinal Beaufort, back in England, therefore arranged (and paid for) a costly military expedition led from England by his nephew, John Beaufort, Earl of Somerset. 'This expedition was to be independent of the duke of York as lieutenant-general, and in the area outside his control.'[1] In effect that somewhat undermined Richard's position as lieutenant in France. It was therefore in a way fortunate for him that the military expedition proved to be relatively unsuccessful. John Beaufort found himself incapable of forcing the French into battle, and he returned to England in disgrace. Even so, in 1443 he found himself elevated by Henry VI to the rank of Duke of Somerset. However, the new duke died in May 1444.

In 1445, when his tenure of the lieutenantship expired, the Duke of York also returned to England. Initially he hoped that he would be re-appointed to his role in France, but instead that post was assigned to another of Cardinal Beaufort's nephews. The individual in question was the younger brother of the late John Beaufort, Duke of Somerset. His name was Edmund Beaufort, and he was then the Marquis of Dorset. Also Edmund was that member of the Beaufort family whose hoped-for marriage with Henry V's widow, Catherine of France, had been ruled out some years earlier by the Duke of Gloucester.

In October 1445, when the Duke and Duchess of York returned to England, Cecily was once again pregnant – but only by about two months. She herself may already have been aware of the fact that another baby was on its way, but the information would probably not yet have been accessible to most people. As we have seen, both of her earlier recorded childbirths in England had apparently taken place at the episcopal palace of Hatfield. That residence had been available for use by the Duke and Duchess of York because the then Bishop of Ely was not actually resident in England. But unfortunately while Richard and Cecily lived in Normandy the situation in respect of the possible availability of the Hertfordshire manor house had changed. Cardinal Louis of Luxembourg had died in 1443. In the following year Bishop Thomas Bourchier had been appointed his successor in respect of the bishopric of Ely. Bishop Bourchier was a cousin of both the Duke and the Duchess of York. However, unlike Cardinal Louis, he was resident in England. Thus the new Bishop of Ely would himself have required the use of his manor house at Hatfield. As a result, following his return to his homeland in October 1445, Richard, Duke of York, now required some other residence within easy travelling distance of London for himself and his family. Two solutions for this need emerged, as we shall see shortly.

For his wife and family, one of the first significant events following their return to England from France was the marriage of their eldest daughter, Anne of York. Born in August 1439, Anne had been just two months past her sixth birthday when her family returned home. But it seems that her parents must already have been planning a suitable marriage for the little girl. Consequently, Anne found herself married to her cousin, the young Henry Holland, who later became the second – or third – Duke of Exeter.[2] It is alleged that the marriage was celebrated in January 1445/6 by Michael Hicks in the ODNB, but unfortunately no source for that proposed date is cited. Moreover, Hicks includes other potential errors in his account, such as the claim that Anne of York had been born at Fotheringhay.[3]

Born on 27 June 1430, Henry would have been just over nine years older than his little bride. Henry's mother, Lady Anne Stafford, had died in September 1432, when her son was only two years old. The little boy had subsequently been given two successive stepmothers by his father, John Holland, Duke of Exeter, who was still alive when his son was married. Like the Duke of York, the Duke of Exeter had served his cousin, the young King Henry VI, in France. Thus the two fathers had probably begun planning the marriage of their children before the Duke of York returned home.

The effect which her marriage had upon Anne is unclear. Normally a child bride would have been transferred to the care of her father-in-law and his (in this case third) wife until she attained the teenaged years at which her young husband would have been allowed to consummate their union. It is therefore probable that initially Anne was given into the care of her father-in-law. However, John, Duke of Exeter, died in August 1447. At that point, Anne's own father, Richard, Duke of York, was appointed the guardian of her young husband, Henry Holland. It is therefore probable that, even though Anne may initially have left her parents' home after her marriage, she was returned to the care of her own parents in the late summer of 1447, accompanied by her young spouse.

From 1446 to 1448 the Duke of York regularly attended royal council meetings. At first he used the guest house at Waltham Abbey in Essex as his new *pied-à-terre*. Moreover, it seems that on at least some occasions his wife was with him. For example, in May 1446, Cecily seems to have been at Waltham Abbey, because it was there that she reportedly gave birth to her third daughter, Margaret (see above, Chapter 3). Intriguingly, that latest York daughter could well have been named after Henry VI's young queen, Margaret of Anjou, who had been well received by her parents at Rouen roughly two years earlier. It is even possible that the young queen consort acted as one of Margaret of York's godmothers.

Given the apparent use of Waltham Abbey by both the Duke and the Duchess of York, it appears that, following their return to England, that religious house initially succeeded the episcopal manor house at Hatfield as the place where Cecily and her husband normally stayed when Richard needed to be in the vicinity of London and Westminster for English government reasons. Indeed, the situation was explicitly formalised on 26 October 1446, when an 'assignment for life' was made to 'Richard, duke of York, who will come often to London for the king's business and his own, for the livery of him and his horses, of the abbey and town of Waltham, as others have had hitherto there or elsewhere.'[4]

Curiously, however, just four months later the situation changed yet again. On 23 February 1446/7, the Duke of York's older cousin and friend, Humphrey of Lancaster, Duke of Gloucester, died – or was possibly murdered. As

Waltham Abbey Gate.

depicted holding the royal pedigree, in the front of an illuminated manuscript commissioned a year or two earlier by John Talbot, Earl of Shrewsbury, the Duke of Gloucester and the Duke of York appear to have resembled one another not only in their political standing, but also in terms of their facial appearance. But in terms of colouring, the Duke of York was apparently fairer than the Duke of Gloucester. As depicted in the manuscript, Humphrey is shown with mid brown hair, while the image of the Duke of York has fair hair (see plate 14).

These two royal dukes seem to have worked together in support of the reign of the Lancastrian child king, Henry VI. However, they had both experienced difficulties with their Lancastrian relatives of originally illegitimate descent – the Beaufort family. Ironically, that was, of course, the family to which the Duke of York's mother-in-law, Joan, Countess of Westmorland, belonged by birth. Yet in spite of his close relationship to the Beauforts by marriage, as we have seen, the Duke of York had already experienced certain problems with that family in respect of his role in France. He was to encounter further problems with the Beauforts later.

Initially, however, it was the Beauforts' closer royal relative, Humphrey, Duke of Gloucester, the heir presumptive to the English throne, who seems to have experienced the greatest difficulties as a result of the ambitions of some of his Beaufort kindred. Beaufort opposition to Humphrey might well have been one of the factors behind the disgrace in 1441 of his second wife, Eleanor Cobham. The key events in question had taken place while Richard and Cecily were both resident at Rouen in France. Thus neither of them had been present in England to take sides in what took place. However, it has already been established that the Duke of York was the friend of his older cousin, the Duke of Gloucester. Presumably, before he and his wife left for France, both of them must also have become acquainted with Eleanor Cobham, Humphrey's chosen second wife. Despite her low birth, initially Eleanor seems to have been well regarded by her husband's royal relatives, so the Duke and Duchess of York may have thought well of her, though there is no clear surviving evidence in this respect.

One of the key factors behind the eventual destruction of both the Duke and the Duchess of Gloucester was their apparent desire for children. Humphrey had produced two illegitimate children earlier. He was therefore obviously capable of becoming a father. Yet, ironically, he had sired no children by either of his wives. That was a situation with which both Richard and Cecily might have sympathised. Certainly evidence exists to show that later Cecily offered her support to another wife who appears to have experienced some difficulty in becoming a mother, even though the wife in question was eventually to be seen as opposed to the Duke of York (see below).

In respect of the family problem of the Duke and Duchess of Gloucester, it seems that Eleanor's failure to produce a son and heir for her husband made her desperate enough to explore the possible help of magic potions. Her London potion maker was Margery Jourdemayne, who also had other talents. These included a claim on her part to be able to foretell the future.

Maybe one day, in conversation, Eleanor asked Margery how long the young King Henry VI would live. After all, if Henry VI died childless, then Eleanor's husband would succeed to the throne, and Eleanor would suddenly find herself the Queen of England! However, if it became public knowledge, the asking of such a question about the life expectancy of the reigning monarch would have officially counted as treason at that period. And unfortunately for Eleanor Cobham, Margery Jourdemayne was also in the service of other significant people.

One of Margery's other clients was Edmund Beaufort, later Earl (1442), Marquis (1443), and finally Duke (1448) of Somerset. It is said that Margery prophesied to Edmund that he would die at 'the Castle'. But unfortunately, until he was later killed in battle at the Castle Inn of St Albans, Edmund was left speculating as to which castle his fortune teller had meant!

Maybe in the course of his meetings with Margery, Edmund had somehow become aware of the fact that she was also in the service of Eleanor Cobham. He may even have picked up from Margery's gossip the fact that on one occasion Eleanor had asked her an unwise question. Certainly the asking of that dangerous question was revealed (or alleged). As a result, Margery Jourdemayne was arrested and her home was searched.

It was claimed that amongst her possessions a small and partially melted wax image of a man was found. This was said to be a wax figure of the young king, and its partial melting was interpreted as an attempt by the sorceress to make the king ill. The assumption was that the ultimate aim would have been to bring about the death of Henry VI, thereby making Humphrey, Duke of Gloucester the next king, with his wife, Eleanor, as his consort.

Margery was put on trial, found guilty of witchcraft, and was then burned at the stake on 27 October 1441. Meanwhile Eleanor had also been arrested. Although she admitted using Margery's skills in an attempt to help her conceive, she denied all the other charges which were brought against her. However, she was found guilty of treason. First she was forced to do a public walk of penance through the streets of London. Then she was imprisoned for the rest of her life.

All this had occurred six years earlier, while the Duke and Duchess of York were far away in France. However, they must have been aware of what had taken place, and of its outcomes. As had probably been intended, the disgrace of the

Humphrey, Duke of Gloucester, and his second wife, Eleanor Cobham. Nineteenth-century engraving, based on a medieval manuscript illustration.

Duchess of Gloucester also destroyed her husband politically. Humphrey lost all power and influence. Then, on 20 February 1446/7, he too found himself arrested for treason. His subsequent death, at Bury St Edmunds, was perceived by some contemporaries as a probable murder engineered by the Beauforts, though in reality Humphrey may actually have died from natural causes.

Ironically, whatever it was that had brought about his death, one outcome of Humphrey's passing was the final acquisition of a permanent London residence on the part of the Duke and Duchess of York. This was because it seems that in his will Humphrey bequeathed his own London home – Baynard's Castle – to his dear cousin, Richard. The text of Humphrey's will does not survive, but it seems that a will did exist, and that its terms were carried out.[5] In the case of

Baynard's Castle, 'it came to the hands of Henry VI, and from him to Richard Duke of York'.[6] It was a fine up-to-date home, because 'in the year 1428, the 7th of Henry VI, a great fire was at Baynard's Castle, and that same Humphrey, Duke of Gloucester, built it of new.'[7] At the same time Richard was widely perceived as having now succeeded the Duke of Gloucester as the heir presumptive to the English throne. Suddenly the Duke and Duchess of York now found themselves as the second highest ranking man and woman in the kingdom.

But despite the fact that he and his family now had their own abode in the capital, Richard's good relationship with his cousin, the late Duke of Gloucester, now made his role in English government far from clear. Moreover, his status as heir presumptive to the throne was apparently contested by Edmund Beaufort, currently Marquis of Dorset, who, in 1444, had replaced the Duke of York as Lieutenant of France.

One outcome of all this was the fact that the Duke of York and his family may have begun to spend more time in other places which were part of Richard's family inheritance. For example, in the summer of 1447 his wife, Cecily, seems to have been residing at Fotheringhay Castle. That was where she reportedly gave birth to her son, William (see above, Chapter 3). For Cecily's husband, London was now a potentially troublesome location. Those who now held power on behalf of Henry VI – the Earl of Suffolk and the Marquis of Somerset – were not Richard's friends, and they seem not to have wanted him to continue to hold any power, either in England or in France. A bizarre outcome of this was the fact that, on 30 July 1447, the Duke of York unexpectedly found himself formally appointed Lieutenant of Ireland.

Curiously the person whom the Duke of York replaced in that post was John Talbot, Earl of Shrewsbury, one of the leading English generals with whom he had worked so effectively in France. Although Talbot's first wife had been Cecily Neville's cousin, Maud, his second wife was Margaret Beauchamp. Margaret's younger sister, Eleanor, was the wife of Edmund Beaufort. It therefore seems that the Marquis of Somerset (who was soon to be elevated to the rank of duke) felt that he needed the effective military experience of his Talbot brother-in-law to support him in his new post in France.

Initially, the Duke of York did not leave England to take up his Irish post in person. Instead he appointed Richard Nugent, Baron Devlin, to act as his deputy in Ireland. Meanwhile, Richard himself mostly remained in England. As for Cecily, in November 1448 she is reported to have been resident at Westminster, where she was staying at Neyte, a manor belonging to the Abbot of Westminster. It was there that she reputedly gave birth to her son, John (see above, Chapter 3).

However, her husband appears to have gone back to Rouen in February 1448/9. Possibly Cecily accompanied her husband on his short visit back to France. Either way, the fact is clear that on one winter's night – either in France (in February) or in England (late in January) – the York couple must have made love once again. The fact that they made love at about that time is a *sine qua non*, because that was when their next son, George (later Duke of Clarence), was conceived.

Whether the baby was conceived in England or in France, Cecily now found herself embarking on yet another pregnancy. For her, as probably for her mother before her, that must have long since come to seem the norm of her married life. Meanwhile, in May 1449, she herself may have reached the age of thirty-four. Curiously, there are only two mentions of Cecily by name in the Patent Rolls of King Henry VI. The first of these dates from ten days after her possible thirty-fourth birthday. On Tuesday 13 May 1449 a licence was granted:

> for 20 marks paid in the hanaper, for Richard, duke of York, and Cecily his wife to grant to John, bishop of St Davids, and Griffin ap Nicholas, esquire, their heirs and assigns, the castle, manor, town and lordship of Nerberth in the march of Wales, held in chief.[8]

A month later, in June 1449, Richard finally set off for Dublin. In England at this time he was probably still widely perceived as a loyal servant of the Lancastrian regime. However, he was no longer popular with the powers behind the throne of Henry VI, the chief of whom was William de la Pole, who had recently been upgraded to the rank of Duke of Suffolk.[9] Thus the Duke of York now decided to take up his lieutenancy in Ireland in person, in spite of the fact that his appointment there had not generally been perceived as a compliment. Indeed, some contemporaries described the post as an exile or a banishment.[10] Nevertheless, in Ireland Richard was likely to be well-received. He had inherited lands there from his Mortimer ancestors. From them he had also inherited Anglo-Irish noble ancestry – including direct descent from native Irish royalty.

The last two Earls of March of the Mortimer family had both died in Ireland.[11] The Duke of Suffolk may have found himself hoping that the Duke of York would follow the example of his two Mortimer predecessors in this respect. Suffolk, who had been formally appointed a member of the royal council in November 1431, had become an influential figure there in the mid 1430s, and subsequently profited from the Duke of Gloucester's opposition to Cardinal Beaufort to take over power there. But of course, in spite of his friendship with

Domnall Mór Ua Briain, King of Thomond
|
daughter m William de Burgh
|
Richard Mór de Burgh, Lord of Connaught
|
Walter de Burgh, Earl of Ulster
|
Richard Óg de Burgh, Earl of Ulster
|
William Donn de Burgh, Earl of Ulster
|
Elizabeth de Burgh, Duchess of Clarence
|
Philippa of Clarence, Countess of March and Ulster
|
Roger Mortimer, Earl of March and Ulster
|
Anne Mortimer, Countess of Cambridge
|
Richard, Duke of York

The Royal Irish Ancestry of the Duke of York

the Duke of Gloucester, Richard, Duke of York had so far shown no sign of attempting to seize power for himself. So one possible motive for such a hope on Suffolk's part may have been the fact that he was then experiencing illegal rivalry in East Anglia from John Mowbray, Duke of Norfolk.[12] The Duke of Norfolk was the son of Catherine Neville, the elder sister of Cecily. He was therefore a nephew by marriage of the Duke of York, for whom he was later to show strong support and friendship.

It is often thought that Suffolk may have been supported in his negative hopes in respect of the Duke and Duchess of York by the young girl from France whom Suffolk and his wife, Alice Chaucer, had virtually fostered. This was Henry VI's consort, Margaret of Anjou, who was now about nineteen years of age. However, firm evidence does exist which appears to prove that Queen Margaret continued to show favour to the Duke and Duchess of York until 1453 by granting them gifts (see above, Chapter 4).

Yet attempts certainly seem to have been made by someone close to the throne to prevent Richard from reaching the Irish capital.

> Royal commands were dispatched to Cheshire, to the Welsh Marches and the seaports in Wales that the Duke was not to reach his destination. Among those sent to waylay him was Sir Thomas Stanley, of an old Cheshire family, whose sons would repeat the act against York's sons.[13]

However, in spite of this the Duke of York and his family found themselves well-protected *en route*. Thus they arrived safely at their destination.

Cecily definitely travelled to Ireland with her husband. And for those who saw the couple on their journey it must by that time have become obvious that the Duchess of York was once again pregnant. 'On July 6 the Duke of York landed at Howth "with great pomp and glory", accompanied by his wife and a number of troops.'[14] He was honourably received in Dublin, where 'the Earls of Ireland went into his house, as did also the Irish adjacent to Meath, and gave him as many beeves for the use of his kitchen as it pleased him to demand.'[15]

Meanwhile in France, in August 1449, fighting recommenced between the French and the English. The English forces now found themselves commanded by Edmund Beaufort, who had recently been upgraded from Marquis to Duke of Somerset. But in spite of his recent promotion, he proved useless as the English military commander. As a result, by the following year virtually all the English possessions in northern France had been lost.

On 21 October 1449, at Dublin Castle in Ireland, Cecily gave birth to her son, George (see above, Chapter 3). Previous writers have suggested that the other York children would probably not have accompanied their parents to Dublin. For example, it has been suggested that the fact that Henry Holland was granted livery of his land on 23 July 1450, may imply that he and his little wife, Anne of York, were then in England. However, it seems questionable whether the granting of livery would have required the young couple to be physically present. It has also been claimed that in 1449 Cecily's two sons, Edward and Edmund, were already established at Ludlow Castle. They were certainly based there later, but there is no particular reason to suppose that Ludlow was already their residence in 1449. It has also been suggested that Elizabeth of York might have been boarding in another noble household, while the very young Margaret of York might simply have been left behind in the nursery at Fotheringhay Castle, under the supervision either of the future Edward IV's former nurse, Anne of Caux, or of the future Richard III's nurse, Joan Malpas.[16]

There appears to be a widespread assumption that Fotheringhay Castle was always the principal York family residence. But there is no real evidence for that view. Incidentally, it has also been suggested that Anne of Caux nursed all the York children. In reality, however, she definitely seems never to have nursed the

Dublin Castle.

future King Richard III, because in 1484, when he renewed her annual grant, he only named her as Edward IV's nurse.[17] Moreover, in 1483 Joan Malpas (Peysmersh) was granted an annuity by Richard III for her service to him and his mother in his youth.[18] As for the view that Fotheringhay Castle was the main family residence, and that York children may simply have been left there under domestic care, that appears to be based largely on the dubious Worcester Annals List 2, which suggests that most of the offspring were born there. However, Worcester Annals List 1 suggests that there was a lot of movement, and that various children were born in different locations, depending on where their parents were based at the moment when their offspring came into the world.

Presumably, in reality, the family nurses accompanied the Duke and Duchess of York in their movements. After all, when Cecily travelled to Ireland, she must have known that another baby was on the way. She would therefore have needed trustworthy women in her entourage, so that they would be on hand to assist her when the next child was born. It would probably also have seemed much safer for the couple to take their children with them to Richard's loving ancestral home of Ireland, rather than leave them behind in an England which (at the highest level, at least) now seemed to be rather hostile in respect of the Duke of York and his family.

The York family trip to Ireland clearly reveals how significant were its ancestral links with that country. The official residence of the Lieutenant of Ireland was Dublin Castle. Therefore that was probably where Cecily resided from the summer of 1449 until after little George was born. However, her husband left Dublin for Trim and then marched on through Ulster. His trip included his first viewing of his own large hereditary Irish home, Trim Castle, where he and his family were subsequently to spend some of their time in Ireland. Nevertheless, the Duke of York had returned to Dublin by October, for a meeting of the Irish Parliament, so probably he was back at Dublin Castle prior to the birth of his third living son, George.

As for his wife, Cecily, who had remained at Dublin Castle, it seems that she too:

> had made an impression on the Irish heart, as when O'Byrne presented her with two hobbys'. … [Thus] it was a highly popular event when on October 21, 1449, the viceroy's third son was born in Dublin. … The bond already formed between the House of York and Ireland was doubly strengthened by this event. The young prince was looked upon as 'one of ourselves', an Irishman by birth as well as descent, and the devotion to his name was shown years later when Lambert Simnel was crowned King in Dublin in the belief that he was Clarence's son, Edward of Warwick.'[19]

It seems to have been in the third week of October that Cecily produced the little boy who may have been her ninth child. As usual she will have been closeted in her private suite – this time at Dublin Castle – during the last weeks of her pregnancy. Subsequently, following her safe delivery, she would once more have been required to spend some weeks in seclusion. The popular belief was that

Seal of Cecily Neville (17th century engraving).

until mothers were 'churched' they were bound to become victims of attacks by evil forces if they dared to venture out of doors.

Meanwhile her new-born son was baptised in Dublin's Dominican Priory Church of St Saviour.[20] This Blackfriars' church stood just across the river Liffey, about half a kilometre northwest of Dublin Castle. Once again, the christening party would have been led by the three godparents, bearing Cecily's latest offspring. On this occasion the identity of the godmother is not recorded, but the baby's two godfathers were rival Irish aristocrats: James Fitgerald, 6th Earl of Desmond and James Butler, 4th Earl of Ormonde.[21]

At the door of the church the party would have been received by a priest – possibly the Dominican Prior himself – who would have blessed the infant and put a few grains of salt into his mouth. This *sal sapientia* was symbolic of wisdom. Then the priest would have led the party through the church door, to the font, where the godparents were required to profess Christian religious belief on behalf of their godson. Then, one of them would have held the naked boy over the font while the priest poured holy water over the baby's head and gave him his Christian name. The little boy was given the name of George. Possibly it was derived from one of his mother's nephews, Canon George Neville (who was later to be appointed Bishop of Exeter and then Archbishop of York). Cecily's Neville relationships seem to have been valued. Indeed, it was certainly sometimes the case that members of Cecily's family acted as godparents for the children of others. Two years later, Cecily herself was to become the godmother of one of her great nieces, Isabel Neville, who would later marry Cecily's son, George (see below, Chapter 6).

After Cecily had re-emerged from her apartments at Dublin Castle and been purified by her churching, she and those of her children who were with her in Ireland seem to have settled at the family Castle of Trim. This was a splendid property which the Duke of York had inherited from his Mortimer ancestors. The family seems to have liked Trim Castle, because Richard now spent both time and money on its restoration.

Chapter 6

The End of Maternity

Meanwhile, across the seas in France the English were being defeated, while in England, the Duke of 'Suffolk's tottering regime had more or less collapsed … [so that] on 28 January, the king and the lords reluctantly agreed to imprison Suffolk in the Tower of London.'[1] A trial ensued, and demands were made for the Duke of Suffolk to be executed. He himself attempted to escape to Flanders. But on the way his boat was seized by a ship called *Nicholas of the Tower* and Suffolk was put to death by his captors as a traitor.

Subsequently, in England a rebellion took place against the government of Henry VI (May–July 1450). The rebellion in England was led by a man who is usually called John (or Jack) Cade, but who seems himself to have used the name John Mortimer. In reality there is:

> no evidence at all that he had any family ties with the aristocratic Mortimers. His decision to assume the name John Mortimer looks to have been a ploy to gain public support by the suggestion that he was connected to the duke of York, a magnate popularly regarded as neglected by the king and, moreover, one untainted by allegations of misgovernment.[2]

However, despite the lack of evidence for a Mortimer connection, it does seem that Jack Cade might possibly have had contact of some kind with the Duke and Duchess of York some years earlier.

> According to the royal proclamation issued for his capture in the summer of 1450, he had worked in sorcery, was a former soldier who had fought at one time for enemy France, and was a murderer, who had fled the household of Sir Thomas Dacre in Sussex after killing a pregnant woman.[3]

This means that Cade had earlier been in the service of Cecily's half-sister, Philippa Neville, and her husband, Sir Thomas Dacre. But of course he may not have been well regarded by the Dacre family and their relatives.

> The duke of York's enemies were later to try to implicate the duke as a moving figure behind Cade's rebellion, but this is unlikely to have been the case. Had he been so, he would surely not have waited until at least two months after the rising was over before returning to England from Ireland'.[4]

Nevertheless, after Cade's rebellion 'several of Cade's grievances were echoed by the Yorkist lords who revolted against Henry VI'.[5]

It was only in September 1450, eleven months after the birth of his latest son, George, that the Duke of York suddenly made a decision to leave Ireland and return with his wife and children to England. There seem to have been two reasons for his decision. The first point was a need he had for more troops and more funding in order to consolidate the English position in Ireland. But although he had put his request to London some months earlier, he had received no response. The second point was the government situation back in England. There, Edmund Beaufort, Duke of Somerset, a distant cousin of the Duke of York, and a much closer cousin of his wife, Cecily, now seemed to be assuming a strong position, which the Duke of York resented.

> It is clear that York's return from Ireland in September 1450 was precipitated by Somerset's own return in August, following the English defeat at Formigny and his surrender of Caen. They clashed in the parliament of November 1450, Somerset's castle of Corfe was ransacked by York's tenants, and he himself was attacked by men of York's retinue and ended up in the Tower of London, probably under compulsion, since the king had to intervene to secure his release in December.[6]

As has been seen, York had already experienced a certain rivalry with Edmund Beaufort's elder brother and predecessor, John Beaufort, Duke of Somerset (died 1444), in respect of his government of France. Now it seemed that John's younger brother, Edmund, was trying to put himself forward as the potential heir presumptive to the English throne, should King Henry VI die without a direct heir. However, the understanding of the Duke of York, and of many other people, was that, following the death of the Duke of Gloucester, York himself was now the Lancastrian heir to the throne.[7] It was also said by a contemporary that 'the comones of this lande hated this duk Edmond and loued the duk of York, because he loued the communes and preserued the commune profyte of the londe.'[8]

Baynard's Castle.

On St Faith's Day – Tuesday 6 October 1450 – William Wayte wrote to John Paston: 'Syr, and it plese, I was in my Lorde of Yorks howse [presumably Baynard's Castle], and I herde meche thynge more thanne my mastyr [Judge Yelverton] wrytyth un to yow of.'[9] 'This letter must have been written just after the Duke of York came over from Ireland in 1450, when he demanded that justice should be fairly administered against persons accused'.[10] It therefore seems that in the first full week of October 1450 the Duke and Duchess of York were resident in the London abode which Richard had inherited a few years earlier from his cousin, the previous Lancastrian heir presumptive, Humphrey, Duke of Gloucester.

However, it seems that Richard did not remain in London, because it was probably later that same week when 'my Maister Calthorp hadde writyng fro my Lord of York to awayte on hym at his coming in to Norffolk to be oon of his men.'[11] And 'my Lord shall be atte Walsingham on Sonday nest comynge [possibly Sunday 18 October], a from thens he shall go to Norwych.'[12] Perhaps

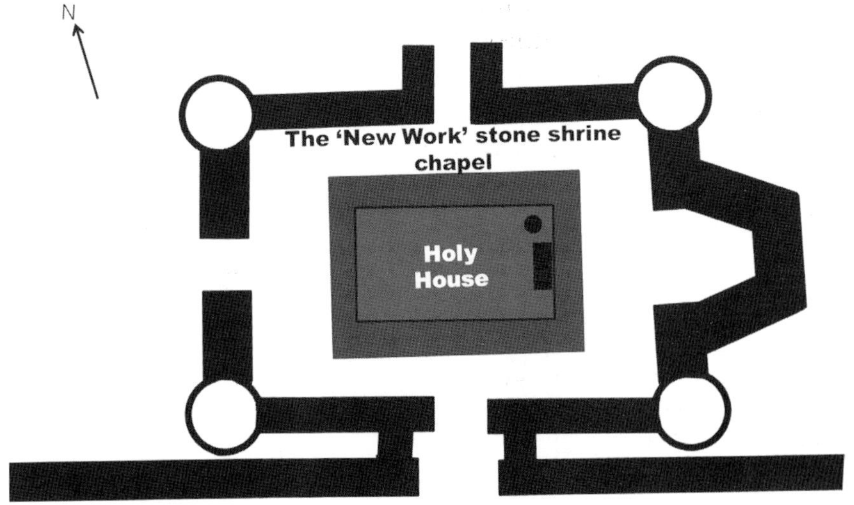

Plan of the 'New Work' stone shrine, built round the Holy House of Walsingham c.1450–1460. Based upon the excavation of 1961.

significantly, it may well have been in 1450 that the decision was taken to build a new shrine chapel at Walsingham. The original shrine chapel, 'the Holy House', had been built of wood in about 1061. That timber building was now about five hundred years old. Subsequently the large Augustinian Priory Church had been built – and later rebuilt – beside it, on its southern side. However, it was in about 1450 that work began on a new stone shrine chapel, enclosing the original timber Holy House.[13] Possibly Richard and Cecily were responsible for that decision and for that work to update the facilities at the shrine.

A trip to East Anglia definitely does seem to have taken place, because on Friday 16 October the Duke of Norfolk, who may then have been on the way to Walsingham with his mother's younger sister's husband, reported from Bury St Edmunds that 'oure unkill of York and we have fully appoynted and agreed of such ij persones for to be knights of shire of Norffolk as oure said unkill and we thinke convenient and necessarie for the welfare of the said shire.'[14] One of the two candidates who had been selected on this occasion was the Duke of Norfolk's cousin, John Howard, who later became Sir John Howard (1461), Lord Howard (1469/70), and finally the first Howard Duke of Norfolk (1483).

Richard, Duke of York and his wife, Cecily Neville, were of more or less the same generation as John Howard, a Suffolk-born gentleman who was to prove to be a very important Yorkist supporter. Indeed, Howard was a distant relative of both the Duke and the Duchess of York. Since Cecily and her husband were both great grandchildren of Edward III, they shared King Edward I with John Howard as a common ancestor.

It was apparently via his Mowbray cousin, the third Duke of Norfolk, that John Howard came to know and be known by the Duke of Norfolk's uncle by marriage, Richard, Duke of York. As we have seen, Richard had certainly come to know John Howard by the 1450s, despite the fact that at that time Howard was then still a relatively insignificant figure. Evidently he seems to have been perceived as a trustworthy and loyal servant by the Duke of York. John Howard's connections with both the Duke and the Duchess of York were to prove long lasting. His role in respect of Cecily will be examined later (see below, Chapter 7). It proves that she too must have met John Howard and got to know him in the 1450s.

Obviously it is therefore tempting to believe that the Duchess of York accompanied her husband to East Anglia, and on his pilgrimage to Walsingham – a holy place with which Richard had a tremendous family connection through his maternal line of Mortimer ancestors and their antecedents. That connection made the Duke of York the hereditary patron of the shrine. Indeed, it is even just possible – though by no means certain – that he was descended from, or related to, the gentlewoman Rychold (probably pronounced Rik-hold),[15] who had reportedly received apparitions of the Blessed Virgin at Walsingham in 1061, together with her request for the foundation of the Holy House, to receive future pilgrims. Cecily was certainly familiar with the Walsingham shrine, as she shows in a letter written almost three years later (see below).

Of course, Cecily may already once again have been about three months pregnant in October 1450 (see above, Chapter 3), because it is possible that in the following April she gave birth to her son, Thomas, who died soon afterwards. And the birth (and death) of Thomas may have taken place at Baynard's Castle in London. That was because on 11 November 1450, after the pilgrimage to Walsingham and other business in the Eastern Counties had been completed, a letter was written at Westminster which reported that 'it is seid here that the Duke of York and the Duke of Norffolk shulln not come here this vii nyght.'[16] Presumably the writer meant that they were then known to be on their way back to the capital, but that the return journey was thought likely to take them more than a week.

Meanwhile, the Duke of Somerset had become the effective head of Henry VI's English government. Edmund Beaufort had begun attending council meetings as soon as he returned to England in August 1450. In September he was given the post of constable, which effectively made him the military commander. Early in the following year he was also appointed captain of Calais.

Given that his return to England followed on from his defeat in France it seems very strange that Henry VI should have chosen to trust his cousin Somerset as England's military commander. One possible explanation could be that it was not the king himself who made this decision, but his consort, Margaret of Anjou. She definitely seems to have favoured Somerset, and by 1451 she was paying him an annuity of 100 marks. It is even possible that she had a love affair with him.

The fact emerged earlier that in the 1430s Edmund Beaufort had a love affair with another French-born queen consort of England. The queen in question had been Henry V's widow and Henry VI's mother, Catherine of France. Catherine had loved Edmund Beaufort so much that she sought permission to marry him. But consent for a second marriage was denied her by a parliament meeting in Leicester. The opposition to her planned Beaufort marriage had been led by Humphrey, Duke of Gloucester. Even so, it is possible that Catherine's second son, Edmund, Earl of Richmond, was fathered by the man whom his mother loved, and whose christian name he shared.

Although he had failed to marry Queen Catherine, and had subsequently wedded Eleanor Beauchamp, by whom he produced quite a large family, Edmund Beaufort now seems to have become closely associated with the new English queen consort, Margaret of Anjou. It may therefore have been Margaret who backed Edmund's tenure of power in England – a position from which it initially proved impossible for the Duke of York to topple him.

Meanwhile Richard wished to secure official recognition of his role as heir presumptive to the throne of his young cousin, Henry VI, who was still childless, and whose mental level already seemed to be such that he had no real control of his kingdom. Richard's chamberlain, Sir William Oldhall from Norfolk, was chosen as Speaker of the House of Commons, and the Commons backed Richard and opposed Edmund Beaufort. But although Edmund Beaufort was then arrested, shortly afterwards the king (or queen) had him released.

The following year was a difficult one for Richard and Cecily. In September 1451 Cecily, presumably accompanied by her husband, apparently stayed for a while at Warwick Castle. There, Cecily's nephew, Richard Neville, was now residing, together with his wife, Anne Beauchamp. As a result of his marriage to Anne, Richard Neville had recently acquired the title of Earl of Warwick (though his tenure of some of the Warwick lands was disputed by the husbands of some of Anne's siblings, notably, Edmund Beaufort, Duke of Somerset, who was married to Anne's half sister, Eleanor Beauchamp). In September 1451

Anne produced Richard Neville's first child – a daughter who was given the name of Isabel – and Cecily became one of the baby girl's godmothers, a fact which is recorded by the underlined words in the later papal dispensation which permitted Cecily's son, George, to marry Isabel:

> *Dispensatio Pauli PP iii [sic for ii] de matrimonio contrahendo inter nobilem virum Georgium Ducem Clarencie & Isabellam filiam nobilis viri Ricardi Nevill Comites Warwici, licet ipse Georgius & Isabella secundo & tertio & tertio & quarto consanguinitatis gradibus coniuncti sunt, Ac etiam licet mater ipsius Georgij eundem Isabellam de sacro fonte levavit. Datum Rome apud sanctam Petrum pridie Idus Martij Anno 1468 7 Edwardi 4ti.*[17]

Later, the York family travelled on north-westwards from Warwick. They spent the Christmas of that year at Ludlow Castle in Shropshire, with their children. It may possibly have been at this point that Richard and Cecily began establishing their two eldest surviving sons (who were then approaching their ninth and eight birthdays respectively) at Ludlow Castle. Certainly Edward and Edmund were resident there a little later in the 1450s.[18]

Obviously while they were staying at Ludlow Castle the York couple made productive love once more. Thus when England made its way into the year 1452 Cecily again found herself pregnant. As for Richard, by 22 February 1451/2 he had journeyed near to Northampton, preparing to march south and enter London. However, in Northampton King Henry VI – or the power behind his throne – was obviously not reassured by Richard's claim that he wished to remove traitors. Orders were therefore sent out that the Duke of York should be denied entry to London.[19]

Finding himself unable to enter the capital, Richard spent three days camped at Kingston-upon-Thames. The royal government had also hoped to prevent the Duke of York from entering Kent, which had recently been the focus of Jack Cade's rebellion. But that proved impossible. Maybe Richard simply made for his own estate at Erith, near Dartford in Kent.[20] He then met the king and his army at Blackheath. No fighting took place on that occasion, because the Duke of York was simply invited to come and put his complaints against Edmund Beaufort to the king in person. However, that turned out to be merely a cunning way of dealing with the dangerous situation. When he reached the royal camp, Richard found himself disarmed. He was then taken back to London under guard as a virtual prisoner. At St Paul's Cathedral, on 10 March, he was then forced to take a public oath not to rebel again.

The whereabouts of Cecily during this difficult and stressful time is unknown. Possibly when Richard left Ludlow Castle she accompanied him in the direction of Northampton. But it seems unlikely that she would then have followed him down to Kent. By 2 October 1452 it seems that she was probably at Fotheringhay Castle. There she reportedly gave birth to her son, the future King Richard III (see above, Chapter 3).

Probably her husband again spent Christmas with her, and a couple of months afterwards they seem to have made productive love once again, because as 1453 advanced, Cecily once again found herself pregnant. However, this was now a very stressful time both for her and for Richard. Those facts emerge clearly from a surviving petitionary letter which Cecily wrote in 1453 – probably in August or September (see below) – to the Queen Margaret of Anjou, who was then pregnant. The original text of the letter reads as follows:[21]

> Beseecheth with all humbleness and reverence possible your lowly obeisant servant and bedewoman, Cecily, Duchess of York that, whereof the plenty of your good and benign grace it pleased thereunto in your coming from that blessed, gracious and devout pilgrimage of our Lady of Walsingham to suffer the coming of my simple person — replete with such immeasurable sorrow and heaviness as I doubt not will of the continuance thereof diminish and abridge my days, as it does my worldly joy and comfort — unto your most worthy and most high presence, whereunto than [you pleased] full benignly to receive my supplication to the same, made for your humble, true man and servant, my lord my husband, whose infinite sorrow, unrest of heart and of worldly comfort, caused of that that he heareth him to be estranged from the grace and benevolent favour of that most Christian, most gracious and most merciful prince, the king our sovereign lord, whose majesty royal my said lord and husband now and ever, God knoweth, during his life hath been as true and as humble, and as obeisant leigeman, and to the performing of his noble pleasure and commandment as ready, as well-disposed, and as diligent at his power, and over that as glad, as joyful to be thereunto commanded as any creature alive, being specified in the said supplication, I beseech your highness and good grace, at the mercy of our Creator now ready to send His grace to all Christian persons, and of that blessed Lady to whom you late prayed, in whom aboundeth plenteously mercy and grace, by whose mediation it pleased our Lord to fulfil your right honourable body of the most precious, most joyful, and most comfortable earthly

> treasure that might come unto this land and to the people thereof, the which I beseech His abundant grace to prosper in you, and at such as it pleaseth Him to bring into this world, with all honour, gracious speed and felicity, with also of furthermore supplication of blessed and noble fruit of your said body, for the great trust and most comfortable surety and weal of this realm and of the king's true liege people of the same, to call the good speed of the matters contained in this said supplication into the gracious and tender recommendation of your highness. Whereunto I should for the same have without sloth or discontinuance and with undelayed diligence have sued, nor had by the disease and infirmity that since my said being in your highness presence hath grown and groweth, upon me caused not only the encumberous labour, to me full painful and uneasy, God knoweth, that then I took upon me, but also the continuance and addition of such heaviness that I have taken, and take, for the consideration of the sorrow of my said lord and husband; and if it please your good grace not to take to any displeasure of strangeness that I have not diligently continued the suit of my said supplication unto your said highness, caused of the same infirmity not hid upon my wretched body. Wherefore I report me to God; and in reverence of whom, and of his said grace and mercy to you showed, it please [eftsones] unto your high nobility to be a tender and gracious mean unto the highness of our sovereign lord for the favour and benevolence of his hand to be showed unto my lord and husband, so that through the gracious mean of you, sovereign lady, he may and effectually obtain to have the same. Wherein I beseech your said highness that my said labour and pain may not be taken frivolously nor unfruitfully, but the more agreeable for my said lord unto your said good grace. Whereunto, notwithstanding my said infirmity, I should not have spared to have recontinued my said suit, if I could or might have done, that it should have pleased your nobility if that I should so have done the which, as it shall please thereunto I shall not let, not sparing pain that my body now suffice of any possibility to bear, or suffer, with God's grace, whom I shall pray to prosper your high estate in honour, joy and felicity.

The text of the letter itself is somewhat complex in its construction, possibly because Cecily was suffering from depression. It may therefore not be easy for all readers to understand precisely what she is saying. However, the contents of the letter can be summarized as follows.

Cecily is reminding Queen Margaret of Anjou that, on her way back from Walsingham, the queen had received her. At that time Cecily had been feeling low and depressed enough to reduce her life expectation. However, she had been received by the queen in order that she might beseech Margaret's help on behalf of her husband the Duke of York. He was also feeling low and depressed because of being estranged from King Henry VI, despite having always been the king's true, humble and obedient servant. In the letter she was writing, Cecily was now repeating the plea which she had put to the queen at their earlier meeting. By the mercy of God and of Our Lady of Walsingham (to whom Queen Margaret had been praying for the successful outcome of her pregnancy – and Cecily is now praying to God for Margaret – as she should have done for herself had she not been so depressed, because then she herself would not have suffered a painful and difficult labour) Cecily begs Margaret to ask the king to show favour and benevolence to the Duke of York. And she apologises that her own ill health has for a time prevented her from earlier reiterating her request to Margaret, for whose own prosperity Cecily is praying.

Margaret of Anjou's pilgrimage to Walsingham had most probably taken place in May 1453. For the Church, May is a holy month dedicated to the Blessed Virgin Mary. Moreover, at that time Margaret would have been in about the fourth month of her pregnancy. Thus she must have been well aware that a child was on its way – for which she apparently wished to thank Our Lady, and ask for her help, so that the pregnancy should have a successfully productive outcome. At that stage it would still have been safe for her to make a pilgrimage without risking the future of the child she was bearing. At Walsingham the Queen must have seen work in progress on the building of the new stone shrine chapel surrounding the ancient timber Holy House, which may have been commissioned by the Duke and Duchess of York (see above and plate 21 C). The interior decoration of that 'New Work' probably included Nottingham alabaster reliefs depicting the life story of the Blessed Virgin (see plate 21 B).

It appears that at that time Cecily, too, had been pregnant. But it seems that during the summer of 1453 *her* pregnancy had come to a disastrous end, presumably as a result of a premature birth. Since she wrote her letter to Margaret of Anjou before the latter gave birth to her son, in October 1453, the above letter was probably written in about August or September of that year. It is interesting to learn that, within a year of the birth of her son, Richard, (who was later to suffer from scoliosis) Cecily had experienced a catastrophic pregnancy, which apparently resulted in the premature birth and loss of a child. That was obviously a saddening experience for her as a mother, and, together with the political problems then being suffered by her husband, the outcome was ill health and depression for both the Duke and the Duchess of York in 1453.

As for Margaret of Anjou's pregnancy, the cause of it is rather intriguing. Although Margaret had been married to Henry VI for eight years, she had never previously become pregnant. Thus it is possible that the marriage had never really been consummated. Certainly Henry VI was said to be opposed to sexual contact.

It was the young king's childless state which had led Somerset to attempt to contest York's claim to be the heir presumptive to the throne. However, York's claim was generally accepted. Therefore it is possible that Edmund Beaufort may have worked with Margaret of Anjou in an attempt to bring about the birth of an heir apparent. It was presumably in February 1452/3 that the queen became pregnant. And, significantly, Edmund Beaufort is named in her financial accounts for 1453 as her 'most dear cousin'. Moreover, she also praised him for an important – but unspecified – service which he had performed for her.

Margaret's discovery that she was pregnant roughly coincided with the outbreak of further disputes amongst English magnates. The first of these involved Cecily Neville's nephew, the new Earl of Warwick, the Duke of Somerset, and land in Wales. Having married Anne Beauchamp senior, the sister of Henry Beauchamp, Earl (and later Duke) of Warwick, Cecily's nephew, Richard Neville, inherited the earldom of Warwick *iure uxoris*, following the death of his brother-in-law in 1446, and the subsequent death of the latter's daughter and heiress, Anne Beauchamp junior, in 1449.

But, as we have seen, the Duke of Somerset was married to Henry Beauchamp's half sister, Eleanor Beauchamp. He therefore put forward claims to some of the Warwick estates, and the royal council favoured his claim. At the same time, the new Earl of Warwick's Neville family found itself involved in another territorial dispute with the Percy family. Up until this point, in spite of his close relationship to Cecily Neville, Duchess of York, the new Earl of Warwick had shown no sign of particularly favouring his uncle and namesake, Richard. Now, however, that was about to change.

As for Margaret of Anjou's pregnancy, the news of that was greeted with some astonishment. Even King Henry VI later called it miraculous. In those days, of course, there was no way of scientifically proving – or disproving – who was the biological father of Margaret's child. Coupled with the fact that Henry VI later formally recognised the baby as his own son, that made the little boy the heir apparent to the throne of England.

But the triumph of Margaret of Anjou's pregnancy coincided with a disaster. At the end of July 1453 Henry VI left London for the West Country. *En route*, at the royal hunting lodge at Clarendon, he suffered a mental breakdown. Abbot John Whethamstede of St Albans reported that the king was incapable of normal movement, of remembering who he was, or of knowing what he was supposed to do. John Paston considered that the king's mental collapse may have been caused by the disastrous news of the English defeat at the battle of Castillon, at which John Talbot, Earl of Shrewsbury, had been killed.

John Arundel (Warden of the Hospital of St Mary of Bethlehem) tried treating the king with gargles, laxatives, poultices and potions. Henry VI was also bled and cauterised, not to mention attempts which were made to subject him to exorcism. However, none of these treatments cured his condition. Initially Margaret of Anjou and Edmund Beaufort conspired jointly to conceal the king's condition from the public, at least until the outcome of the queen's pregnancy became known. Thus, for about two months the king's incapacity remained concealed.

It was on Saturday 13 October 1453, in the Palace of Westminster, that Margaret produced her son.[22] His birth meant that if the little boy could formally be acknowledged as the king's heir, there could be no more arguments about the succession. But October also saw a meeting of the great council. The queen and the Duke of Somerset would have preferred to exclude the Duke of York from that meeting, but they were unable to do so. Also, there was growing public criticism of the Duke of Somerset, led apparently by Cecily Neville's nephew, John Mowbray, 3rd Duke of Norfolk.[23] Thus the council appointed the Duke of York as Lord Protector of the kingdom. At the same time the Duke of Somerset was imprisoned in the Tower of London.

As for Margaret of Anjou's little son, on the day after his birth he was baptised Edward. The Duke of Somerset was one of his godfathers, and the other was the Archbishop of Canterbury, Cardinal John Kempe, while his godmother was Anne Neville, Duchess of Buckingham, Cecily's sister.[24] Subsequently the little boy was formally created Prince of Wales. In December he was taken to Windsor Castle to be shown to the king.

> At the Princes coming to Wyndesore, the Duc of Buk' toke hym in his armes and presented hy, to the Kyng in godely wise, besechyng the Kyng to blisse hym; and the Kyng yave no maner answere. Natheless the Duk abode stille with the Prince by the Kyng; and whan he coude no maner answere have, the Queene come in, and toke the Prince in

> hir armes and presented hym in like forme as the Duke had done, desiring that he shuld blisse it; but alle their labour was in veyne, for they departed thyens without any answere or countenaunce saving only that ones he loked on the Prince and caste doune his eyene ayen, without any more.[25]

Meanwhile, Cecily's husband was now the effective ruler of England. However, he was not exclusively based in London. For example, on Monday 19 August 1454 Richard – presumably accompanied by Cecily – was at Sandal Castle in Yorkshire. That castle had been granted by Richard's great grandfather, King Edward III, to his son (Richard's grandfather), Edmund of Langley, in 1347. Subsequently it had become part of the inheritance of Edmund's successors as Dukes of York.

At Sandal, Richard wrote a grateful letter to John Paston, first thanking him for his kind and loving help to Prior Thomas Hunt[26] and his convent in respect of Richard's patronage of 'the hows of Our Lady of Walsingham' – a reference which may well refer to the ongoing building work which was then in progress around the ancient wooden Holy House – and secondly asking him to assist appointed persons to take possession of certain Norfolk manors 'in the name and to the use of our ful worshipful nepveu th'erl of Warrewic'.[27] Just over two weeks later, on 6 September 1454, William Paston reported that the Duke of York would not soon be coming back to London.[28]

It may have been at Sandal Castle that, in about October 1454, Cecily and Richard's love-making brought about the start of her last known pregnancy. Shortly after that, around the feast of Christmas 1454, King Henry VI recovered from his mental illness. As a result, the Duke of York's first protectorship came to an end. To his surprise, the recovered king found himself presented with his wife's miraculous son, whom he finally acknowledged as his heir. The king's recuperation not only led to the Duke of York's loss of the protectorship. Another consequence was the release of his rival, the Duke of Somerset, from his imprisonment in the Tower of London. As the year 1455 progressed, the trouble in England grew. Also Cecily gave birth to her last known child, a daughter who was baptised with the name of Ursula, but whose life proved very short.

It was also probably at around this time that plans were made for the marriage of Cecily's second daughter, Elizabeth, who had now reached the age of ten. The husband chosen for her was the twelve year old John de la Pole, Earl of Suffolk.[29] As we have seen, John's father had originally planned to marry the boy to Lady Margaret Beaufort. However, in February 1452/3 that planned marriage had been annulled. Margaret Beaufort's wardship was then granted by Henry VI to his half brothers, Edmund and Jasper. At the same time a marriage was arranged between Margaret and Edmund. Thus young John de la Pole was left without a planned bride. It must have been his mother, Alice Chaucer, who made the new marriage plans on her son's behalf with the Duke and Duchess of York. As we have seen, she was Cecily's cousin. It might therefore have been the two mothers who planned the marriage of John to Elizabeth of York. The actual marriage took place before 1458 (see below, Chapter 7).

Chapter 7

Through the Menopause, into Custody

At royal council meetings held in February and March 1454/5 the Duke of Somerset, who had recently been released from the Tower of London, heard himself officially cleared of all charges. With his reputation restored, Edmund Beaufort then resumed his prominent role in Henry VI's government. Thus the Duke of York and his supporters found themselves confronted with a grave problem. Richard, together with his namesake and brother-in-law, the Earl of Salisbury, and his other namesake and nephew, the Earl of Warwick, feared that moves might be made against them at a great council meeting scheduled at Leicester on 21 May. Therefore they now took to arms and advanced on London.

Probably Cecily was not part of her husband's march. The first reason for that suggestion is the point that the march was military in nature. But another possible motive is the fact that Cecily was in about the seventh month of her current pregnancy. Arguably it might have therefore been about the right time for her not to be travelling, but to be establishing herself at the place in which the forthcoming child would come into the world. Unfortunately, however, in this case the birth location is unrecorded. Some people might assume (as they do in respect of the birth of most of Cecily's children) that her lying-in took place at Fotheringhay. That is one possibility, though it has now been shown that the actual evidence suggests that Cecily was more selective and variable in respect of where she would give birth than most modern writers seem to have thought. Another possibility is that on this occasion she was still at Sandal Castle, where she seems to have conceived the child in question, and where she and her husband are known to have been living in May 1456 (see below). However, it is also possible that Cecily actually did travel part of the way towards London with her husband, but that she then went to stay at the Franciscan Priory at Ware. That was in a location not far from St Albans, which was the route taken by her husband, brother, nephew and their supporters. Cecily appears to have chosen religious houses for her lying-in on at least two previous occasions.

Wherever his wife was, on 22 May 1455 the Duke of York and his supporters arrived at Key Field, beside the town of St Albans.[1] Negotiations proved impossible, and for the first time fighting took place. In the course of it the

Duke of Somerset found himself killed outside the Castle Inn, fulfilling the earlier reputed prediction of the late Margery Jourdemayne. After the battle Somerset's body was interred within the Abbey Church of St Albans, though his burial site was never marked. As for the Duke of York, he formally submitted to his cousin, the king. He was then created Constable of England.[2] Finally he made his way a few miles east from St Albans, to stay at the Franciscan Priory at Ware.[3] Possibly Cecily was waiting for him there.

Wherever Cecily was, a few weeks later she gave birth to her last known child. It was a little girl, who must have come into the world alive, because she was apparently baptised with the name Ursula. However, the baby's life proved very short, and it is recorded that she soon joined the Lord in heaven.[4]

'Just as he had done in the early 1450s, the duke submitted to the king and attempted to rebuild unity. This was to remain his posture and that of his allies right up to the disasters of 1459.'[5] On 15 November 1455 Richard found himself reappointed Protector of England. This effectively deprived Henry VI of his personal authority. However, the Duke of York did not wish to undermine the king's sovereignty. As a result his own position remained insecure. In February 1455/6 the Duke of York was at the Parliament at Westminster.[6] However, on 25th of that month, he once again found himself deprived of his role as Protector.

Just over two months later, on 8 May 1456, the Duke of York had made his way back to Sandal Castle in Yorkshire.[7] He seems to have lived there for over a month, because he was still in residence at Sandal on 7 June.[8] Presumably therefore his wife was with him. Cecily had probably now passed the age of 40. That was the age which Aristotle described as being typical for the loss of female fertility in ancient Greece.[9] In the modern western world most women remain fertile until about the age of 50. But in the third world the menopause is more likely to come in the mid forties. There has been some debate on the question of whether the age at which the menopause started could generally have been some years earlier in medieval Europe than it is today. However, it is not the question of *average* medieval European age which is being debated here. Each woman will start the menopause at an age of her own. For example, in the case of my own two grandmothers, I have heard that one started her menopause much earlier than the other.

In the case of Cecily the surviving evidence appears to show clearly that, after 1455, she never again experienced a pregnancy. Another interesting point is the fact that in 1456 Cecily's eldest surviving child, Anne of York, Duchess of Exeter, would have attained the age of sixteen. It is therefore probable that the marriage of that eldest daughter had now been consummated. It has been suggested that historical evidence indicates that women may tend to start their menopause at an earlier age than the norm if their own daughters are of an age to potentially become pregnant.[10] On the basis of the available evidence in this case, it therefore seems likely that Cecily may have begun to experience menopausal symptoms at about this time.

When the menopause begins, typically women find that their monthly periods become irregular. Initially the periods may become heavier and last longer, though they occur less frequently. Normally flushes and sweats occur more or less continuously. Women may also feel drained, and may sense dryness of the vagina. At night sleeping may present various problems, including night sweats. There can also be mood changes. In physical terms the body may show a slight increase in weight, together with the slowing down of its metabolic functioning. The skin may become somewhat dry, and the hair on the head may thin a little. In the 1450s, Cecily Neville may well have begun to experience some of these symptoms. It has already emerged that in 1453 she had suffered from quite a deep depression, and had experienced a difficult pregnancy. Possibly she now had to cope with more mood changes, together with slight discomfort when her husband wanted to make love with her.

Cecily must have written many letters which unfortunately no longer exist. For example, in the late spring or early summer of 1456 it appears that she explored with either Sir John Fastolf or John Paston the possibility of a Norfolk coastal visit. No letter from Cecily herself on this subject has survived. But on 18 June 1456 Sir John Fastolf wrote from Caister to John Paston 'If you find my Lady of York disposed to visit this poor place, commend me to her, and tell her how it is with me that I cannot receive her as I ought'.[11] It seems that the Duchess of York did visit Caister later that year, because in another letter which Gairdner assigns to 15 November 1456 'My Lady of York has been here, and sore moved me for the purchase of Castre.'[12] Possibly on this trip Cecily had offered prayers for her well-being at the Norfolk shrine of Our Lady of Walsingham which, as we have seen, was under the patronage of her husband. Maybe she had also been to Norwich.

Furthermore, a visit to the eastern counties in the second half of 1456 might have been significant for Cecily and Richard in another way. It was on a date prior to February 1457/8 that their second daughter, Elizabeth of York, who had been born at Rouen in 1444, celebrated her planned marriage to young John de la Pole, Earl of Suffolk. Unfortunately the precise date of their marriage is not on record. But it could well have taken place on the Suffolk border with Norfolk, at the village of Wingfield. The castle at Wingfield was subsequently the principal residence of Elizabeth, John, and their children. Also the couple's

Wingfield Castle, Suffolk.

remains would later be interred at Wingfield Church (see plate 33). That may also be the building within which nuptial mass was offered for them following their joining of hands and exchanging of vows in the church porch.

On 1 February 1457/8 'the Duk of Yorke came to London with hys oune housole onlye to the nombre of cxl hors.'[13] It was not until twenty months later that fighting once again broke out in England. 'York, Warwick, and Salisbury revived the case that evil counsellors around the king were destroying the common weal of the realm and threatening their own security. On this occasion, however, their propaganda cut no ice.'[14]

At that point the Duke of York and his family were once again in residence at Ludlow Castle. There Richard found himself confronted by a powerful number of nobles opposing him in the name of the king. The battle took place on 12 October at Ludford Bridge. The Duke of York found himself deserted by a part of his army, so during that night he and some of his associates fled. On this occasion Richard found himself forced to abandon his wife and their three younger children. However, he cannot have done so without prior discussion. He and Cecily must have agreed, before he left, that her life and the lives of the children would not be threatened, and that she could submit herself to the king, but then plead with him on behalf of her husband.

Incidentally, by the time the battle of Ludford Bridge took place, it appears that the Duke of York may have begun using a white rose as one of his heraldic emblems. The surviving evidence for this dates from 1466, when the Duke had been dead for more than five years. At that time, as part of his inheritance from John Fastolf (who died in November 1459), William Worcester delivered to John Paston 'certain notable jewels and gold jewellery adorned with precious stones, to wit one of the richest jewels, called in English *a White Rose*, late of the Duke of York, set with a precious stone called *a poynted dyamant*.'[15]

Accompanied by his second son, Edmund, Earl of Rutland, the Duke of York escaped back to Ireland. There the two of them spent eleven months trying to put together sufficient men and money for their return to England. Curiously, the account written by Jehan de Wavrin claims that the Earl of Warwick and his admiral visited Ireland for consultation, 'where they found the Duke of York, the Duchess, his wife, and all their children except Edward, Earl of March, who was living in Calais.'[16] Wavrin also claims that later Warwick 'took leave of the Duke of York, of the Duchess and of their children, and set off, together with my lady his mother [Alice Montacute, Countess of Salisbury] who had long been with my lady of York.'[17] Cecily's alleged close friendship with her sister-in-law the Countess of Salisbury sounds interesting. However, in respect of the year 1460, Wavrin's claims must be erroneous.

Meanwhile, at a Parliament held in Coventry, the Duke of York and his leading supporters were attainted.[18] In fact 'the Duke of York, therlis of Marche, Rutland, Warwyk, and of Salesbury wt the said Dukes wif, and many other knyghtes, Squyers and Gentlilmen, were atteynt of high treason.'[19] Subsequently, on Friday 7 December 1459, it was reported from Coventry by John Bocking that 'the Duchess of York come yester-even late' to that city to speak to her sovereign.[20]

Curiously, it is often claimed that Cecily and her younger children had been found on 13 October 1459 standing at the Ludlow Market Cross when the Lancastrians arrived after the battle of Ludford Bridge. But there seems to be no contemporary source for that story. One contemporary account states that

> King Harry rode into Ludlow [fn. 1] and spoiled the Town and Castle, where-at he found the Duchess of York with her two sons (*then*) children, the one of thirteen years old, and the other of ten years old: the which Duchess King Harry sent to her sister Anne Duchess of Buckingham.[21]
>
> [fn.1 " 'The Duke of York, not confiding in his men, was forced to fly from Ludlow into Wales, and leave the town a prey to the King's

soldiers, who burnt and pillaged the same; and the Duchess of York, residing then here, had her wardrobe sifted, and all her furniture spoiled.' *Documents connected with Ludlow*, p. 10."]

According to this version of the story it sounds as though Cecily and her children may simply have remained in their apartments at Ludlow Castle, even though those apartments were ransacked around them by enemy forces.

Certainly it does not sound as though Cecily and the children were immediately arrested. The letter written in Coventry by John Bocking on 7 December 1459, and sent to John Paston and others (see above), suggests that it was the Duchess of York herself who subsequently opted to come to that city and submit there to King Henry VI. Another contemporary account tells a similar version of the story:

> Also that same yere [1459–60] the Duchyes of Yorke com unto Kyng Harry and submyttyd hyr unto hys grace, and she prayde for hyr husbonde that he myght come to hys answere and to be ressayvyd unto hys grace; and the kynge fulle humbely grauntyde hyr grace, and to alle hyrs þat wolde come with hyr, and to alle othyr that wolde come yn with yn viij days.'[22]

As we saw earlier, there are only two mentions by name of Cecily, Duchess of York, in the Patent Rolls of King Henry VI. The second of these dates from Thursday 20 December 1459, precisely two weeks after the arrival of the duchess in Coventry:

> Whereas the king promised Cecily, duchess of York, for the relief of her and her infants who have not offended against the king[23] 1000 marks yearly during her life from certain possessions late of Richard, her husband, in the counties of Northampton, Essex, Hertford, Suffolk, Salop and Hereford, and signed a bill thereof: – the king has granted to John, bishop of Lincoln, Humphrey, duke of Buckingham, James, earl of Wiltshire, John, viscount of Beaumont, Richard Tunstall, knight, William Lucy, knight, William Catesby, knight, and John Barre, knight, the manors and lordships of Nassyngton, Yarwell and Upton, co. Northampton, Erbury, Clarethall, Greys in Cavendish, Hunden, Berdefeld with the borough of Berdefeld, Norfambrige, Lacheley and Thaxsted, the borough of Sudbury, the manors of Wodehall and Leyham, the borough and park of Raylegh, the manors of Thunderley

> and Louedon, and the manor and lordship of Estwodbury, in the counties of Suffolk and Essex, the manor and borough of Pembrigge, the manor of Orleton, a tenement called 'Litel Cowarne', the manors and lordships of Wolfelowe and Nethewode, the manors of Kyngeslane, Malmeshull and Marche and a tenement called 'Nook', co. Hereford, the manors of Staunton Lacy and Ernewode, the manor, lordship and borough of Clebury, the lordship of Cleton and Ferlowe, the manor and lordship of Cheilmerssh and the manor of Huggley, co. Salop, the manors and lordships of Bardesley, Brymesfeld, Mussarder, Wynston, Chorleton, Doughton, Bislegh with Bislegh hundred and Lichelade, co. Gloucester, Whaddon and Cleydon and the manor of Berton, co. Buckingham, and the manor and lordship of Fynmere, co. Oxford, in full recompense of the said 1000 marks, which premises came into the king's hands by an act of forfeiture against the duke of York in the parliament held at Coventry on 20 November last, to hold with the issues thereof to the use of the said duchess for her life; provided they pay to the king any excess of the said sum if the yearly value of the premises exceed the same beyond the charges, fees and annuities issuing therefrom.[24]

Nevertheless, one surviving contemporary source reports that after coming to an agreement with the king in Coventry, Cecily and her three youngest surviving children were not left free to go and live wherever they wished. 'The Duchyes of Yorke was take to the Duke Bokyngham and to hys lady, for they two ben susters, and there she was tylle the fylde was done at Northehampton [10 July 1460], and she was kept fulle strayte and many a grete rebuke.'[25]

A letter written by William Botoner to John Berney in January 1459/60 reports that 'my Lady Duchesse [of York] ys stille ayen receved yn Kent. [While] The Duke of York ys at Debylyn [Dublin], strengthened with his Erles and homagers.'[26]

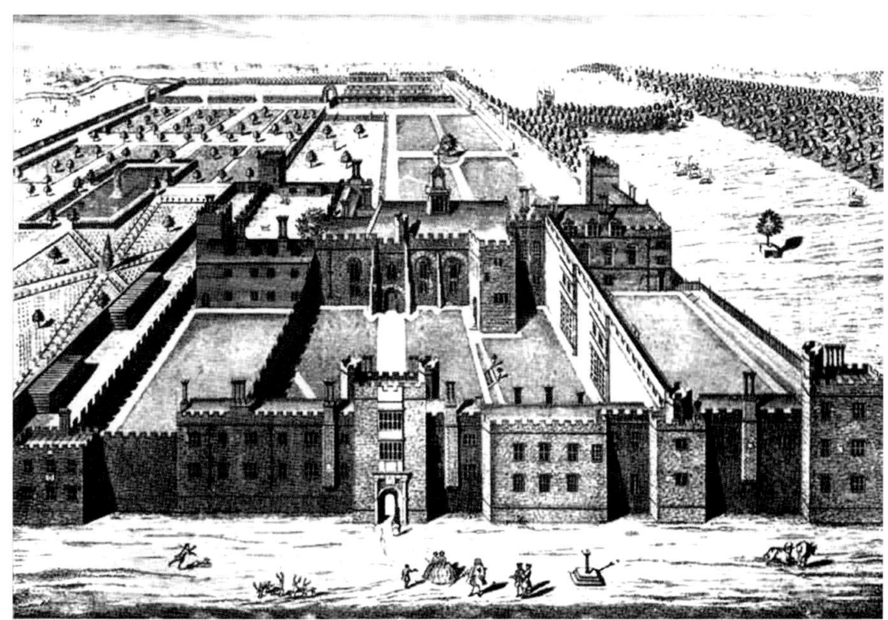

Penshurst Place, Kent.

The principal residence of the Duke and Duchess of Buckingham in the county of Kent was Penshurst Place. That is probably where Cecily and her children now found themselves residing under a degree of constraint for some months.

Chapter 8

The Blue Velvet Carriage to Bereavement

Cecily's eldest son, Edward, Earl of March, together with his mother's brother, Richard Neville, Earl of Salisbury, and the latter's son and namesake, Edward's first cousin, Richard, Earl of Warwick had escaped across the sea to Calais. There they made plans to return to England and seize control. Their aim was to take command of both the king's person and the government. The three earls returned to England at the end of June 1460. They landed in Kent, where Cecily and her younger children seem to have been at that time. Possibly the three earls met her as they travelled from their landing place at Sandwich. Their most likely route would have taken them via Maidstone, so they would have passed just to the north of Penshurst Place Assuredly Edward, Earl of March, was in contact with his mother and his three young siblings shortly afterwards (see below).

Edward, his uncle and his cousin, together with the support they gained after their return to Kent, confronted the royal army at the battle of Northampton on 10 July 1460. There, they captured the person of Henry VI. From that point onwards, control was in their hands. Meanwhile the Duke of York, together with his second son, Edmund, Earl of Rutland, was still in Ireland. As for the Duchess of York, she and her younger children were probably still living with Cecily's sister, the Duchess of Buckingham, at Penshurst Place. However, the change in the political situation no doubt meant that their residence there may now have ceased to resemble imprisonment.

In September 1460 Richard, Duke of York and his son, Edmund, left Dublin and sailed back to England. It seems clear that Cecily heard the news of their intended return before they actually left Ireland. Presumably Richard sent his wife a letter from Dublin, though unfortunately no text of such a message has survived. Undoubtedly he wrote to Cecily on Monday 8 September (Feast of the Nativity of the Blessed Virgin Mary) as soon as he got back from Ireland. Richard landed near Chester, and he then sent Cecily instructions to meet up with him. However, that letter is also lost.

Nevertheless, the Duchess and her younger children promptly left the custody of her sister. The four of them travelled from Kent in the direction of London, *via* Southwark. It seems that they may have travelled in some state,

The signature of Cecily's husband, Richard, Duke of York.

because shortly afterwards, when Cecily left Southwark to rejoin her husband, 'hys lady the duchyes met with hym in a chare i-coveryd with blewe felewette, and iiij pore courssserys ther-yn.'[1] The most likely explanation is that she had travelled in her blue-velvet covered carriage, with its four pairs of horses, when departing from her sister, Anne Neville. Indeed, Cecily's carriage may also have taken her earlier from Coventry to Kent. Incidentally, blue and white were the livery colours of her husband.[2]

It may not yet have felt safe for Cecily and her younger children to enter the capital and take up residence at their own family home of Baynard's Castle. Therefore John Paston II Esquire, who was then resident in Norwich, found himself receiving a letter from his servant, Christopher Hanson. Hanson was a German and a former archer who had been placed in charge of a house in Southwark which was owned by the Pastons. Hanson's letter was sent to Paston about a month after the event to which it refers. The event in question had been the receipt of a request from the Earl of March for temporary accommodation at the Paston home in Southwark for his mother and his three youngest siblings. It seems that the Earl of March was himself staying in the Southwark region at that time, having travelled south from the battle of Northampton via Suffolk and Essex.[3]

Hanson's letter to Paston reads as follows:

> Right worschipfull ser and maister, I recommaund me unto you. Please you to wete the Monday after Oure Lady Day[4] [th]ere[5] come hider to my maister ys plase my Maister Bowser, Ser Harry Ratford, Maister

A fifteenth-century carriage similar to the one used by Cecily Neville in 1460.

> John Clay, and the h[ar]bynger[6] of my lord of Marche, desyryng that my lady of York might lye her untylle the coming of my lord of York, and hir [tw – *crossed out*] sonnys my lorde George and my lord Richard and my lady Margarete hir dow3tyr, whiche y graunt hem in youre name to lye here untylle Mychelmas.[7] And she had not ley here ij days but sche hade tythyng of the londyng of my lord at Chester. The Tewesday next after my lord sent for hir that sche shuld come to hym to Hartford, and theder she is gone, and sythe y-left here bothe the sunys and the dow3tyr, and the lord of Marche comyth every day to se them.[8]

'Master John Clay', one of the servants of the Earl of March who delivered his letter to Hanson, was probably about fifteen years old in October 1460. Three years later he was proposed as a possible husband for a Paston daughter.[9] It seems that he was the son of John Clay Esquire of Cheshunt, Hertfordshire, by his wife, Joan. As for the young lad's father and namesake, he was a known Yorkist supporter, who was subsequently appointed chamberlain of the Duchess of York. At the time when his son delivered the Earl of March's letter in Southwark, the father probably formed part of the entourage of the Duke of York, and had been with him in Ireland. Certainly John Clay senior had been condemned the previous winter by Henry VI for taking part in Richard's rebellion.

It was on Monday 15 September 1460 that Edward, Earl of March, dispatched to Christopher Hanson his request for his mother and his three youngest siblings to be accommodated at the Paston's Southwark house, which stood on the south bank of the river Thames, not far from the southern end of London Bridge. Today the site of this long lost building is occupied by

Southwark Crown Courts, and by parts of the 'More London' development. The house stood on the north side of Tooley Street, just to the west of today's City Hall, and not far from HMS Belfast and 'The Shard'. In 1460 it was known as 'Fastolf Place', because it was a former property of Sir John Fastolf. The Pastons had inherited the house – together with other property – from Sir John.

It had been in 1440 that John Fastolf had acquired two existing adjoining moated houses on the south bank of the Thames, not far from London Bridge and opposite the Tower of London. Little remained of the two earlier houses, so Fastolf rebuilt on their sites, constructing his new 'Fastolf Place'. His new residence had a large, buttressed brick wall surrounding it, which was pierced by at least two gatehouses. Fastolf Place also had its own inlet from the river, into a little private dock, thus allowing access to the property by boat.[10]

Apparently the Duchess of York and her three youngest children were already in the vicinity of Fastolf Place when Edward sent his letter to Hanson. Indeed they may have been staying somewhere nearby with the Earl of March. Thus they may well have arrived at Fastolf Place on the afternoon of Monday 15 September. Initially they were told that they might stay there for two weeks (until Monday 29 September). But on about Wednesday 17 September Cecily heard the news that her husband had landed at Chester. On Tuesday 23 September she received a message from Richard summoning her to join him in Hertford. That same day she left Fastolf Place, travelling in her carriage (see above). Her three youngest surviving children were left behind. In fact they were still staying at Fastolf Place on Sunday 12 October 1460. By that time they had been there for four weeks (twice the length of time which had originally been agreed). On a daily basis their elder brother, Edward, Earl of March, is said to have visited them at Fastolf Place. Obviously, therefore, he must have been living somewhere nearby, within easy travelling distance.

In the weeks during which the three youngest York children stayed in Southwark without their parents it may have been better for them to stay indoors, out of the rain. Contemporary sources reveal that the weather in England during 1460 was the worst for about a hundred years, with a lot of heavy rainfall.[11] Nevertheless, the Duke and Duchess of York did see one of their other children at about this time. In October 1460 Friar Brackley of Norwich wrote to John Paston to inform him that 'the Lady of Suffolk [Alice Chaucer, dowager Duchess of Suffolk] hath sent up hyr sone [John de la Pole, second Duke of Suffolk] and hise wyf [Elizabeth of York] to my Lord of York.'[12] Elizabeth of York, the new Duchess of Suffolk, was now sixteen years old. She had been married – and living with her young husband and his mother

Cecily's Chaucer Relationship

– for more than two and a half years. But although her marriage may by now have been consummated, probably Elizabeth had not yet produced a child. Her eldest son, the future Earl of Lincoln, seems to have come into the world about two years later.

Although Friar Brackley's letter was written from Norwich, it contained reference to plans for a forthcoming Parliament, to be held at Westminster. It is therefore probably the case that, at the time when the letter was written, the Duke and Duchess of York were already in London, probably at Baynard's Castle. It is also likely that their two eldest sons, the Earl of March[13] and the Earl of Rutland were with them. As for their daughter, Elizabeth of York, and her husband, John de la Pole, they were presumably sent from East Anglia to London to see the Duke and Duchess of York at Baynard's Castle.

In October 1460 the Duke of York formally submitted to parliament his claim for the English crown.[14] This asserted that Henry IV and his son and grandson had been Lancastrian usurpers of the crown of King Richard II, and that, as the living heir of Richard II's senior uncle, Lionel, Duke of Clarence, Richard, Duke of York had a superior claim to the throne than King Henry VI. Hitherto the Duke of York had never put forward such a claim, which, if it was accepted, would now put him on the throne as King Richard III of England, with his wife as Queen Cecily.

Since Cecily had been with her husband during the weeks following his arrival in England, she must have been well aware of his plans before they became public. Presumably she must also have supported what he was doing. The Duke and Duchess of York had now been together in a very productive relationship for many years. And although in her youth Cecily may have felt what was then the normal loyalty to her cousin, King Henry VI, since then the situation in England had become very stressful for her, as her earlier letter to Henry's consort, Margaret of Anjou, revealed. Also she knew well that her husband had never previously aimed to oppose Henry, or claim the throne from him.

> York marched into London, seized the king, and entered parliament on 10 October, announcing that he intended 'to challenge his right' to the crown (Johnson, *York*, 214). The Lords' response was unpromising: they went into conclave at Blackfriars and sent the young earl of March to persuade his father to accept a negotiated settlement. By 13 October York had been brought to abandon his plans for an immediate coronation, and a few days later he submitted his claim for discussion in parliament. An accord emerged on 31 October, and its central feature was to leave Henry VI on the throne, while settling the succession on York and his sons. It is possible that even after this York attempted to get his way by inducing Henry to abdicate. He must have realized that, like the treaty of Troyes on which it was apparently based, the accord promised immediate war with the disinherited heir. In any event, the king was moved to safety and the duke was obliged to accept the terms agreed in October, at least for the time being. Acting more or less as protector he marched north in early December to deal with the forces of the prince of Wales and Queen Margaret, which had regrouped in Yorkshire after the defeat at Northampton. Venturing forth from his castle at Sandal on 30 December 1460, in what may have been an uncharacteristic attempt to surprise his enemy, York was set upon by an unexpectedly large Lancastrian force. In the ensuing battle of Wakefield, he and his second son, Edmund of Rutland, were killed. As a macabre riposte to Duke Richard's recent pretensions, his head was severed from his body and displayed on the walls of York bearing a paper crown.[15]

Although the Duke of York had marched north accompanied by his second son, Edmund, Earl of Rutland, by no means all the members of his family who had been with him at Baynard's Castle went with the two of them. For example, Edward, Earl of March was sent westwards by his father, to Gloucestershire and the Welsh border.[16] Probably on that journey Edward had a meeting with the lovely Eleanor Talbot, Lady Boteler, daughter of his mother's relative, and his father's late collaborator in France, and predecessor in Ireland, John Talbot, Earl of Shrewsbury. Young Eleanor had recently been widowed, but remained alone, residing in the Warwickshire manor houses which had been granted to her and her late husband by the latter's father, Lord Sudeley.

It is also obvious that the putative Queen Cecily had neither accompanied Richard and Edmund to the north of England nor accompanied Edward to the west. She appears to have remained in London, at Baynard's Castle. There she had apparently been rejoined at some point by her three youngest children, whom she had earlier left staying at Fastolf Place in Southwark.

However, Cecily's eldest brother, Richard Neville, Earl of Salisbury, did accompany her husband and her son Edmund to the north. He was not killed with them in the battle of Wakefield, because initially he managed to escape the battlefield. However, he was then captured and taken to Pontefract Castle. There he was reportedly put to death by the local common people.

When the disastrous news of what had happened to her husband, her second son and her eldest brother reached Cecily, she must have been enormously shocked and deeply distressed. Nevertheless, she forced herself into rapid action for the protection of her two youngest surviving sons. 'Thenne the Duchesse of York, heryng ther losse of that ffeeld, sent over the See hir ij yong Sones George and Richard which went vnto Vtryk.'[17]

The Burgundian chronicler, Jehan de Wavrin, who met the two young Yorkist boys during their exile in the Low Countries, guessed their ages as nine and eight respectively – correctly in the case of Richard, but erroneously in the case of George.[18] George was actually eleven years old, though he apparently looked younger – most likely because he was shorter than the normal average height – a feature which he may have inherited from his mother. Richard was eight years old and, unlike George, he must have been of about the right height for his age. Presumably young Richard had inherited his height genes from his father and namesake rather than from his mother.

As for Cecily's unmarried youngest daughter, Margaret, she was fourteen and a half years old. Although she was later to go and live in the Low Countries, thanks to her marriage with the Duke of Burgundy, at this point she was not sent there with her two younger brothers. Instead she appears to have remained with her mother at Baynard's Castle as the English calendar year of 1460 lumbered its way to an end through its final difficult months of January, February and March.

Half of that time was taken up by the annual penitential season of Lent. For six and a half weeks no meat could be eaten. Also the sky still seems to have been weeping: an activity which it may now have shared with the widowed and bereaved Duchess of York. It had been very wet in 1460 (see above) and after Christmas the weather did not improve. The final three months of 1460 (in terms of the English calendar) proved stormy. Francesco Coppino, Bishop of

Terni, and the Apostolic Legate, reported that he had encountered 'a violent storm' while crossing from Tilbury to Holland, where he arrived on 10 February 1460/61.[19] A few weeks later, in a letter written from Brussels on 15 March 1460/61, the diplomat Prospero Camuglio noted that 'the sea between here and England has been stormy and unnavigable ever since the 10th.'[20] Morever, it also seems to have turned cold during these winter months. Indeed, on the last Sunday in March (the first Sunday of the English New Year of 1461) there was a snowstorm.

Chapter 9

The First Reign of Edward IV

Though the Duke of York and the Earl of Rutland had been killed at the battle of Wakefield, the Earl of March had fought another battle near the Welsh border, at which he had been victorious. The Yorkists had therefore by no means been beaten. Returning to London via Warwickshire, following his victory at the battle of Mortimer's Cross, young Edward may have paid another visit to Eleanor Talbot, Lady Boteler, towards the end of the second week of February 1460/1. That was the last full week during which pleasures were supposed to be enjoyed, because the following Wednesday (17 February) marked the beginning of the penitential season of Lent. At that convenient moment in terms of the religious calendar young Edward found himself once again in the vicinity of Eleanor's Warwickshire manors while travelling from the Welsh border back to London, where he would claim the throne. Possibly therefore it was in the second week of February 1460/1 that Edward first tried to make love to Eleanor. But if so, in spite of his recent military victory, this time he must have found himself defeated. It seems that his girlfriend was too devout and too virtuous to indulge him in sexual pleasure outside of marriage.

Subsequently Edward met Eleanor's uncle – his mother's nephew, and his own first cousin the Earl of Warwick – at Burford, to the west of Oxford. He then went on to London, where he arrived around 26 February and presumably rejoined his mother. He found himself heartily welcomed in the capital. There, in the second week of Lent, on Wednesday 4 March, he was formally acclaimed King of England as Edward IV. In the eyes of Londoners, the Lancastrian period was now regarded as having ended. Thus, former servants of Henry VI and his government now changed their allegiance. Among those who did so was Henry VI's 'clerk and servant, Robert Stillyngton, doctor of laws',[1] Dean of the London free chapel of St Martin le Grand,[2] who seems previously to have been a loyal servant of the Lancastrian sovereign.[3]

However, not all the opposing forces had yet been dealt with. Therefore young Edward had to set off for the north, where his father and his younger brother had been defeated and killed, to put down the military forces there who remained loyal to Henry VI. 'Before the battle of Towton, having been recognised as king in London, Edward had publicly expressed his trust in his mother when he recommended the Duchess to the mayor and assembled notables of the city, presumably as his representative whilst he was absent fighting the Lancastrians.'[4]

So once again, Cecily remained behind in London, together with her daughter, Margaret. It was on Easter eve – Saturday 4 April 1461 – at 11 o'clock, that she received a letter from her son, Edward, recounting to her his victory in the snow, at the battle of Towton, on Palm Sunday, followed by his triumphant reception at the city of York.[5] At York he had rescued the head of his father, which had been impaled by the Lancastrians upon Mickelgate Bar. Edward then respectfully dispatched his father's head to Pontefract for burial with his body.

Although Cecily and her unmarried daughter, Margaret, were then still living at Baynard's Castle, at that point Cecily's two youngest surviving sons, George and Richard, were still out of the country. The two young lads remained in exile in the Low Countries until the final days of April. They then set sail from Calais, probably arriving back in their homeland around the middle of May. On Saturday 30 May 1461 (the vigil of the feast of the Holy Trinity) the two boys were received at Canterbury Cathedral.[6] Once they had reached the capital it is virtually certain that initially they rejoined their mother and sister at Baynard's Castle. Subsequently, however, the new sovereign of England, their elder brother, King Edward IV, made different arrangements for his siblings. After all, despite their young age they were now persons of potential importance. George, in particular, had suddenly become one of the most highly significant members of the royal family. Since his elder brother, the king, was still childless, George was now the heir presumptive to the English throne.

On Monday 1 June 1461 manors to the value of 5,000 marks a year were granted to Cecily Neville by her son, the new King, as follows:

> Grant for life to the king's mother Cicely, duchess of York, in full recompence of her jointure, to the value of 5,000 marks yearly, of the manors of Letchelade, Berdesley, Brymmesfeld, Musardere, Wynston, Chorlton, Doughton and Byslegh with the hundred of Byslegh, co. Gloucester, the manor and lordship of Sevenhampton, the hundred of Hieworth with the borough of Hieworth, the town or borough of Cricklade, the manor of Chelworth, the manor and lordship of Old Wotton with the borough of Wotton, and the manors of Fastern, Tokenham, Compton, Wynterbourne and Somerford Caynes, co, Wilts, £25. 12s. 8d, yearly from the fee farm of the town of Andever, and the manors of Hokemortymer and Worthy-mortymer, co. Southampton, the manor and lordship of Neubury with the borough

of Neubury, the manor of Wokefeld, and the manor and lordship of Stratfeld Mortymer, co. Berks, the manor and hundred of Pymperne, the manor of Tarent Goundevile, the town or township of Waymouth, a tenement called 'Helwell', the manors of Stuple and Criche, the hundreds of Roughburgh, Russhemore and Hasellore with courts and perquisites of courts, the manor and town of Wike, the manor and island of Portelond, the manors of Mershewode and Gussecho Bowne, and the manor and lordship of Wareham with the town of Wareham, co. Dorset, the manor of Odecombe, the manor of Milverton with the borough of Milverton, and the castle of Brugewater and the manor of Heygrove with the borough of Brugewater, co. Somerset, the manor of Whaddon Nasshe with the chase of Whaddon, the manor of Steple Claydon, the manor of Wendover called 'Wendover Foreyn' with the borough of Wendover, and the manors of Salden and Boerton, co. Buckingham, the manor of Fynner, co. Oxford, the manor and lordship of Huchen and the manors of Ansty, Staundon, and Popsale, co. Hertford, the castle and manor of Fodrynghay and the manors of Nassyngton, Yerwell and Upton, co. Northampton, the castle, town and manor of Staumford, the manor and lordship of Depyng, £11. 6s. 9¾d. yearly from the fee farm of West Depyng, the manors and lordships of Kelby and Grantham, and an inn called 'le George' in Grantham, co. Lincoln, the manors and lordships of Great Walsyngham, Little Walsyngham and Bircham, co. Norfolk, the castle, manor, lordship and honour of Clare with the borough of Clare with appurtenances in the counties of Suffolk, Essex, Norfolk, Hertford and Cambridge and other counties, the manors of Erbury and Honden, co. Suffolk, the manors and lordships of Latcheley, Clarethall, Berdesfeld and Thaxsted, with the boroughs of Berdesfeld and Thaxsted, co. Essex, the town of Sudbury, co. Suffolk, the manor of Wodhall and a third part of the manor of Leyham, co. Essex, the manor of Southfrith with the wood and park there and the manors of Depford, Stroude, Erith, Tonge, Swannescombe, Kyngesdown and Shillyngeld, co. Kent, the manors of Purbryght, Shire and Drayton; £4. 17s. 4d. yearly from the fee farm of the city of Chichester, co. Sussex, £12. rent in Bottesham, co. Cambridge, and the courts and leets of the honour of Gloucester with their perquisites in Bottesham, Royston, Litlyngton, Moredon, Malrede, Thadlowe, Abyndon, Arnyngton, Harleton and Toft co. Cambridge, with the fees and parts of fees late of the king's father, Richard, duke of York, there and elsewhere in that county, the

> leets and courts of Wolley and Grandysdon, co. Huntingdon, with their perquisites, the manors of Brymmesgrove, Kyngesnorton and Clyfton, £70. 17s. 10d. yearly from the fee farm of the town of Wyche, and the manor of Odyngley, co. Worcester, an inn or tenement called 'Baynardescastell' in London, £400. yearly from the customs of wools, hides and wool-fells in the port of Eyngeston on Hull, £289. 6s. 8d. from the like customs in the port of London, £100. yearly from the issues of the county of York, the manors and lordships of Mawardyn and Marcle, co. Hereford, and 50 marks yearly from the issues of the forests of Exmore, Rachiche and Mynedepp, cos. Somerset and Devon, from 30 December last, on which day the said duke died, with knights' fees advowsons, wards, marriages, escheats, views of frank-pledge, courts, woods, parks, warrens, chaces, fairs, markets, fisheries, liberties, wreck of sea and other appurtenances.[7]

For a list of these manors &c, by county, and with updated spellings, see Appendix 1.

Returning southwards after the battle of Towton, Edward IV travelled via Durham, York, Lincoln, Coventry, Warwick, Daventry and Stony Stratford. Probably on the way he secretly married – and bedded – Eleanor Talbot. The most likely venue for this secret marriage is in the county of Warwick, either at Eleanor's manor of Fenny Compton or at her manor of Burton Dassett. The most probable date is Monday 8 June 1461. A week earlier, on Monday 1 June, it seems that Edward was at Lichfield.[8] From 3–6 June he was in and around Coventry.[9] On Sunday 7 June he was in Warwick.[10] By Tuesday 9 June he had reached Daventry.[11]

Probably the secret marriage took place at one of Eleanor's manor houses, just as Edward's later secret wedding with Elizabeth Widville was contracted at *her* family manor. According to his later statement as made in 1483, the ceremony was carried out by Canon Robert Stillington, a former servant of King Henry VI (see above). Though Edward probably married Eleanor in early June 1461, the fact was not made public. However, it is possible that Eleanor accompanied her new husband on his journey towards the capital, as a member of his entourage. It is also possible that his mother subsequently became aware of the relationship when her son got back to the capital.

Writing more than half a century later, Sir Thomas More asserted that in 1464 'the king's mother objected openly against his marriage [to Elizabeth Widville], as it were in discharge of her conscience, that the king was sure [committed] to Dame Elizabeth Lucy [*sic*] and her husband before God.'[12]

The only provable error in More's statement is the name of the woman cited as Edward IV's true wife. More also claimed that same name (Elizabeth Lucy) was the basis behind the offering of the English throne to Edward's younger brother, Richard III, in 1483. However, that is demonstrably erroneous. The person cited as Edward IV's legitimate wife in 1483 was unquestionably Eleanor Talbot, Lady Boteler.[13] Moreover, there is no evidence that a woman called Elizabeth Lucy really existed, or had a relationship of any kind with Edward IV.[14] Thus, in reality, Thomas More's account of how Cecily Neville claimed in 1464 that her son's relationship with Elizabeth Widville was illegal because Edward was already committed to another woman could only have been based upon Edward's earlier secret marriage to Eleanor Talbot. That means that if More was telling the truth, Cecily must have been aware of her eldest son's relationship with Eleanor.

On Tuesday 12 June the young king appears to have reached the royal manor house of Sheen,[15] which had been built almost half a century earlier by King Henry V. Maybe he initially stayed at this private residence outside of London (about ten miles from the capital) because Eleanor was in his entourage at that stage. Later Edward seemed to have enjoyed staying at Sheen with Elizabeth Widville. The young king may not have seen his own closest relatives immediately. Possibly he sent for his mother and his youngest sister and brothers to join him at Sheen the following day. Or he may have waited to see them until Sunday 14 June, when he apparently went to stay for a week or so at the Lambeth Palace of his cousin, Thomas Bourchier, Archbishop of Canterbury,[16] which would have required a shorter journey on their part. It was apparently at Lambeth Palace that Edward prepared for his coronation. On Friday 26 June, he made his state entry into London, and on Saturday 27 June his brothers, George and Richard, were made Knights of the Bath.[17]

Edward IV's coronation was celebrated on Sunday 28 June at the Benedictine Abbey of Westminster.[18] It was carried out at minimum cost because the royal treasury was empty. George, Edward's younger brother and heir presumptive, was appointed to act as Steward of England at the coronation, which he must have attended, even though Lord Wenlock had also been appointed to assist him in view of his youth.[19] The surviving accounts of Edward's coronation offer no information as to whether the ceremony was also attended by other surviving close relatives. For example, there is no solid proof that Cecily Neville attended her son's coronation. However, it seems impossible that she would not have done so. After all, she had probably attended earlier coronations, and if her husband had not lost his life at the battle of Wakefield, she herself would presumably at some point have been crowned as his consort. Moreover, she had not, at this stage, had any known disagreements with her eldest son. However, as a dowager Duchess, she would have had no special role to play at the coronation of a young king, and would probably simply have witnessed the ceremony.

In the immediate aftermath of his coronation, on 10 July 1461, Edward IV remunerated the clergyman who had recently aided him in respect of his relationship with Eleanor Talbot. 'Master Robert Stillyngton, king's clerk, … dean of the king's free chapel of St. Martin le Grand, London, archdeacon of Colchester … and of Taunton',[20] and prebend of the king's free chapel of St Stephen at the palace of Westminster, was rewarded by confirming his life tenure of all the posts he held. This confirmation was granted by the young king just over four weeks after the most likely date of the secret marriage ceremony which Stillington later claimed to have carried out between Edward and Eleanor in Warwickshire. Before the end of the year Stillington also found himself requited much further by the king. He was appointed keeper of the privy seal, and became a government diplomat, serving Edward as an ambassador.[21]

Only limited evidence survives of the king's mother and her activities at this time, in spite of the fact that she was now officially the first lady of the land (given that her son had as yet no recognised consort). At this early stage of his reign it seems that Edward IV still had a good relationship with his mother. He had recommended her to the mayor of London prior to his departure for the battle of Towton (see above). On Tuesday 20 October 1461 Richard Foweler and William Flette were appointed by the king to collect all arrears and rents from farmers and tenants of the manor of Stoke (Bucks.) for the dowager Duchess of York.[22] In November 1461 she seems to have accompanied Edward to the palace of Westminster, where he was required to open parliament on 4 November.[23] And on 23 February 1461/2 the king confirmed Cecily's jointure income.[24]

Obviously she continued to use Baynard's Castle in London as her home in the capital city, although she also travelled about the country, visiting her other estates, as was the norm for those of her status in the fifteenth century. For example, in August 1462 she went to Canterbury, where she was given two horses, and was feasted, together with wine.[25] But she was at her London home on 27 May 1463, on which date she wrote – and signed – the following letter to the mayor of Folkestone:

> The Kyngys Moder, Duchesse of York.
>
> Trusty and welbeloved, we grete you welle. And whereas we understand that it hathe pleased my lord and son the Kynge, and also our cousin tharchebisshope of Caunterbury, entendering the righte of oure welbeloved Chapellaine, Thomas Banys, to wryte for hym unto

> you and othe[r], for to see hym reioyce such lyvelodeas he oughte of righte to have; we desire and pray you that, according unto the tenure of the letters of oure said lord and son, and cousin, aforesaid, ye put you in devoyr to the performing of the same, and with the more diligence, at oure especiall contemplacion, as we trust you. And that no personne vexe, inquiet, nor trouble hym, as we may for his sak thank you in in[*sic*] tyme to comme.
>
> Yeven under our signet, in our place at Baynardys Castelle in Londone, the xxvii day of Maye.
>
> To our trusty and wellbeloved The Mayre and Jurattes of Folkestone, and to everiche of theyme.[26]

The published version of this letter also has a note which states that 'there is a scrawl in the margin, in large characters, which, we may guess, was intended for her signature, "Ceycily"'.[27]

Unfortunately it is not clear precisely where Cecily was living during the period from January 1461/2 until August 1462. During those months Edward IV mainly travelled from London and Westminster, through Hertfordshire, Cambridgeshire, Huntingdonshire, Lincolnshire, Leicestershire, Nottinghamshire, Northamptonshire and Warwickshire, though he was also briefly in Canterbury with his mother in August 1462, when she was feasted and given horses (see above). This is the period during which Edward is said to have been having a love affair with his own second cousin, Henry Beaufort, Duke of Somerset. The handsome Henry was also ironically the first cousin of Eleanor Talbot. However, his closest blood relationship with the young king was via the latter's mother – Cecily herself. It is unclear whether Cecily had any direct knowledge of what her eldest son was up to at this time. But a contemporary chronicle reported that:

> the king made very much of [Henry]; so much that he lodged with the king in his own bed many nights, and sometimes rode hunting behind the king.... The king loved him well.[28]

So it seems that their relationship was a matter of public knowledge – which eventually brought about an attack on the Duke of Somerset by local people in Northampton. Therefore it may well have disturbed the Duchess of York.

One piece of evidence in respect of Cecily's movements around the country emerges from the fact that, after her husband was killed at the battle of Wakefield, a close link evolved which brought John Howard into the service of his widow.

Howard, a cousin of Cecily's nephew, John Mowbray, 3rd Duke of Norfolk, had already been serving the York family for some ten years, and his personal link with the future Yorkist King Edward (then the Earl of March) had clearly been established by the summer of 1460.[29] The large number of manors and castles granted by the new king to his mother included the manor and Castle of Clare, and the town of Sudbury, both of which are in Suffolk.[30] In 1461 these were not far from John Howard's home at Tendring Hall, Stoke by Nayland.

It must have been shortly after 1 June 1461 (the date upon which she received all the manors from her son) that Cecily Neville appointed John Howard as her steward of the honour of Clare. For that post he subsequently received from her an annual payment of £17.[31] His appointment as her Clare steward meant that John Howard had now become a formal member of Cecily's client network. It was probably in the same month in which he was knighted by Edward IV. About five years later, Sir John Howard[32] drafted a letter, defending the interests of a Sudbury widow. The woman in question was one of Cecily's tenants and her intended second husband was Howard's own servant and tenant. In his letter Howard proudly referred to Cecily as 'the hy an myty prynses, my lady, the Kenges moder, to wome I hame steward.'[33]

Of course, Cecily cannot have resided permanently at Clare Castle. She had many other properties, and these included Baynard's Castle (though she had not yet acquired Berkamsted Castle in Hertfordshire – see below). Nevertheless, it does appear to be the case that she lived at Clare on a regular basis during the 1460s. Her visits there may have formed part of an established cycle of annual movements. Cecily definitely seems to have been living at Clare Castle on Saturday 8 October 1463.[34] Possibly she was there again in the summer of 1464, when she issued a certificate that Lawrence Gerard, Master of the College of Russheworth [*sic* – Rushford], near Thetford in Norfolk, had paid homage for military service in the honour of Clare.[35] She was also there in June 1465, because the surviving household records of Sir John Howard include the following note:

> Item, the xj day of June my mastyr spent for costys at Clare, whan he rode to my Lady of Yorke, viij s.[36]

Two months later Howard paid half a gold angel (3s. 4d.) to the Duchess of York's secretary for the writing of three warrants,[37] but of course that does not prove that Cecily was then at Clare in person.

It is also possible that Cecily may have been at Clare Castle in July 1467, when Sir John Howard received her youngest son, Richard, Duke of Gloucester, in

Colchester and then took the young prince on to his mother's town of Sudbury, and to Bury St Edmunds – possibly visiting Cecily at Clare *en route*.[38] In other words it seems that Clare Castle may have been one of Cecily's normal residences in summer and autumn during the years 1463 to 1467.

Cecily may also have left an intriguing memento of her visits on site in Clare. A small originally enamelled gold reliquary crucifix set with pearls was found during railway construction work at the castle site in 1866 (see plate 24).[39] Since this piece of jewellery had been created around the middle of the fifteenth century, it must have been lost at Clare Castle during Cecily Neville's tenure of that property. Cecily herself later showed strong signs of religious devotion. She would have been the logical owner of a fine little reliquary crucifix, containing small pieces of wood and stone which are thought to be relics of the True Cross and of the rock of Calvary. Indeed, it seems that Cecily Neville may have shared with her Suffolk steward, John Howard, a particular devotion to the Holy Cross.

Further evidence of Cecily's possible interest in this cult may be the fact that her daughter, Margaret of York is reputed to have been born at Waltham Abbey, home of the shrine of the Holy Cross of Waltham (see above, Chapter 3). As for Sir John Howard, he visited Waltham Abbey in February 1463/4.[40] He is also known to have patronised the shrine of the Holy Rood of Dovercourt, in Essex. Howard spent time at Dovercourt and the adjacent town of Harwich working on shipbuilding on behalf of King Edward IV.[41] On 27 August 1463 he offered 8d. at the Dovercourt shrine.[42] On 5 May 1481, Howard's second wife, Margaret Chedworth, offered 4d. at the same shrine.[43] Also, on 25 February 1482 Howard's servant, Thomas Dalamar, reported that 'I took Hew Wryte, for dressing of the rood at Dovercourt 21s., with xxx sterys of gold, prise viijd. a piece.'[44] It is probable that the Howards made other donations to the Dovercourt shrine in the intervening years, but unfortunately their household accounts for much of that time have not survived.

On 12 February 1462/3, Cecily Neville granted a tenement in Worcestershire to Alexander Holt, esquire, serjeant of her pantry, and to his wife, Katherine.[45] On 23 March 1462/3, her son-in-law, John de la Pole was created Duke of Suffolk by Letters Patent, thereby elevating her daughter, Elizabeth, to the rank of Duchess of Suffolk.

According to the surviving Paston correspondence, on 13 November 1463, Margaret Paston, in Norwich, was planning a marriage for her daughter with the eighteen year old son of Sir John Cley. The proposed husband was almost certainly the 'Master John Cley' who had delivered a message from the Earl of March to the Paston household in Southwark three years earlier, seeking hospitality for the Duchess of York and her three youngest children (see above).

At that time the young Cley's father and namesake had only been an esquire. However, his Yorkist loyalty had subsequently been rewarded by Edward IV with a knighthood. Also, Sir John Clay had then found himself appointed the chamberlain of Cecily Neville, Duchess of York.[46]

In the early years of the reign of her son, Edward, Cecily was treated as the senior female member of the royal family in respect of the offering of prayers for royalty on behalf of individuals to whom royal grants were made. Existing prayers for Cecily's good estate while she lived, and for her soul after her death, were confirmed on 19 July 1461.[47] New prayers of the same category were commissioned on 10 and 16 July 1461,[48] on 6 September 1461,[49] on 29 November 1461,[50] on 16, 17 and 26 December 1461,[51] on 22 February 1461/2,[52] on 23 February 1461/2,[53] on 11 August 1462,[54] and on 21 March 1464.[55] In these years the format of such commissioning was to request prayers for the good estate of the king and of Cecily his mother, and prayers for their souls after death. Prayers were also normally requested for the soul of the king's dead father, Richard, Duke of York, and occasionally also for that of his brother, Edmund, Earl of Rutland.

However, by May 1465, the provisions had changed.[56] Prayers were then requested first and foremost for the king and for his recently acknowledged consort, Elizabeth Widville. Cecily now found her name moved back into third place. Similar commissions of this new formula continued for a time.[57] What is more, gradually a situation arose in which the king's mother came to be omitted entirely from such request for prayers.[58] The implication is that following his public acknowledgement of his secret marriage to Elizabeth Widville, Edward IV began to drift apart from his mother.

The young king's movements about his realm show that he had been in the vicinity of Northampton in July 1462, in July, August and/or September 1463, and in January 1463/4.[59] Since her mother and father had a manor in that area, it is possible that he might have met Elizabeth Widville on any (or all) of those occasions. It has been widely asserted that the couple first met because Edward had confiscated the property of Elizabeth's late husband, Sir John Grey, who had been an anti-Yorkist. However, that is misleading. In reality the property had not been confiscated by the king. However, there was an on-going family controversy over its ownership based upon a conflict between Elizabeth Widville and her mother-in-law. Thus, through Lord Hastings, Elizabeth sought the king's help.

It seems that, when she met the young king, he found himself attracted to her in a similar way as he had previously found himself attracted to Eleanor Talbot. Reportedly, like Eleanor, Elizabeth was asked to let the young king make love to her, but refused. Thus Edward IV seems to have felt himself forced to propose a secret marriage once again. This second secret marriage was reportedly celebrated at the manor house of Grafton Regis, on 1 May 1464.

> In moste secrete maner, vpon the firste daye of May,[60] kynge Edwarde spousyd Elizabeth, late the wyfe of sir John Graye, knyght, whiche before tyme was slayne at Toweton or Yorke felde, whiche spowsayles were solempnyzed erely in ye mornynge at a towne named Graston [Grafton], nere vnto Stonyngstratforde; at whiche mariage was no [moo] persones present but the spowse, the spowsesse, the duches of Bedforde her moder, y preest, two gentylwomen, and a yong man to helpe the preest synge. After which spowsayles endyd, he went to bedde, and so taried there vpon. iii. or. iiii. houres, and after departed & rode agayne to Stonyngstratforde, and came i^n maner as though he had ben on huntinge, and there went to bedde agayne. And within a daye or. ii. after, he sent to Graston [Grafton], to the lorde Ryuers, fader vnto his wyfe, shewynge to hym y^t he wolde come & lodge with hym a certeyne season, where he was receyued with all honoure, and so taryed there by the space of. iiii. dayes. In whiche season, she nyghtly to his bedde was brought, in so secrete maner, that almooste none but her moder was of counsayll. And so this maryage was a season kept secret after, tyll nedely it muste be discoueryd & disclosed, by meane of other [proposed brides] whiche were offeryd vnto the kynge, as the quene of Scottes and other.[61]

Like the alleged earlier Talbot marriage, Edward IV's Widville marriage initially remained a secret. Only four months later, in September 1464, did the king make his connection with Elizabeth Widville public. The revelation was made at a meeting of the royal council at Reading. At that time Cecily's nephew, the Earl of Warwick, was proposing a royal marriage between Edward and the French king Louis XI's cousin and sister-in-law, Bona of Savoy. But the factor which induced Edward IV to make public his connection with Elizabeth Widville may well have been the premise that, at that point, four months after their secret alliance, Elizabeth was (or was claiming to be) pregnant by him.[62]

Of course the revelation must have surprised Cecily Neville as much as it surprised her nephew, the Earl of Warwick, and other relatives of the young King. As has already been shown (see above), some fifty years after the event Sir Thomas More wrote that Cecily openly objected to her son's so-called marriage with Elizabeth Widville, and asserted that Edward was already committed to

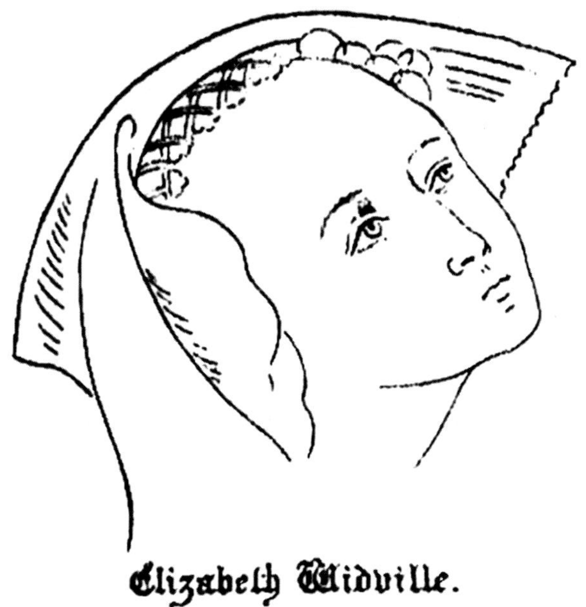

Elizabeth Widville, copied in 1789 from a fifteenth-century stained glass window at Thaxsted Church, Essex.

another woman. Although Thomas More put forward the apparently invented name of 'Elizabeth Lucy', in reality no such person seems to have existed. Significantly, however, More also claimed that 'Elizabeth Lucy' was the partner of Edward IV who was named by the Three Estates of the Realm in 1483 as Edward IV's legitimate wife. In reality, of course, the woman named on that later occasion was Eleanor Talbot.

It therefore seems that if Cecily did claim in 1464 that her son was already married to another woman whom she named – and perhaps personally consulted – the woman in question must really have been Eleanor. However, it seems that by that time Eleanor Talbot had already chosen to devote herself to a religious life as a tertiary.[63] Therefore it may well be that, in spite of apparent support for her partnership with Edward IV on the part of the young king's mother, she herself declined to assert that she was the true consort of Edward IV (as Thomas More later claimed in respect of *his* alleged candidate, 'Elizabeth Lucy'). Obviously what really happened between Edward IV and his mother in September 1464, in respect of his public announcement that he was married to Elizabeth Widville, cannot now be established with absolute clarity. However, on the basis of the hypothesis which I have advanced, it is not surprising that the relationship between Edward IV and his mother suddenly seems to have started to become less close.

On 23 March 1464/5, only five months after he had revealed his secret alliance with Elizabeth Widville – followed by whatever consequences that unveiling had brought about between him and Cecily Neville – we find for the first time Edward IV contemplating his mother's future demise. On that occasion provision was drafted by the young king for the future tenure of the Castle of Bridgewater in Somerset 'on the death of the king's mother, Cicely, duchess of York, who holds the said castle, lordship and manor for life.'[64]

It is possible that Cecily may have attended the subsequent coronation of Elizabeth Widville as Edward's queen consort at Westminster Abbey (26 May 1465).[65] Unfortunately, in this respect, as in the case of all the other coronation ceremonies which she lived through, no clear and specific evidence of Cecily's presence survives. Nevertheless, it is undoubtedly the case that Cecily subsequently became one of the two godmothers of the royal couple's first living child, her granddaughter, Elizabeth of York.

> 1465/6
> This year in the month of February, and in the fifth year of King Edward, the Queen was delivered of a daughter (*Elizabeth*), the which was christened in Westminster, the 11th of February 1466, to whom was godfather the Earl of Warwick, and godmothers were Cecily, Duchess of York, and Jacomyne (*Jacqueline*) Duchess of Bedford, Mothers to the King and Queen.[66]

Although her godmotherly role in respect of her granddaughter is clear, a question remains of how Cecily might have felt about the arrival of this little girl. After all, up until this point, for the past five years the heir to the English throne had been Cecily's son George.

As for George himself, he had now been required to act for a second time as steward – this time at the coronation of Elizabeth Widville. But his performance of that office does not mean that the young lad thought well of the new queen consort. Both he and his elder brother, the king, must have been well aware that questions had been raised regarding George's role as heir presumptive by the acknowledgement of the Widville marriage, followed by the birth of Elizabeth of York. At this point, of course, in English history, there had never been a reigning queen of England. The only person who had ever claimed that position – the Empress Matilda – had never actually secured recognition for her tenure of that role, despite the fact that her son had subsequently succeeded to the throne as King Henry II.

Nevertheless, the role in England of George (whom his brother had created Duke of Clarence) was now becoming uncertain. Indeed, his elder brother was clearly aware of this, because he attempted to win another position for George, by promoting plans for a marriage between the Duke of Clarence and the Burgundian heiress presumptive, Marie. Unfortunately the Burgundian court apparently preferred to negotiate instead a marriage between Marie's father, the Count of Charolais, and Edward and George's sister, Margaret of York, presumably in the hope of producing a male heir apparent for the duchy. The potential project of a Burgundian marriage for George therefore produced no result.

Meanwhile, Cecily must have been aware that a relationship was developing between her nephew, Richard Neville, Earl of Warwick, and his young cousin, George (Duke of Clarence). Warwick had definitely felt insulted by Edward IV's publication of his marriage to Elizabeth Widville. He also opposed the projected Burgundian marriage of Margaret of York (which was strongly supported by Elizabeth Widville and her family). Warwick would have preferred to arrange a French royal marriage for Margaret. He also explored with King Louis XI of France the possibility of granting some Burgundian lands and titles to his young cousin, George. This idea was opposed by Edward IV, but of course, George himself welcomed the idea. Thus by the early summer of 1467 George was known to be siding with his elder cousin, Warwick, and to be at odds with his brother, the king.

Cecily's own earlier problems in respect of Edward and his secret marriage were now apparently augmented by the fact that one of her younger sons was now experiencing problems with the king. One outcome of the friendship between George and his cousin, the Earl of Warwick, was the fact that the latter began proposing a marriage between his own daughter and heiress, Isabel Neville, and young George. This idea was initially opposed by Edward IV. However, it seems that Cecily supported the idea of George's marriage to Isabel, and was at odds with the king in that respect (see below, Chapter 10).

All this appears to have had certain consequences for Cecily and her life. It has already been noted that from 1465 onwards she was downgraded, and eventually removed, in respect of the prayers requested for members of the royal family. Edward IV also seems now to have become less interested in promoting Cecily's practical actions and needs. For example, at her manor of Kennington, in Kent, on 20 May 1468, the Duchess of York granted keepership of her great park at Bardfield (near Braintree in Essex) to John Serle and his son

Thomas. But her grant was only confirmed by Edward IV seven years later (at Canterbury on 10 June 1475) when all the intervening troubles seemed to have been resolved.[67] Also, on 8 June 1468 a grant was made for life by the king to his mother of the manor of Newhall and other specified lands.[68] However, that grant then became invalid because of the total lack of any follow-up action on the part of Edward IV to confirm the donation.

In addition, on 7 July 1468 Cecily was granted the right to export wool and other produce for the next two years.[69] However, this grant – requiring activity on her part – was merely in lieu of a more positive award which had theoretically been made to her on 1 June 1461. The earlier grant should have given the king's mother an addition to her annual income comprising the sum of £400 a year from the customs paid at the port of Kingston on Hull together with a small additional sum from the port of London. However, it seems that Cecily had never actually received anything from the earlier grant!

Most significantly of all, in February 1468/9, Cecily was required to surrender Fotheringhay Castle and its estate to Edward IV.[70] It was in response to her surrender of that property that, on 4 March 1468/9, she was given instead the manors of Berkhamsted and Kings Langley in Hertfordshire, together with Berkhamsted Castle,[71] and on 29 June she was granted some properties in

Berkamsted Castle, Herts.

Suffolk which had formerly been held by her husband.[72] At some unrecorded earlier date, Cecily had rewarded a man named John Walker for his loyal service to her late husband, and to her son, the king, by appointing him the porter of Fotheringhay Castle. Fortunately from Walker's point of view, on 28 October 1469, when the king had taken over Fotheringhay, he did confirm that Walker was to retain for his entire life the office which Cecily had granted him.[73]

Chapter 10

Cecily's Sons in Conflict

In the summer of 1467, Duke Philip of Burgundy's bastard son, Antoine, came to London, leading an important Burgundian delegation. This was in connection with the planned marriage of his half-brother, the Count of Charolais, with Cecily Neville's unmarried daughter, Margaret of York. In honour of the Burgundian envoys an impressive tournament was arranged at Smithfield by Elizabeth Widville's family, which strongly supported the Burgundian marriage plan for Margaret. It was Elizabeth's brother, Anthony Widville, Lord Scales, who was to represent England in this contest, and challenge his Burgundian namesake. Elizabeth and her Widville family presumably supported the Burgundian alliance because of the origin of her mother, Jacquette of Luxembourg.

There is no evidence as to whether Cecily herself, or her youngest son, Richard, Duke of Gloucester, attended the event at Smithfield. Cecily's relationship with Elizabeth Widville and her family may well have been not very warm, because it appears that Cecily had sought to persuade Edward IV that he could not be legally married to Elizabeth (see above, Chapter 9). Elizabeth clearly hated anyone who questioned the validity of her royal marriage (see below, Chapter 12). However, Cecily's middle son, George, Duke of Clarence was definitely made to attend the tournament. He was required to be there as an attendant for Anthony Widville.[1] Since, in the context of the house of York, George was the senior living male prince of the blood royal, finding himself required to act in this way as an attendant for a social inferior was a role which he cannot have appreciated. As will emerge shortly, he clearly disliked the Widvilles and the role they had assumed in the ruling of England.

As for Cecily's nephew, Richard Neville, Earl of Warwick, he definitely was not present at the London tournament. He had consistently opposed the Burgundian alliance proposed for his cousin, young Margaret, by Elizabeth Widville. Thus, instead of attending the event at Smithfield, he sailed across the Channel to France. Despite Edward IV's view of foreign affairs, which simply seemed to follow the advice and views of Elizabeth Widville, Warwick was still seriously attempting to promote a positive relationship between his cousin, the

The sons in italics all died violent deaths.

All her sons died before their mother.

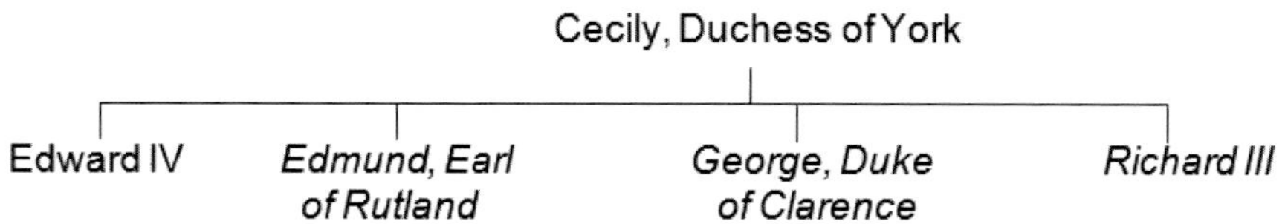

Cecily's Experience as a Mother

Yorkist king, and France. Having already failed to do this by arranging a suitable royal marriage for Edward IV, he was now seeking to arrange a French royal marriage for Margaret. He reached Rouen on 6 June 1467.

Two days after Warwick's arrival in Rouen, and possibly partly in consequence of that French trip, Cecily's younger nephew, Warwick's brother, George Neville, Archbishop of York, who had hitherto been serving as Edward IV's chancellor, received an unexpected and astonishing visit from his cousin the king. Edward called on the Archbishop at the inn in Charing Cross where he was staying, and demanded that the great seal of England should be handed back to him. The king was accompanied on this occasion by a number of lords, including his brother, the Duke of Clarence. In their presence the archbishop had to hand back the great seal to his sovereign in its white leather bag.[2] The dismissal from his government post of the Earl of Warwick's brother underlined the rift which existed – and which had now become visible – between Edward IV and these Neville cousins. As for the great seal, Edward IV transferred that to Bishop Robert Stillington of Bath and Wells. Stillington thereupon resigned the privy seal (which he had held hitherto) to Thomas Rotherham, Archdeacon of Canterbury.[3]

It seems likely that the king took his own brother, George, to witness the sacking of their cousin of the same name in order to ensure that the Duke of Clarence should be fully aware of the fact that if his friendship with the Earl of Warwick continued he too might now find himself on the wrong side politically. However, if that was Edward's intention, clearly it did not produce the required result (see below).

Meanwhile, nine days later, on Monday 15 June 1467, the situation in Burgundy suddenly changed dramatically. Duke Philip the Good died. He was succeeded as Duke of Burgundy by his legitimate son, Charles, hitherto the Count of Charolais. On receiving this news the Burgundian delegation left London for home. They were escorted to the Kent coast by Cecily's Suffolk steward and friend, Sir John Howard. The Burgundian representatives departed from Dover on 24 June – the Feast of the Nativity of St John the Baptist.[4] Ironically, on that very same day the Earl of Warwick, arrived back in England from France. He landed at Sandwich. There he received the offensive news that his brother the Archbishop of York had been dismissed from the chancellorship.

Warwick was accompanied by French ambassadors, who came with proposals for a French alliance. These men included the bastard of Bourbon, the Bishop of Bayeux and Master Jehan de Poupincourt. They accompanied Warwick via Canterbury to London.[5] However, only one member of Edward IV's court came to greet them. The person in question was Edward's brother, George, Duke of Clarence.[6] 'When the Earl of Warwick caught sight of the Duke of Clarence he greeted him very warmly, as he wanted to speak to him. The said duke received the ambassadors most honourably, as he very well knew how to do.'[7]

Shortly after the French ambassadors arrived, plague broke out in London. This was not uncommon at that period, in the warm days of summer. To escape the risk of infection, those who were able to do so left the capital for the countryside. The king himself went to Windsor Castle. As for the Earl of Warwick, he seems to have gone to the Eastern Counties, accompanied by both of Edward IV's younger brothers.[8] The king's youngest brother, Richard, Duke of Gloucester, had been under the guardianship of his cousin and namesake, the Earl of Warwick, since 1464. Initially the three cousins travelled together to Cambridge. It seems that while they were there Warwick took advantage of the intimacy to seek to win over George, Duke of Clarence, as his ally. Wavrin chronicles a conversation which took place in the summer of 1467 between Warwick and his cousin, George, though he does not specify where the conversation took place. Wavrin's record of the discussion exists thanks to the fact that Warwick had subsequently reported it to the French ambassadors.[9]

Initially, Warwick complained about the lack of attention which had been paid by the king to the French ambassadors. George, who perhaps misunderstood what his cousin meant, protested that he was in no way to blame for that. However, Warwick then made it clear that he was already very well aware of that fact, and was definitely not criticising George. After that the two cousins began to focus in their conversation upon the distressingly prominent role played in Edward IV's government by Elizabeth Widville's father and siblings. It rapidly became clear that George found that situation distressing. In fact, he longed for action of some kind to be taken to address the problem, and he asked the Earl of

Warwick what they could do about it. Warwick then proposed that the Duke of Clarence should himself take over the leading role in Edward IV's government. At this stage, in 1467, Warwick was not, of course, thinking of deposing Edward IV. For the moment his sole aim was the removal of the Widville family as the power behind the throne. However, he also proposed a marriage alliance between himself and the Duke of Clarence by offering George the hand of his elder daughter, Isabel Neville.

For the Earl of Warwick this marriage plan had the possible advantage that one day it might make the elder of his two daughters the queen consort of England. After all, in the summer of 1467 Elizabeth Widville had only produced one living child for Edward IV, and that child was a daughter – Cecily Neville's godchild, Elizabeth of York junior. Since Elizabeth had not produced a son for Edward IV, arguably the Duke of Clarence was still the heir presumptive to the English throne. Although Elizabeth Widville was in the final stages of another pregnancy, and would probably produce another child some time in August 1467,[10] it was by no means certain that would be a son. Also, since the objective of Warwick and the Duke of Clarence was to remove the Widvilles from power, presumably their work was meant to include questioning Elizabeth's right to be Edward's queen. That would obviously have the aim of removing Elizabeth herself, as well as the rest of her family.

A marriage between George and Isabel Neville would require a papal dispensation, firstly because her father was his first cousin, so they were very close blood relatives, and secondly because his mother was Isabel's godmother. Where Cecily herself was while the alliance was being built up between her son George and her nephew, Richard, Earl of Warwick, is not known for certain. However, it seems probable that she was in the Eastern Counties, not a hundred miles from Cambridge. This suggestion is based upon the fact that shortly after Warwick took her two younger sons to Cambridge, Cecily seems likely to have been visited by her youngest son, Richard, Duke of Gloucester, at Clare Castle.

Initially, of course, Richard had travelled to Cambridge with his brother, George, and their cousin, the Earl of Warwick. Later, however, though George stayed with the Earl of Warwick, Richard seems to have parted from them. This seems to have been the time when he went on a sight-seeing and hunting trip in Essex and Suffolk, in company with his mother's steward, Sir John Howard. There are two pieces of evidence in support of this: first, the fact that although George and the Earl of Warwick remained together after the visit to Cambridge, the Duke of Gloucester was then no longer with them; and second, the surviving draft of a letter which was written at about this time by Sir John Howard:

> My right especial good lord (*after all due recommendation*)[11] please you to wit yesterday my lord of Gloucester came to Colchester, and as I was in communication with his lordship of divers matters, among others I did[12] remember your lordship to my lord, promising you I found my lord as well disposed toward you as any lord may be to another; save my lord speaketh it largely,[13] whereof I was[14] right glad to hear it.
>
> Furthermore, my lord hath desired me to be with him at Sudbury, Lavenham and Saint Edmundsbury, and further if I might; but I durst promise him no further, for I was not in certain how hastily ye would have me: wherefore I pray you send me word by what day ye will have me there, and I shall not break it, by the grace of God, who have my right good lord in his blessed safeguard.
>
> Written on Mary Magdalene's day [22 July].[15]

The 'good lord' to whom this letter was addressed was probably Howard's young cousin, John Mowbray, Duke of Norfolk, Cecily Neville's great nephew, and the husband of Eleanor Talbot's younger sister, Elizabeth. He and his wife were probably also not feeling friendly towards the Widville family.

As the letter shows, first the Duke of Gloucester visited Sir John Howard in Colchester. Then the two of them travelled on into Suffolk. The road from Colchester to Sudbury would have taken them past Howard's local manor house

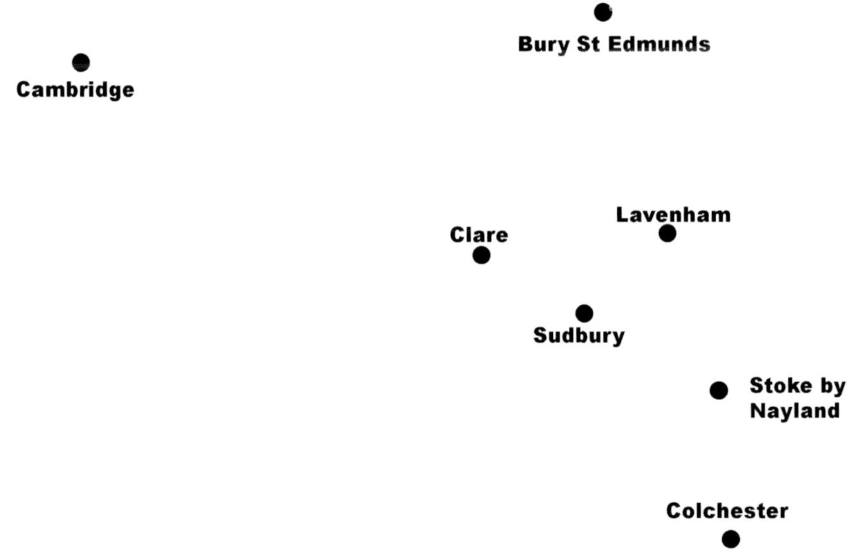

The area visited by Cecily's son, Richard, Duke of Gloucester, in the summer of 1467.

at Stoke by Nayland. The letter makes it clear that they then visited the Earl of Oxford's estate at Lavenham, the Sudbury area itself, and Bury St Edmunds. They were still together when the letter was drafted, and the Duke of Gloucester was proposing further visits. Thus, together with her steward, John Howard, he may well have gone on to visit his mother at Clare Castle. Certainly he was in the right vicinity.

An interesting sequel is the fact that if Cecily was at Clare in the third full week of July 1468, she might also have met her middle son, George, and her nephew the Earl of Warwick, while they were in that neighbourhood – though unfortunately no correspondence survives to support *that* possibility. If so, given the focus of their conversations at that time, it seems probable that she would have discussed the political situation with both of them. After all, as will emerge shortly, it appears that Cecily supported the anti-Widville campaign of her middle son and her nephew, which sought to drag her eldest son, Edward IV, back to what his closest blood relatives would have perceived as authentic Yorkism, as opposed to 'Widvillism'!

The following year found Cecily staying in Kent. The surviving evidence shows that in May 1468 she was residing at her manor of Kennington (see above, Chapter 9). In the following month the marriage procession of her daughter, Margaret, left London, travelling via Kent to Margate. Although the Earl of Warwick had opposed the Burgundian alliance, he was required to lead Margaret from the Royal Wardrobe through London. Also both of Cecily's younger sons accompanied the sister with whom the two of them had spent most of their childhood. It therefore seems likely that at some point Cecily, too, must have taken part in the departure ceremonies and wished her youngest surviving daughter well. This could either have been in London or somewhere in Kent. Unfortunately, however, no surviving records of the marriage mention the bride's mother or the role she took. The Canterbury Chronicle of Brother John Stone merely mentions that Edward IV, accompanied by his sister, Margaret, and his two younger brothers, George, Duke of Clarence and William [*sic* for Richard], Duke of Gloucester, together with various other earls, barons and knights, arrived at Canterbury Cathedral on Wednesday 22 June 1468. They attended mass the following day, and in the afternoon they all rode on to the Thanet district, where Margaret took ship at the appropriately named port of Margate. At Sluis ('Sclwce') she was married to Charles the Bold, Duke of Burgundy, on Sunday 3 July, by Richard Beauchamp, Bishop of Salisbury.[16]

A number of English aristocrats travelled with Margaret, including absolutely all of the surviving members of Eleanor Talbot's family. Since Eleanor Talbot died suddenly, in her thirties, on 30 June 1468, while all her living relatives had been separated from her and sent away to the Low Countries, the inclusion of every single member of her family in Margaret of York's entourage may well have been politically significant. The fact that Elizabeth Widville and her family were behind Margaret of York's marriage plans may also be significant in this respect. It is possible that by this time Elizabeth was not only aware of the fact that the legality of her marriage to the king was disputed, but also knew that he had made an earlier secret marriage contract with Eleanor, whom it would therefore be advisable to get rid of.

In 1469 Cecily once again found herself staying in Kent. There she met her son George, her nephew, Richard, Earl of Warwick, the latter's daughter, Isabel Neville, and other relatives at the port of Sandwich. This meeting took place in connection with another set of marriage plans. On Tuesday 14 March 1468/9 a papal dispensation had been granted in Rome, which gave George permission to marry Isabel Neville. It had been obtained thanks to the assistance of the king's proctor at the papal curia, Dr James Goldwell. Having obtained the papal dispensation, the Duke of Clarence and the Earl of Warwick planned to sail to Calais to celebrate there the marriage between George, and Isabel. In April 1469 the Earl of Warwick sought the king's permission for him to go to Calais, and campaign from there against Channel pirates, and Edward IV agreed to this.

Detailed information of what occurred in Kent (and Calais) in the summer of 1469 has survived in the form of a record kept at Canterbury Cathedral Priory by a member of the monastic community, Brother John Stone. First Brother John reports the arrival at Canterbury of the Duke of Clarence:

> Item this year [1469] on the 7th day of the month of June, that is to say feria iiii [Wednesday],[17] on the eve of the Translation of St. Aelphegus, Martyr, Lord George, Duke of Clarence and brother of Edward IV, King of England and France, came to Canterbury, between about the fourth and fifth hours after none,[18] and was welcomed at the door of the church in the name of the Most Holy Trinity by Prior John Oxne[19] – decently clothed in a green cope – and by the community. And he stayed for two nights in the chamber of the Lord Prior with a numerous entourage; and on the following feria vi [Friday 9 June] he departed from Canterbury towards Sandwich.[20]

On Friday 9 June George's cousin and namesake, the Archbishop of York, arrived in his turn at Canterbury Cathedral.[21] There he honoured St Augustine and St Thomas Becket. Three days later he went on to bless a fine new ship which his brother, the Earl of Warwick, had commissioned. He named the vessel *Trinity*. The Duke of Clarence and the Earl of Warwick were both present at that event, together with Thomas Kempe, Bishop of London, and the Prior of Canterbury Cathedral.[22]

As for Cecily herself,

> on the next feria iiii [Wednesday 14 June] the Duchess of York, mother of the most illustrious King Edward IV, came to Canterbury, and stayed in the chamber of the Lord Prior, and used his[*sic*] as the Duke of Clarence had done, but with not so many attendants. And on the following day [15 June] she departed from Canterbury towards Sandwich, to her son, that is to say, to the Duke of Clarence; And on the next feria ii [Monday 19 June] she returned to Canterbury. And on the following day [Tuesday 20 June] she was at vespers, and on Sunday she attended high mass and second vespers, and on Monday [26 June] she left Canterbury.[23]

It is absolutely clear, therefore, that Cecily had been to Sandwich to see her middle son, George, her nephews the Earl of Warwick and the Archbishop of York, and her great niece, god-daughter, and prospective daughter-in-law, Isabel Neville, and that she had spent five days with all of them at Sandwich. Since all the other people involved were definitely on the side of the Duke of Clarence and the Earl of Warwick and their anti-Widville policy, and supported George's planned marriage with Isabel Neville, it appears that Cecily must also have been backing them. Thus it seems that she too was in favour of their marriage plan, of the removal of the Widville family from power in England, and of attempting to draw her eldest son the king back to what his family saw as authentic Yorkist policies.

The Duke of Clarence and the Earl of Warwick returned to Canterbury from Sandwich on Wednesday 21 June, and on Thursday 22 June they departed from Canterbury in the direction of Queenborough Castle (Sheppey).[24] However, on Tuesday 4 July Clarence, Warwick, the Archbishop of York, and the Earl of Oxford were all back at Canterbury Cathedral. On 5 July an offering was made by the Archbishop of York at the shrine of St Thomas Becket, and Brother John (who, of course, was not present at the ceremony in person) claims that on the following Sunday (9 July 1469) Archbishop George Neville solemnised the marriage of his namesake, George, Duke of Clarence, and Isabel Neville in Calais.[25] Another source claims that the marriage was celebrated on Tuesday 11 July, and I do not know which of the two dates is correct.

> Be it knowen and remembred, that the Tewesdaye, the xith daye of the moneth of July, in the translation of Seint Benet the Abbot, the ix yere of the raigne of our soveraine Lord Kinge Edwarde the Fourthe, in the castelle of Calais, the seid Duke tooke in marriage lsabell, one of the daughters and heires of the seid Richard erle of Warwik; whiche that tyme was prefent there; and v other knyghtes of the garter, and many other lordes and ladies, and wurshipfull knightes, well accompanied with wife and discreete esquires, in right greate numbyr, to the laude preysinge of God, and to the honoure and wurship of the world: and there abode after the daye of the matrimonye fivedayes; and then shipped into Ingland, leavinge the seid Duchesse at Caleis aforesaid; and went hymself and the seid Erie to the citie of London, and soe forthe northwarde.[26]

The possibility that Cecily may also have sailed from Sandwich with the wedding party has been considered. For example, Hicks has suggested that she may have been present in Calais at the marriage of George and Isabel.[27] Unfortunately, however, there is no solid evidence to clarify that point. And while the above account mentions that many lords and ladies were present, it does not specifically name George's mother.

Meanwhile, a rebellion against Edward IV – or rather against the Widvilles – had begun in the north of England, led by a man known by the pseudonym of 'Robin of Redesdale.' It later emerged that this rebellion had been planned by the Earl of Warwick the previous year. When George's marriage to Isabel had been celebrated, the Duke of Clarence and the Earl of Warwick also made public their desire for reform in England. They put out their own very firm manifesto against the Widville family, criticising their 'disceyvabille covetous rule'.[28] The two of them then sailed back to Sandwich, and returned to Canterbury where they successfully mustered a number of Kentish supporters. Leaving Canterbury in mid July, they rode on to London, 'where they waited for their men and sometimes got news of the progress of the northerners.'[29] Subsequently they made for Coventry, and on Wednesday 26 July 1469 both Clarence and Warwick confronted men loyal to Edward IV and his existing government at the battle of Edgecote.

> The erle of Warweke ... sent with owt lingering unto the duke of Clarence, who was hard by with an army, that he wold bring his forces unto him, signyfying withal that the day of battayle was at hand. Uppon this message the duke reparyd furthwith to the earle, and

> so they both having joygnyd ther forces marchyd to a village caulyd Banbery, wher they understoode ther enemyes to be encampyd. Ther was a feyld fowghte,[30] Therle of Pembrowghe was taken, all his army slane and discomfytyd. Emongest this number was killed Rycherd earl Ryvers, father to Elyzabeth the queen, and his soone John Vedevill.[31]

To many people in England – possibly including Cecily – executing two members of the Widville family may have seemed like an excellent start to the process of restoring a genuine Yorkist government. However, obviously the work had not been completed. Thus, in September 1469, Jacquette, Duchess of Bedford and Countess Rivers, found herself being focused on as the next intended victim. One of the Earl of Warwick's retainers, Thomas Wake, provided Warwick with a damning piece of evidence against her, in the form of an 'image of lede made lyke a man of armes, conteynyng the lengthe of a mannes fynger, and broken in the myddes, and made fast with a wyre.'[32] It was claimed that this proved Jacquette's involvement in witchcraft.

Meanwhile, the anxious king had been asking advice from his supporters as to whether he should himself take up arms against the northern rebels. Perhaps significantly, Lord Hastings, Lord Mountjoy, Sir Thomas Montgomery and other allies of Edward IV all advised him to do nothing.[33] It seems likely that the fact that the rebellion was focused on the removal from power, not of Edward IV himself, but of the Widville family, was clearly understood and quite widely appreciated. Apparently at this stage even the king himself refused to believe that his brother, George, and his cousin, the Earl of Warwick, meant to ruin him.[34]

However, the sequel to the battle of Edgecote proved to be the capture of Edward IV himself. The king was staying at Olney, and it was there that he suddenly found himself made a prisoner.

> The king heard the news of this [the battle of Edgecote], which greatly displeased him, he felt that he had been betrayed, and prepared all his men to go and confront his brother the Duke of Clarence and his cousin of Warwick, who were coming before him. They were between Warwick and Coventry when they received the news that the king was coming to see them. ... it was not then to be believed that his brother of Clarence, nor his cousin of Warwick would think of treason when meeting him in person; wherefore the king proceeded to a village nearby and there he lodged all his men not far from the place where the Earl of Warwick was staying. At

> about midnight the Archbishop of York came to the king with a large party of armed men. He went right up to the king's lodging, saying to those who guarded his person that he needed to speak to the king, to whom they announced him; but the king sent him a reply that he was resting and that he should come in the morning when he would be happy to receive him. Which response did not please the archbishop, so he again sent his messengers to the king a second time, to say that he had to speak to him. When they did this the king ordered that he should be allowed in, in order to hear what he wanted to say, for he had no doubts regarding his loyalty. When the archbishop had entered the chamber, where he found the king in bed, he quickly said to him 'Sire, get up', from which the king wished to excuse himself, saying that he hadn't yet had any rest. But the archbishop, false and disloyal as he was, said to him a second time: 'You must get up and come to my brother of Warwick, for you cannot resist this.' And the king, thinking that nothing worse could happen to him, got dressed, and the archbishop led him without making much noise to the place where the said earl and the duke of Clarence were, between Warwick and Coventry.[35]

Although he was not mistreated further, Edward IV found himself effectively imprisoned at Warwick Castle during the second week of August 1469. Subsequently he was moved north, to Middleham Castle. At this point it may have seemed to many people that the plans of the Earl of Warwick and his son-in-law, the Duke of Clarence, had proved utterly successful. After all, given that the reigning monarch was now in their hands, they appeared to have made themselves the effective power behind the throne.

But to move things further forward a Parliament seemed necessary. Provisions were therefore made for one to meet in York on 22 September. It was probably with that intention in mind that Edward IV was allowed to depart from Middleham and go to York. However, the planned Parliament never actually met. As for Edward IV, he moved on from York to Pontefract. It was now clear that he was no longer a prisoner. Thus, in October 1469, he made his way south to London. At first all still seemed to be well, for in London the king granted 'a general pardon to all manner of men, for all manner (of) insurrections and trespasses',[36] and a council of the peers of the realm began meeting. By the end of the first week of December 1469 the Earl of Warwick and the Duke of Clarence had joined Edward IV and his council in London. At this point Cecily seems to have played a role in attempting to completely reconcile the two parties, for on Tuesday 6 March 1469/70 George, Duke of Clarence, met his brother, the king, at their mother's London home, Baynard's Castle.[37]

However, in some quarters the earlier capture of Edward IV had brought about a reversion to Lancastrian loyalty. That further complicated the situation in England, leading to the battle of Losecoat Field, fought on 12 March 1469/70. The Earl of Warwick and the Duke of Clarence told Edward IV that they were marching north to support him against the Lancastrians. However, just before his execution, the captured Lancastrian captain, Sir Robert Welles claimed that Warwick and Clarence were his partners in the rebellion.

Warwick and his family, including the Duke of Clarence then fled into the West Country, meeting up in Exeter on 3 April 1470. Although Isabel, Duchess of Clarence was then nearing the end of her first pregnancy, they set sail for Calais. However, a rapid message from Edward IV ensured that they were not allowed to land there. Thus Isabel gave birth to her first child on the ship. Either the baby was born dead, or died soon after birth. Because they were not allowed to land at Calais, eventually they sailed on to Normandy. They were honourably received by King Louis XI, and the Earl of Warwick himself had now clearly changed sides. He reconciled himself with Margaret of Anjou, and deserted Edward IV, becoming a Lancastrian.

How Edward's brother, George, Duke of Clarence, felt about this we have no way of knowing. However, his later contact with his mother and sisters suggests that he must always have felt uneasy about the new situation, one result of which was the fact that in May 1470 'King Edward proclaimed that his brother, George Plantagenet, Duke of Clarence, and Richard Neville, Earl of Warwick, together with some of their followers, were banished.'[38] Meanwhile, in France the government was now definitely anti-Yorkist and supported the restoration to the English throne of Louis XI's cousin, Henry VI. The French government sought every possible means of undermining the claim to the English throne of Edward IV. As a result, a story seems to have been invented, implying that Edward had no right to the English throne because he had never really been of royal birth. This was a tale which very much insulted Cecily. Indeed, it must have greatly distressed her, because twenty-five years later, in her last will, she denied the claim that Edward had been a bastard.

Chapter 11

The Blaybourne Bastardy Myth

The story of the 'Blaybourne bastardy' is the curious myth which claims that Edward IV was not really the son of Richard Duke of York. The allegation is that he was borne by Cecily Neville as a result of a love affair, which she had conducted during her husband's absence, with an archer whose surname was Blaybourne.[1] Clearly this story had never been current during Edward's childhood, because Richard, Duke of York unquestionably accepted Edward as his son and heir. Proof of his belief in this respect exists in his surviving letters to King Charles VII of France, written in 1445, when he was attempting to arrange a splendid French royal marriage for 'Edouart of York, my eldest son.'[2]

Some historians have claimed that the bastardy myth was first publicised on the mainland of Europe by Richard Neville, Earl of Warwick, in 1469.[3] No contemporary evidence ever appears to have been cited in English language publications to back that assertion. However, Armstrong referred to a source, albeit without actually quoting it.[4] The item in question is a letter written by Sforza de Bettini, Milanese ambassador at the French court, to his sovereign, Galeazzo Maria Sforza, the Duke of Milan. The letter was written from Amboise on 8 August 1469. It states that :

> This Most Christian lord King [Louis XI] has lately received advice concerning an important piece of news in England. It seems that the Earl of Warwick, who is a great and mighty lord in that country, having given his daughter as wife to the Duke of Clarence, brother of the King of England, has been rather inventive, claiming that the said King of England is a bastard, so the crown and sovereignty do not legitimately belong to him, but should duly and directly be transferred to the aforesaid Duke of Clarence.[5]

This is a very interesting letter. It clearly states that the source for the bastardy allegation was the Earl of Warwick. But of course, Sforza de Bellini is not suggesting that he himself had heard the Earl of Warwick making such a statement. Sforza de Bellini was the Milanese ambassador at the French court, so his source for the information on this front which he had received during the summer of 1469 can only have been King Louis XI. Thus it seems that the French king was disseminating the story that he had received this important news. However, both in the past and in the present day, governments readily tell lies whenever they think that it may be in their own interest to do so. Therefore the story that the Earl of Warwick had claimed that Edward IV was illegitimate might possibly have been an invention of the government of Louis XI.

Undoubtedly the position of the French government in relation to the Yorkist regime of England in the 1460s was basically hostile. This is clearly revealed by a command which Louis XI sent to the Philip the Good, Duke of Burgundy, in June 1462. In that document, King Louis wrote:

> Dear and beloved uncle. Our dear and beloved cousin the Queen of England [Margaret of Anjou] has recently come before us to report and reveal to us the great injuries, inhumanities and other enormous excesses and related crimes which have been and are daily committed by Edward of March, his allies and accomplices, against our dear and well beloved cousin Henry, King of England, their natural lord and sovereign.[6]

The wording of this message makes it obvious that Louis XI's government still recognised Henry VI as the legitimate King of England. Edward IV is simply referred to as the Earl of March. Thus, in spite of the fact that he had seized the throne, he was not accepted by the French regime as the true sovereign of England. In other words, the French government was utterly opposed to Edward and his Yorkist government.

Other surviving evidence appears to confirm that the bastardy story concerning Edward IV actually first spread within the kingdom of France. Between the battle of Ludlow Bridge and the battle of Northampton a poem supporting the Yorkist cause seems to have been written 'in May 1460, previous to the landing of the Earls of March, Salisbury, and Warwick, in Kent.'[7] At that time the Duke of York, who is briefly mentioned in the poem, was still alive, but was based in Ireland. However, the poem chiefly concentrates on three other Yorkist leaders: Edward, Earl of March (later Edward IV), his uncle, Richard Neville, Earl of Salisbury, and his cousin, Richard Neville, Earl of Warwick. In May 1460 these three earls were based on the European mainland, in Calais. But they were planning an invasion of England. Although the poem claims to have been inspired by Yorkist support as seen in London, in reality it was a piece of political propaganda, and could well have been written in Calais, as part of the three earls' preparation for their invasion of England.

In respect of Edward, Earl of March, the poem says:

E for Edward, whos fame þe erþe shal sprede,
Be-cause of his wisdom named prudence,
Shal saue alle Englond by his manly-hede,
Wherfore we owe to do hym reuerence.

M for Marche, trewe in euery tryalle,
Drawen by discretion þat worthy and wise is,
Conseived in wedlock, and comyn of blode ryalle,
Joynyng vnto vertu, excluding alle vises.[8]

It is interesting that in respect of the young Edward, one of the key points put forward in the poem appears to be the affirmation of his legitimacy. This might possibly suggest that in the Calais area, on the European mainland, there was already some gossip current upon this point as early as May 1460. If so, Edward's cousin, Richard Earl of Warwick would presumably have heard the gossip at that point. In May 1460 he appears to have supported its denial. Later, however, he may have chosen to make use of the story in a different way, for his own possible advantage.

Unfortunately, however, there is also one small but significant piece of doubt and confusion in respect of the date of the poem. Although most of the evidence (in terms of its contents) suggests that it was originally written in May 1460, the last verse in the surviving manuscript version[9] refers to 'Edward, kyng most ryalle'.[10] This suggests that the existing manuscript may contain a version of the poem which was produced at a later date, after Edward IV had become king. The fact that the last verse also mentions that its aim is 'to destroy treson, and make a tryalle, / Of hem þ^{t} be fauty',[11] implies that the surviving text (which includes the naming of Edward as *king*, together with confirmation of his legitimacy) may be a version which was written in about 1469–1470, when Edward's tenure of the throne was being opposed. If so the existing text of the poem – with its assertion that Edward was born legitimately – could be of about the same date as the letter from Sforza de Bettini (see above), which is the earliest surviving documentary source for the story that Edward IV was alleged to be illegitimate.

Much later, in the 1490s, it was reported that in 1475 Charles the Bold, Duke of Burgundy, had felt very angry with his brother-in-law, the English

Charles the Bold, Duke of Burgundy (19th century engraving of a 15th century portrait).

monarch, because Edward IV had then just concluded a treaty with King Louis XI of France. Reportedly Charles therefore stamped the ground, swore, and shouted that Edward IV's real name was Blaybourne, and that he was the son of an archer.[12] Accounts of the Duke of Burgundy's conduct were subsequently related to his cousin and enemy, King Louis XI, who 'laughed heartily and told [the narrator] to speak up and to repeat his story again because he was becoming a little deaf.'[13]

The earliest record of the bastardy story in *England* is to be found in the records of the act of attainder against Edward IV's brother, George, Duke of Clarence, in 1477/8. This claims that George had said 'that the Kyng oure Sovereigne Lorde was a Bastard, and not begottone to reigne uppon us.'[14] Of course, this was by no means a *publication* of the story in England, since the report merely figured in the parliamentary records.

A few years later, in 1483, Domenico Mancini reported that Edward IV's mother had been so angry about his secret marriage with Elizabeth Widville

King Louis XI of France (19th century engraving of a 15th century portrait).

that she 'offered to submit to a public inquiry, and asserted that Edward was not the offspring of her husband.'[15] But of course, Mancini's text was, once again, a French government report rather than an English document. After all, Mancini was acting as a French diplomat or spy, and his report was written for the French regime. Once again, therefore, what he wrote by no means circulated the story in England. What is more, there is no reason to believe that Mancini himself had ever met or spoken to the Duchess of York. Thus his claim is merely a second-hand story. However, reportedly one of his chief sources of information in England comprised members of the Widville family. And that family (in the person of Elizabeth Widville) must have been behind the earlier inclusion of the bastardy allegation in the parliamentary record of the act of attainder against the Duke of Clarence.

By the 1490's (possibly because the then king of England – Henry VII – and some of his key supporters had earlier been living in France, and had heard the myth there) the bastardy story seems to have become a little more widely known in England. It was probably at about that time that a note asserting that Edward had been conceived in the chamber next to the chapel in the Palace of Hatfield was added to one of William Worcester's reports of the boy's date of birth (see below).[16] Presumably that addition to the original text was a deliberate attempt to deny the bastardy story. Also, in 1495 his mother's will (see below, Chapter 15) stated specifically that Edward IV was her husband's son. Obviously by that time Cecily Neville must have been aware of – and upset by – the bastardy myth. However, like the parliamentary record of 1477/8, Cecily Neville's will was, at that time, in no way a public document.

It was also in the late 1490s that Philippe de Commynes recorded his account of how the Blaybourne story was cried out in anger by Charles the Bold in 1475 (see above). However, although that story figures on *one single page* of his memoirs, everywhere else in his account Commynes consistently calls 'the Duke of York, father of the late King Edward',[17] and treats Edward IV as a legitimate prince.

In the sixteenth century, Polydore Vergil (who, like Domenico Mancini, was not a native of England, even though he served there), claimed that Edward IV's brother, Richard III, had promoted the bastardy story. Writing in the period 1505–1534, Vergil asserted that, as Duke of Gloucester, Richard:

> being blinde with covetousnes of raigning … had secret conference with one Raphe Sha, a divyne of great reputation … to whom he utteryd, that his fathers inherytance ought to descend to him by right, as the eldest of all the soones which Richard his father Duke of York had begotten of Cecyly his wyfe: for as much as yt was manyfest ynowghe … that Edward who had before raignyd, was a bastard, … praying the said Sha to instruct the people therof in a sermon at Powles Crosse.[18]

Vergil then went on to claim that 'ther ys a common report that King Edwards chyldren wer in that sermon caulyd basterdes, and not King Edward, *which is voyd of all truthe*.'[19]

However, Vergil's version of the story appears to be absolute rubbish. Fabyan's *Chronicle* of 1516 reports very clearly that the sermon at Paul's Cross argued 'that *the childyr of King Edward* were not rightfull enherytours unto the crowne.'[20] The veracity of Fabyan's version of the story is very clearly backed up by the act of parliament (known as *titulus regius*) of 1484. The case for offering the crown to Richard III is there stated clearly. And it was definitely not based upon any allegation that King Edward IV himself had been a bastard. It was based upon Edward's bigamy and the consequent illegitimacy of his children by Elizabeth Widville.

More recently, arguments have been advanced by some modern historians to the effect that the evidence of his date of birth and the evidence of his place of baptism both back up the story that Edward IV was not the true son of the Duke of York, but was a bastard. As was seen earlier, first, it is argued that nine months before Edward was born the Duke of York would not have been in the right location to have fathered him. Secondly, a completely groundless legend has been invented, claiming that Cecily was attracted to tall men (like archers), but that the Duke of York was too short for her. Thirdly, it is claimed that if Edward had been the Duke's son and heir he would have been baptised at Rouen Cathedral.

Edward IV was born in France, at the Castle of Rouen. Modern sources all claim that his date of birth was 28 April 1442. This is based on the following statement from the *Annals* of William Worcester:

> 1442 Edward, King of England and France, the second son and heir of Richard, Duke of York, was born, on Monday [*sic*] 28 April after midnight in the second hour of the morning, at Rouen – who was conceived in the chamber next to the chapel in the Palace of Hatfield.[21]

Unfortunately this statement is clearly inaccurate, because 28 April 1442 was not a Monday but a Saturday. Therefore at least one element (and possibly more than one) of 'Monday 28 April 1442' has to be incorrect. But of course there is no way of knowing which element (or elements) need changing. By crossing out 'Monday' and substituting 'Saturday' one would produce the claim that Edward IV was born on *Saturday* 28 April 1442 and that might appear superficially to be acceptable. However, it is equally possible that the error was not the day of the week as reported by William Worcester, but the month. In that case the correction might need to read 'Monday 28 *May* 1442'.

In that case Edward would have been born about a month later than is normally supposed – and the estimated date of his conception would then also need to be altered!

The only other correct possibilities for Monday 28 in this period – Monday 28 January 1442/3 or Monday 28 October 1443 – are both ruled out by Cecily Neville's conception date of her next child, Edmund (Earl of Rutland), as the table of her conceptions shows (see above, Chapter 3).

Sadly, in another part of his text regarding Edward's date of birth, William Worcester muddles things even further by changing his number, and recording Edward IV's birth date as *27* April.[22] In other words the truth is that we have no evidence to prove precisely when Edward was born. That being so, any attempt at presenting arguments as to where the Duke of York would have been geographically when the baby was conceived is simply ludicrous. Yet Michael Jones, who has put forward the strongest modern argument in favour of the bastardy of Edward IV, has completely overlooked that problem in respect of the documentary evidence, and simply asserts that 'Edward was born on 28 April 1442.'[23] As for Jones' assertions regarding the stature and appearance of both the Duke of York and his wife, they have been shown to be based upon no solid evidence. His view of the manly stature which Cecily found attractive is also groundless. (See above, Chapter 4.)

The argument about where the little boy was baptised is also ludicrous. First, we do not know for certain where the baptism took place. Laurence Stratford claimed that:

> A note in MS in the British Museum speaks of his being christened in the Cathedral Church of Rouen, all the prelates and clergy being present 'in pontificalibus' But against this must be set the fact that the Chapter Book of Rouen Cathedral has no entry of any such event, while permission for the reception and baptism at the Cathedral of his younger brother Edmund is recorded on May 18, 1443, as also that of his sister Elizabeth on September 22nd, 1444. There is an entry under the date of October 30th, 1442, giving permission to the Duke of York to use certain ornaments and vestments from the Cathedral 'to decorate the Chapel of the Castle of Rouen' for the celebration of the feast of All Saints. It is, therefore, reasonable to suppose that Edward was baptised in the Chapel of the Castle. His mother's brother, Richard, Earl of Salisbury, with Lord Scales and Lady Say, were his sponsors.[24]

Stratford then goes on to suggest that Edward may have been baptised in the chapel of the castle in *October* 1442. If the baby really was born in April – or even in May – that is extremely unlikely. In the medieval period the baptism of a new-born child would never normally have been delayed for six months.

Unfortunately, in spite of the fact that the truth is uncertain, as with Edward's alleged birth date, there appears to be a popular impression that we know the facts. In respect of his baptism the general belief seems to be that Edward was not baptised in the cathedral; that this means that his baptism was not seen an important event by the Duke of York, and that therefore Edward must have been a bastard. But this ignores the genuine written evidence of the Duke of

York's letters of 1445 (cited above). It also ignores the fact that, in the fifteenth century, baptism was taken very seriously as a *religious* event. If a child showed any signs of weakness (s)he was therefore rapidly baptised in order to save his or her soul. Holding a grandiose public ceremony was of very small importance when compared to the issue of salvation. It is therefore possible that Edward seemed a little weak when he was born, and that for this reason his baptism was carried out immediately, in the closest convenient location. In this context the fact that the Duke and Duchess of York had probably already lost at least one child – Edward's elder brother, Henry – would have been a significant factor.

Chapter 12

The Second Reign of Edward IV

In the first months of 1470, Cecily's second son, George, found himself obliged to be out of the country in France. George returned to England in September 1470, together with his cousin and father-in-law, the Earl of Warwick. Then in the following month Cecily's other two sons, Edward IV and Richard, Duke of Gloucester, found themselves forced to flee the country to the Netherlands, because Warwick had restored Henry VI to the English throne. This must have been a very strange time for Cecily, who found herself more or less alone in England in terms of her family of children. Only her two elder daughters, the Duchess of Exeter and the Duchess of Suffolk might have been around if she felt she needed children to talk to.

But the Duke of Clarence found himself in a very strange situation. Initially he and his cousin, the Earl of Warwick, had focused on removing the Widville family from power in England, and bringing Edward IV back to proper Yorkism (as they perceived it), making the Earl of Warwick and the Duke of Clarence the chief powers behind the throne. Warwick had also married George to his elder daughter, Isabel, and the second part of his aim was that George should once again be recognised as the heir to the throne, with the Widville marriage dismissed as illegal, and its children removed from the royal inheritance. Thus Warwick hoped that one day his own daughter would be queen, and that his own grandchildren would ultimately succeed to the crown of England.

But when Edward IV reclaimed the right to make his own decisions, and allied himself, not with his brother, George, and his cousin the Earl of Warwick, but with Elizabeth Widville and his daughters by her, George had ended up in a quandary. He was still linked to Warwick, but Warwick had now been forced to change his plans. Thus he was re-allying himself with the Lancastrians, and aiming to restore Henry VI to the throne. Logically, Henry VI would one day be succeeded by his acknowledged heir (and possible son), Edward of Westminster. Therefore Warwick now had to arrange new measures to ensure that one day his own heirs would reign. This time he did so by organising a marriage between his younger daughter, Anne, and the Lancastrian Prince of Wales. Although he also ensured a Lancastrian agreement that, if Edward of Westminster ultimately proved childless, George, Duke of Clarence, should be acknowledged as the

Lancastrian heir to the English throne, George's chance of one day becoming the king of England was not really improved thereby. The overall outcome was that George suddenly found himself now a Lancastrian instead of a Yorkist, but with very little personal advantage from his point of view.

It was in this context that Philippe de Commynes has preserved on record the fact that an intriguing piece of diplomacy was set in motion.

> Now I was at Calais negotiating with Lord Wenlock ... He told me moreover that it would be easy to reach a settlement because that day a lady had passed through Calais, on her way to my lady of Clarence in France. She was bearing an offer from King Edward to open peace talks. He spoke the truth, but as he deceived others he himself was deceived by this lady, for she was going to carry out a series of negotiations which in the end were prejudicial to the earl of Warwick and all his supporters.
>
> Assuredly you will never learn more from anyone than from me about all the secret schemes or ruses which have been carried out in our countries on this side of the channel since then, or at least about those which have happened in the last twenty years. This woman's secret business was to persuade my lord of Clarence not to be the agent of the ruin of his family by helping to restore the Lancastrians to authority, and to remind him of their ancient hatreds and quarrels. He should consider very carefully whether Warwick would make him king of England when the earl had married his daughter to the prince of Wales and had already done homage to him. This woman exploited the situation so well that she won over the duke of Clarence who promised to join his brother, the king, as soon as he came back to England.
>
> This woman was not a fool and she did not speak lightly. She had the opportunity to visit her mistress and for this reason she was able to go sooner than a man. And however cunning Lord Wenlock was this woman deceived him and carried out this secret assignment which led to the defeat and death of the earl of Warwick and all his followers.[1]

Unfortunately the identity of the lady in question is not on record. However, it is interesting to find that a woman was now playing the key diplomatic role. What is more, other evidence also exists which proves that their mother and sisters were all actively involved in the attempt to reconcile Edward IV and the Duke of Clarence. Hicks has claimed that Cecily urged George to be Yorkist.[2] He cites no source for that statement. Nevertheless, contemporary evidence does exist which shows that Cecily and her three daughters all strove to reconcile Edward and George.

> By right covert wayes and meanes were goode mediators and mediatricis, the highe and myghty princis, my Lady theyr mothar; my Lady of Exceter, my Lady of Southfolke, theyre systars; my Lord Cardinall of Cantorbery; my Lord of Bathe; my Lord of Essex; and, moste specially my Lady of Bourgoigne; and other, by mediacions of certayne priests, and other well disposyd parsouns. Abowte the Kynges beinge in Holland, and in other partes beyond the sea, great and diligent labowres, with all effect, was continually made by the high and mighty princesse, the Duches of Bowrgine, which at no season ceasyd to send hir sarvaunts, and messengars, to the Kynge, wher he was, and to my sayd Lorde of Clarence, into England; and so did his verrey good devowre in that behalf my Lord of Hastings, the Kyng's Chambarlayne, so that a parfecte accord was appoyntyd, accordyd, concludyd, and assured, betwixt them; wherein the sayde Duke of Clarence full honourably and trwly acquitted hym.[3]

The key players named here include Cecily Neville and her three living daughters, Anne, Duchess of Exeter, Elizabeth, Duchess of Suffolk and Margaret, Duchess of Burgundy. Three other relatives – cousins of both Edward IV and George – were also involved, namely the Archbishop of Canterbury, the Earl of Essex, and Lord Hastings (cousin by marriage). As for the final key player mentioned in the above source, he was Robert Stillington, Bishop of Bath and Wells.

In theory, given that George was supposed to be close to the Lancastrian throne of Henry VI, and had been recognised as second in line to succeed him, Henry's restoration should not have proved threatening in the long term, either to Cecily or to her daughters. Yet their action appears to indicate that real family feeling existed amongst the female members of the house of York. It also seems that both Cecily and her daughters must have felt concerned about the future of the other two sons, Edward IV and Richard, Duke of Gloucester. After all, *their* two lives would have been disasters had Henry VI remained on the English throne.

In due course Edward IV and his youngest brother, Richard, returned to England. Finding the county of Norfolk potentially dangerous because it was controlled by the Earl of Oxford, while their cousin the Duke of Norfolk was detained in London, Edward and Richard eventually landed in the north of England. They then marched southwards towards London. Meanwhile, although he had promised to return to Yorkist allegiance, George had by no means deserted his father-in-law, the Earl of Warwick.

> The Duke of Clarence, beinge right desyrows to have procuryd a goode accorde betwixt the Kynge and th'Erle of Warwyke; not only for th'Erle, but also for to reconsyle therby unto the Kyngs good grace many lords and noble men of his land, of whom many had largly taken parte with th'Erle ... made, therefore, his mocions, as well to the Kynge as to th'Erle, by messagis sendynge to and fro, bothe for the well above sayde, as to acquite hym trwly and kindly in the love he bare unto hym, and his blood, whereunto he was allied by the marriage of his dowghtar.[4]

Regrettably, in the end George found that his father-in-law could not be won back to the side of Edward IV, presumably because Warwick was now absolutely convinced that there was no possible way of getting Edward to give up his Widville alliance.

On Tuesday 9 April 1471 Edward spent the night at St Albans. The next day his men took over the Tower of London, and on Maundy Thursday (11 April) Edward IV rode to St Paul's Cathedral and assumed custody of his rival, King Henry VI. Edward then rode on to Westminster. There he found Elizabeth Widville hiding in sanctuary, together with their children. Significantly, these included one new arrival because, during his exile in the Low Countries, 'she had browght into this worlde, to the Kyngs greatyste joy, a fayre sonn, a prince, where with she presentyd hym at his comynge.'[5] The couple then joined Cecily, who was in residence at her London home of Baynard's Castle. Wavrin reports that Edward IV stayed at Baynard's Castle with his mother, attending divine service on Good Friday (12 April) and the Easter Vigil Mass on the following night (Holy Saturday – 13 April).[6]

Since Cecily is known to have been living at Baynard's Castle in April 1471, and since we know she had been there just over a year earlier (see above, Chapter 10), it may well be that she had remained based in the safety of her London castle all through the disturbing months of conflict between her sons, coupled with the Lancastrian restoration of her cousin, King Henry VI. Significantly, it seems that she had also remained at Baynard's Castle through other disturbing months at an earlier period in her life (1460–1461), so perhaps she felt it was her safest abode during times of trouble. Interestingly, her earlier stay there had culminated in the beginning of Edward IV's first reign. Likewise on the present occasion, Cecily's stay at Baynard's Castle culminated in her son's restoration and the beginning of his second reign.

Cecily's father, Ralph Neville, Earl of Westmorland, with his two wives. His second wife, Cecily's mother, Joan Beaufort, is on the right hand side of the engraving (on the Earl's left).

Restored image (break in the glass and outer wire protection removed) of the medieval stained glass window fragment at Penrith which was claimed in the 19th century to be of Cecily Neville, but which is actually a portrait of her mother, Joan Beaufort, Countess of Westmorland, probably produced in the late 1390s (see the caption of plate 3 and the text of the Introduction).

The medieval stained glass window fragment at Penrith which was claimed in the 19th century to be of Richard, Duke of York, but which is actually a portrait of his father-in-law, Ralph Neville, Earl of Westmorland. This image was produced in the late 1390s, because he was portrayed with his second wife (married in 1396), and was depicted with a hairstyle (long hair) and originally wearing armour (see the text of the Introduction) both of which dated from the reign of Richard II (deposed in 1399).

King Henry IV, elder half-brother of Joan, Countess of Westmorland, from a medallion based upon his tomb effigy.

John Beaufort, Earl of Somerset, elder brother of Joan, Countess of Westmorland, from his tomb effigy at Canterbury Cathedral.

Cardinal Henry Beaufort, Bishop of Winchester, middle brother of Joan, Countess of Westmorland, from the Coventry Tapestry, courtesy of St Mary's Guildhall and Coventry City Council.

Some of Cecily's immediate family. From right to left: her father, the Earl of Westmorland; her brothers (including Bishop Robert Neville), and her half brothers and three of her half sisters on her father's side. From the Neville Book of Hours, f. 27v, © Bibliothèque Nationale de France. These portraits must have been painted after 1427, when Robert Neville was appointed Bishop of Salisbury, and probably date from about 1430 (see the caption for plate 8). By that date Ralph Neville, Earl of Westmorland, was actually deceased (d. 1425). The men are all depicted with their hair in the very short style which was fashionable in the first third of the 15th century.

The rest of Cecily's immediate family, presumably also painted after 1427, probably in about 1430 (see the caption to plate 7). From right to left: her mother, the Countess of Westmorland (apparently depicted as a widow); Cecily herself (then aged about 15, and already the Duchess of York); her full blood sisters: Catherine, Duchess of Norfolk, Anne, Duchess of Buckingham, and Eleanor, Countess of Northumberland, and two of her half sisters on her mother's side. From the Neville Book of Hours, f. 34v, © Bibliothèque Nationale de France.

A drawing of the tombs of Cecily's grandmother, the Duchess of Lancaster (rear), and of her mother, the Countess of Westmorland (front), at Lincoln Cathedral, as seen in about 1640, before they lost their brasses. GNU Free Documentation License.

Pope Martin V, who must have granted the dispensation which allowed the marriage of Cecily Neville and Richard, Duke of York.

The Sainte Chapelle, Paris. Here, in December 1431, Cecily, then aged 16, may have attended the reception of the ten year old King Henry VI, prior to his French coronation.

The adult Cecily Neville and Richard, Duke of York in terms of their probable relative heights.

Cecily Neville as depicted in about 1430, aged about 15 and already married to the Duke of York, redrawn from the Neville Book of Hours, © Geoffrey Wheeler.

Richard, Duke of York, as portrayed in 1444/5, at the age of about 34. By this time it seems that for younger men longer hair was starting to come back into fashion. Redrawn from British Library, Royal 15 E VI f2v.

Cecily's sister, Anne Neville, Duchess of Buckingham, as originally depicted in the north window of Lichfield Cathedral (F. Sandford, *A Genealogical History of the Kings and Queens of England*, London 1707, p. 332)

Cecily's second cousin, Alice Chaucer, Duchess of Suffolk, from her tomb at St Mary's Church, Ewelme ('Creative Commons').

The Lancastrian cousin, colleague and benefactor of Richard, Duke of York and his wife, Cecily Neville: Humphrey, Duke of Gloucester. It was Humphrey who bequeathed the London home of Baynard's Castle to Richard and Cecily.

Cecily's Lancastrian first cousins also included King Henry V (redrawn from a fifteenth-century portrait at the National Portrait gallery, © M.H.).

The child king Henry VI in 1433, praying before the shrine of St Edmund, from a tapestry at the cathedral of Bury St Edmunds, based on a fifteenth-century manuscript illustration.

Cecily's Lancastrian first cousins also included Joan Beaufort, who became the consort of James I, King of Scots (Melrose Abbey).

Cecily's Lancastrian first cousins also included Edmund Beaufort, Duke of Somerset (St Mary's Collegiate Church, Warwick).

Ruins of the pulpit in the refectory at Walsingham Augustinian Priory, from which readings were given during the eating of meals. Probably both the Duke and the Duchess of York sat in the Refectory during their Walsingham pilgrimages.

Alabaster relief of St Anne teaching the Virgin Mary to read. This may have been commissioned by the Duke and Duchess of York as part of the decoration for the new Walsingham shrine chapel.

Part of a finial from one of the pinnacles of the new Walsingham shrine chapel, found during the 1961 excavation of the site.

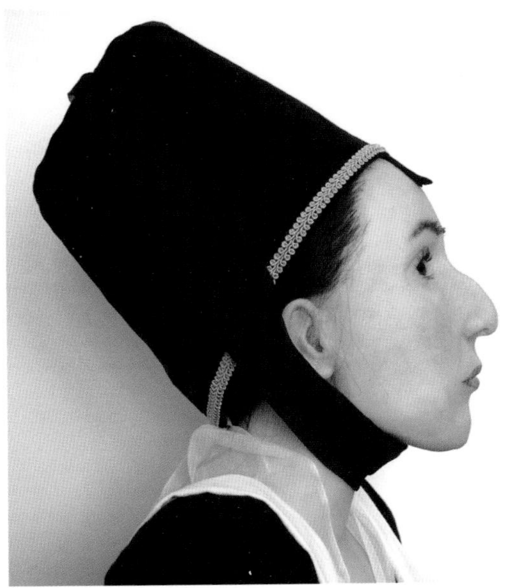

Eleanor Talbot, Lady Boteler? A facial reconstruction based on the CF2 skull found at the Carmelite Priory site in Norwich, © Amy Thornton, University of Dundee.

Elizabeth Widville, Lady Grey. Copy of a contemporary portrait.

A copy of the Clare Crucifix, commissioned by the author in 2012 for interment with the bones of Cecily's youngest son, King Richard III. The original reliquary crucifix was found on the site of Clare Castle in the nineteenth century, and may well have belonged to Cecily.

Cecily's eldest surviving son, Edward IV. Redrawn from an image produced in the 1470s.

Cecily's middle daughter, Elizabeth of York, Duchess of Suffolk, from her alabaster tomb effigy at Wingfield Church, Suffolk.

Cecily Neville's seal, as used in 1477, and its Latin inscription.

Sigillū · dñe · cecilie · ux'is · ueri · hered' · anglie · ⁊ · francie · et · dñi · hib'nie · matris · reg' · Edwardi · quarti · ducisse ebor'.

Cecily's youngest surviving daughter, Margaret of York, Duchess of Burgundy: copy of her 1468 marriage portrait.

Cecily's youngest son, Richard III, from the Coventry Tapestry, courtesy of St Mary's Guildhall and Coventry City Council.

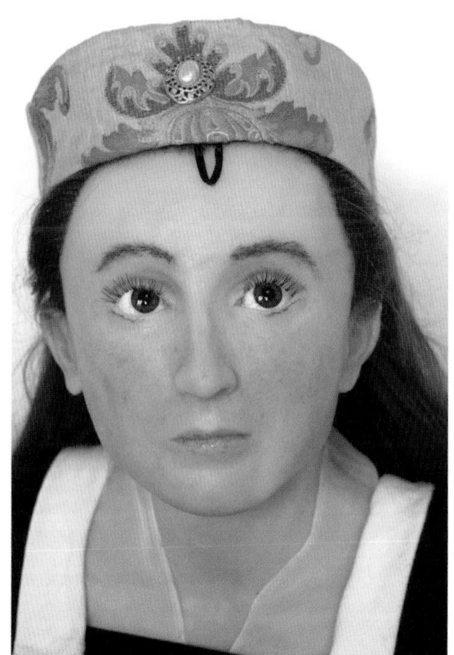

Facial reconstruction of Anne Mowbray, Duchess of York and Norfolk, the great granddaughter of Cecily's eldest sister, Catherine Neville, the niece of Eleanor Talbot, and the wife of Cecily's grandson, Richard of Shrewsbury, © Amy Thornton, University of Dundee.

Cecily's first cousin once removed, Margaret Beaufort, Countess of Richmond and Derby, the mother of Henry VII.

Henry VII, nineteenth-century engraving based on a contemporary portrait.

The sixteenth-century tomb commissioned at Fotheringhay Church for Cecily Neville and her husband, Richard, Duke of York, by their great great granddaughter, Elizabeth I.

The alabaster tomb of Cecily's son-in-law and daughter, the Duke and Duchess of Suffolk, at the former collegiate church of Wingfield in Suffolk. Cecily's original tomb in the choir at Fotheringhay was of about the same date, and may have resembled this.

The all-female line of descent discovered by the present author in 2004, which revealed the mtDNA sequence of Cecily Neville and her children.

Plans of the upper and lower jaws of Richard III – showing no evidence of congenitally missing teeth.

The right and left hands and lower arms of Cecily Neville's youngest maternal uncle, Thomas Beaufort, Duke of Exeter (died 1426/7). His well-preserved body was found close to the wall of the ruins of the Lady Chapel at the Abbey of Bury St Edmunds in February 1772. The hands were cut off and presented to the Royal College of Surgeons. Unfortunately they have since been lost. Their mtDNA would have matched that of Cecily Neville, Richard III, and Joy Ibsen, and their Y chromosome might have revealed interesting facts about the late medieval English royal family.

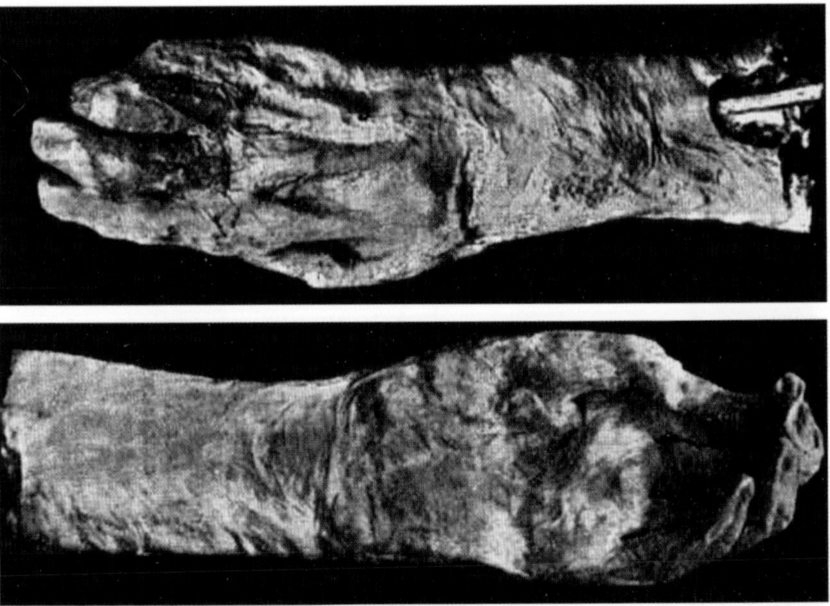

Subsequently her three sons fought together at the battle of Barnet. But sadly for George – and perhaps also for his mother – that battle ended in the death of George's father-in-law, and Cecily's nephew, Richard Neville, Earl of Warwick. Cecily herself may subsequently have beheld Warwick's dead body because, on the day after the battle, his corpse was displayed very close to Baynard's Castle, at St Paul's Cathedral.

> On the morrow aftar, the Kynge commandyd that the bodyes of the dead lords, th'Erle of Warwicke, and hys brother the Marques [of Montagu(e)], shuld be browght to Powles in London, and in the churche there, openly shewyd to all the people; to th'entent that, aftar that, the people shuld not be abused by feyned seditiows tales, which many of them … would have made aftar that, ne [= he?] had the deade bodyes there be shewyd, opne, and naked.[7]

In theory the York family conflict was now at an end. But of course, in reality, problems still remained. The Widville marriage which George disliked had not been ended. As for his potential role as heir presumptive to the throne, that had now been thoroughly undermined by the birth of a living son of Edward IV and Elizabeth Widville. And while in one sense George now had a good claim to the inheritance of the Earl of Warwick, via his marriage to the Earl's eldest daughter, Isabel, a younger Warwick daughter, Anne, also existed. She had been married in France to the Lancastrian Prince of Wales who was subsequently killed at the battle of Tewkesbury. However, it subsequently emerged that an apparent attachment existed between Anne and George's own younger brother, the Duke of Gloucester. That led to the start of another family inheritance dispute in the summer of 1471 between George and Richard in respect of their respective claims to the Warwick inheritance.

On Sunday 16 February 1471/2 Edward and Elizabeth received both the younger brothers at Sheen, though they were 'nott alle in cheryte. …The Kynge entretyth my Lord of Claurance, ffor my Lorde of Glowcester; and as it is seyde, he answerethe that he may well have my Ladye hys suster in lawe, butt they schall parte no lyvelod.'[8] Although at that point it sounds as though George was at least willing to let Richard marry Anne, at some point in 1472 the Duke of Clarence appears to have changed his mind. We are told that he then hid his sister-in-law, Anne Neville, disguised as a cooking maid, in a house in London. But the Duke of Gloucester rescued her and took her to sanctuary at St Martin's Church. 'At last their most loving brother, king Edward, agreed to act as mediator' between his quarrelling brothers.[9]

The Bridge, Lechlade, Gloucestershire.

It also seems that Edward IV had now readopted caring for his mother. On 8 November 1472, he granted her the patronage of the hospital of St John the Baptist, which stood beside the bridge across the river Thames at Lechlade in Gloucestershire. She was required to found there a chantry chapel comprising three priests, and dedicated to the Blessed Virgin Mary. The three priests were to pray in the chantry chapel for King Edward himself, for Elizabeth Widville, for Cecily, and for the soul of the king's late father. Thus Cecily's name had now been restored to figure once again on the list of royal prayers. Cecily was also to grant £10 a year from the income of the hospital, to John Twynyho of Cirencester. Twynyho would then found on the same site a second chantry chapel, dedicated to St Blaise (with just one priest), to pray for the same specified members of the royal family.[10]

John Twynyho's family seems to have played a significant role in Cecily's life, and in the fate of her middle surviving son, George, about five years later. It seems that the man in question was the son of Ankarette Hawkeston and of her husband, William Twynyho (see the Family Tree). In 1477, Ankarette was arrested at her Somerset manor house on the orders of

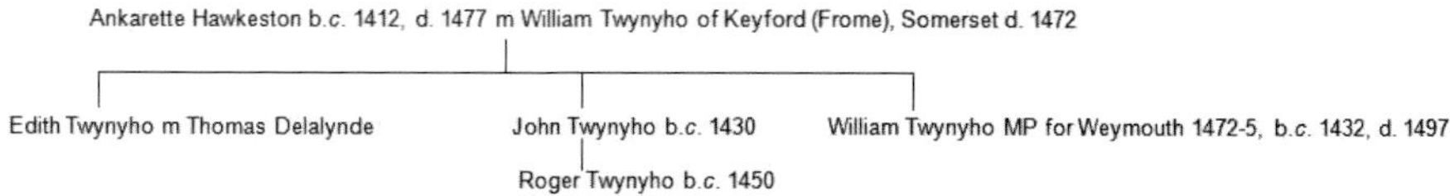

The Twynyho Family

George, Duke of Clarence, for the murder of his wife (and Cecily's great niece), Isabel Neville. Ankarette was then transported via Cirencester to Warwick,[11] tried for murder, and then executed. Roger Twynyho, son of the John Twynyho who was Ankarette's son was then to lead a campaign to have George's judgement against his grandmother reversed.[12] Although that move on Roger's part was not the direct cause of George's eventual execution, for Cecily it must have been tied up with the other distressing moves which were then being taken against her middle son. However, that part of the story came later.

On 13 November 1472, land formerly held by her late husband was surrendered to Cecily.[13] Subsequently, at her Castle of Berkhamsted, on 25 June 1473 (confirmed on 28 June 1474), the Duchess of York granted to Ralph Kyrisshawe, esquire, 'one of the sewers of her chamber' the role of keeper of her park at Marshwood in Dorset.[14] Similarly, at Berkamsted, on 13 December 1473 (confirmed on 1 November 1475), Cecily granted to her servant, Richard Gylmyn, esquire, sergeant at arms, and to John Gylmyn, yeoman of her chamber, the keepership of her park and chase of Suthfrith (South Frith, near Tonbridge in Kent).[15]

Like her Suffolk steward, Sir John (Lord) Howard, Cecily Neville at times required the services of lawyers. Indeed, the surviving evidence shows that both Cecily and John Howard sometimes employed the same lawyers. The records indicate that some of Howard's lawyers later went on to serve Cecily and other members of the royal house. Indeed, some of them were subsequently given high-status legal appointments by the Yorkist government.[16] For example, it seems that both Howard and Cecily were used to employing James Hobart. Also both of them seem to have employed John Catesby. And while John Sulyard is not recorded as having worked directly for Cecily, he did work for John Howard, and he was also employed by Cecily's son, Richard, Duke of Gloucester, in a case which involved both him and his mother (see below).

James Hobart (1440–1517) is a typical example of these lawyers. He was the younger son of Thomas Hobart of Monks Eleigh, Suffolk. He had an older brother, William, who, like Thomas, became a local merchant and member of the

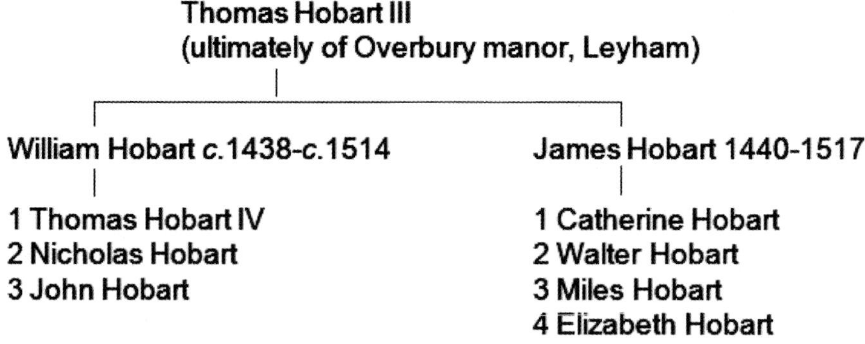

Hobart Family Tree (simplified)

Hadleigh Clothmaker's Guild. Apparently there were connections of some kind between the Hobarts and Sir John Howard in the 1460s. Soon after his accession to the throne, Edward IV had granted the newly knighted John Howard the northern part of the manor of Leyham.[17] Howard in turn enfeoffed Thomas Hobart of this manor, which was subsequently (1468) inherited by Thomas Hobart's elder son, William.

In addition James Hobart regularly received livery from John Howard. The livery in question was sometimes that of John Howard himself, sometime that of his cousin, the Mowbray Duke of Norfolk, and sometimes that of King Edward IV. For example, on 7 April 1464 'my mastyr gaff to Jamys Hobard a longe blakke gown off Puke, the wych coste my mastyr 42s.'[18] Black was then the colour of Howard's own livery.[19] On 24 May 1465 two yards of crimson (Mowbray) livery cloth was delivered by Sir John Howard to James Hobart.[20] On 31 May 1465 'my mastyr gaff to Jemes Hoberd ij yerdes and a quarter [of blake damaske, prise of the yerde 7s.']'[21] In December 1466: 'my mastyr owyth hym [Bolstrode] for ij yerdes and di. of ray, for James Hoberd, be my lordes comaundement, 6s. 5d.'[22] 'Ray' was striped cloth. In this case it is clear from the context that the stripes were of murray and blue, the livery colours of Edward IV. In1467 Hobart again received one and three quarter yards of Howard black livery cloth.[23]

On 7 February 1464/5 John Howard made various payments to lawyers (Alyngton, Thomas Yonge, serjeant-at-law, John Catesby, and John Sulyard) of which 3s. 4d. went to James Hobart, who also passed on payments to Yonge and Catesby.[24] By 1474, at least, John Catesby had become a member of the 'learned council' of Howard's employer, Cecily Neville, Duchess of York.[25]

Later, Hobart helped John Howard when the newly created Duke of Norfolk was required to supply men-at-arms for King Richard III. On 26 February 1483/4 'James Hobard hath graunted my Lordes grace, that he shall fynde the kynge iij men and armour to my Lord at his proper cost, which shall awayte uppon my said Lord; and he hath promised my Lord to gete hym as many men as he can gete, to the nombre of [blank].'[26] In addition Hobart undertook to supply a further two men at the duke's expense.[27] A list of grants made by Richard III includes 'an annuyte of x markes for terme of his lif of the fre farme of Ipswhicche' to James Hobard.[28]

But in spite of his close connection with the Mowbrays and with John Howard (to whom, as we have seen, he had supplied at his own cost men at arms for Richard III's array) James Hobart not only survived the eclipse of Howard and the house of York, but actually prospered after Bosworth – as was also the case, both with other lawyers and with other former Yorkist supporters (see below). Henry VII promoted Hobart to the privy council in 1486, at which time he was also appointed attorney general. Hobart was knighted in 1503.

In March 1473/4 Cecily Neville wrote a letter to her youngest son, Richard, Duke of Gloucester, concerning her servant, John Prince, whose property, called 'Gregory's' had been cheated away from him by people who had also attempted to get Richard on their side.

> Right trusty and entirely well beloved son, we greet you heartily well, giving you God's blessing and ours. And whereas it is come unto our knowledge that since our departing you have been sued unto by our wellbeloved servant, John Prince, as is according to his duty. By whose report we understand to the accomplishment of your promise made unto us at Syon you have showed him the favour of your good lordship and the more especially at our contemplation *[sic]*, we thank you therefore in our most hearty wise, praying you that no man intromitt [meddle] with our said servant's matter, saving only our counsel learned and yours, as our faithful trust is in you. And whereas your servant Sir Robert Chamberlain, kt, intendeth to have interest therein, we pray you to commend him the contrary, remembering the said promise made between us and you, which we doubt not shall be observed on your part. Son, we trusted you should have been at Berkhamsted with my lord my son [King Edward IV] at his last being there with us, and if it had pleased you to come at that time, you should have been right heartily welcome. And so you shall be whensoever you shall do the same, as God knoweth, whom we beseech to have you in governance.

Written at our Castle of Berkhamsted, the 15th day of March.
To the Duke of Gloucester.[29]

The year date of this letter is not contained within the letter itself. However, the document appears to refer to the resolution of an issue concerning John Prince. An earlier letter concerning the same issue also survives (see below). It was written by Cecily to the Essex authorities in February, and bears the regnal year date 13 of Edward IV (1473/4). Thus the above letter to the Duke of Gloucester must have been written in March 1473/4.

Cecily's earlier letter concerning the case of John Prince reads as follows:

> Cecilie, mother &c, to the justices of peas, sheriffs, constables, bailiffs and all others the Kenges ministers in the c[ounty] of E[ssex], gretyng:
>
> Where now late, that is to sey the Sonday [*blank*] day of Fevers the xiij yere [1473/4] of our most dere and biloved son E[dward] the iiij[th], by the grace of God Kyng of Yngland and of Fraunce and Lord of Irlond, oon Thomas Wethiale[30] by a feyned pretence with others entered in to the londe of our welbiloved servant J[ohn] P[rince], called 'Gregoryes', contrarie to the lawes and peas of our said son, and incontinent, therof enfeoffed our right dere biloved son, R[ichard], Duc of G[loucester], with others, souly for maintenance of the said feyned title, as we be credibly enformed. Wherof pitefull compleynt aswell unto us as to our seid son the duc of G[loucester] on the bihalf of our seid servant Joh[n] P[rince] hath be made. And we both therunto takyng respect and tendre consideracion, have comuned togiders, and for paccificcie of bothe partiers, be concluded that aswell two of our lerned counseill to be elect by our said servant, as two of the lerned counseill of our seid son the duc of G[loucester] to be elect by the seid Th[omas], shall have the title and enteresse of both the same partiers in the seid londe in examynacion, accordyng unto conscience and to the Kynges lawes, the same our son permittyng us nothyng to doo or maintene them,[31] whether our both counseill juge fynally the seid title or not, but suffre the Kynges lawes for to have there verry cource after the due ordre of the same. Yeven &c.[32]

Althought it is not easy to identify, it seems that the disputed property of 'Gregoryes' lay somewhere in the county of Essex. Cecily also drafted a third letter to officials in Essex about the proposed solution to the problem. This third text is dated about a week after the letter addressed to her youngest son, who must therefore have responded very quickly to his mother – something for which she herself thanked him in the very loving letter which she addressed to him in person (see above).

> Trusty and welbeloved we grete you well. And forasmyche as we and our right dier said entierly welbeloved son of Gloucester ar fully agried that the mater betwex our welbeloved servant, John Prince, and our Thomas Withiale, be put in the determynacion of John Catesby and Roger Towneshend (elect and named be us) and of Guy Fawefox[33] and Sulyard or elles Pigot[34] (named and ellect be our said son) we be fully acertayned ye will confourme you to the said appoyntement, and when we wrot unto you but late for the said mater, we be credibly enformed ye be well disposed theron, and the bothe(?) at the contemplacion of us, wherfor we thank you. And for the contynuaunce of the same, if ther be any thing we may doo for you herafter, ye shall fynd us right agreable to your desir. Yeven, &c, the xxij day of March.[35]

The existence of a draft bond in the sum of £200 from John Catesby and Roger Townshend confirms that the adjudication did indeed take place as planned by Cecily Neville, and that John Sulyard, 'gentleman', together with Guy Fowler [*sic*], 'serjeant-at-law', did act in the matter for her son, the Duke of Gloucester.[36] This is an interesting example of an attempt to settle a dispute peacefully and amicably.[37] However, it is also extremely interesting that, in her letter to her son Richard, Cecily speaks to him in the most affectionate way, and expresses regret at not seeing more of him.

In the context of the employment of lawyers, it is also worth considering the career of John Sulyard, the primary lawyer who acted on Richard, Duke of Gloucester's behalf in the John Prince case, and was well known to Cecily Neville. Sulyard frequently worked for John Howard, and there are numerous records of payments to and on behalf of John Sulyard in the surviving Howard accounts.[38] John Howard and John Sulyard were probably of much the same age, and Sulyard's direct service to Howard seems to date from the 1460s, when Howard was rising from relative obscurity and becoming a figure on the national stage. Chronologically, the evidence may imply that Sulyard was first employed by the Mowbrays. Subsequently he began to work directly for John Howard. Howard in turn introduced him to Cecily Neville (who had employed Howard as her steward of the honour of Clare), and to the young Duke of Gloucester, in whom Howard also took an interest.[39]

On 28 December 1464 John Sulyard received from Howard a payment of 3s. 4d.[40] About six weeks later, on 6 February 1464/5, there was another payment, this time of 8s. 4d.[41] On this occasion Howard also bought both Sulyard and Hobart a drink, at a total cost of 2d.[42] On the following day Sulyard received a further 3s. 4d,[43] and Howard visited Lincoln's Inn, and paid 1d. for apples for Sulyard and James Hobart.[44] On 15 March 1464/5 'my master gaff to Solyardes man 4s. 2d.'[45] On 5 April 1465 Sulyard was paid 8s 4d, and 'also Boteler, Solyardes man', received 20d.[46] Both references are presumably to John Butler, who is considered separately below.[47] On the Sunday after Easter (21 April) 1465 'my master gaff to Solyard for syttenge uppon his comyscion at Loppames [Lopham, Norfolk] … 10s.'[48] This concentrated series of payments to Sulyard between December 1464 and April 1465, which suggests the possibility that Howard was assiduously cultivating the connection, is nowhere repeated in the Howard accounts. We must remember, however, that the surviving Howard accounts are not complete. The fact that Sulyard was paid 4s. on 13 May 1467 'for inrollynge of ij wryttes, one ageyn Sulyard and a noder ayeyn my mastyr' certainly indicates that he continued to serve John Howard.[49]

By the late 1460s Howard was becoming a significant presence in the town of Colchester, and it is possible that his influence there lay behind John Sulyard's appointment as *Legisperitus* for the Borough in 1473.[50] Sulyard held this post again in 1476, 1477, 1480 and 1481. Records for the intervening years are not extant, but probably his tenure was continuous from 1476 until about 1482. However, by 1484 at the latest he had been succeeded by another of Howard's lawyers, Thomas Appleton.[51]

After the death of John Mowbray, fourth Duke of Norfolk, in 1476, Sulyard continued to serve on commissions with former Mowbray clients. In addition to his Norfolk links, he had now established himself at Wetherden in Suffolk, and in about 1480 he began to rebuild the south aisle of Wetherden Church.[52] In 1483 Richard III appointed Sulyard to a commission headed by three people: John Howard (then newly created Duke of Norfolk); Howard's son and heir, Thomas, and the king's brother-in-law, John de la Pole, Duke of Suffolk. This was a commission of which the king's cousin, Alexander Cressener (the son by her second husband of his mothers' half-sister, Margaret Neville, who had died twenty years earlier and been buried at Clare Priory), was also a member. At the same time Richard also numbered Sulyard among the notables of Suffolk, in a list which included John Howard, Duke of Norfolk, and his son Thomas Howard, Earl of Surrey.[53] In the same year Sulyard went on the Home Circuit with Chief Justice Bryan.[54] On 22 October 1484 Richard III appointed Sulyard one of the Justices of the King's Bench.[55]

Interestingly, like other lawyers who had been close to Howard and who had served the house of York, Sulyard later seems to have survived the advent of Henry VII without any difficulty. Lawyers, after all, were still required by the new regime. On 20 September 1485 Henry VII confirmed Sulyard as a Justice of the King's Bench, and it was probably also from Henry VII that he received his knighthood. He is described as 'knight' in surviving records from 4 July 1486 onwards. On 10 November 1487 Henry VII appointed him one of the stewards for the coronation of his queen, Elizabeth of York.

Sulyard married twice. His first wife was Anne Hungate, and the second, Ann(e) Andrew(es), the daughter of John Andrew(es) of Baylam, and the granddaughter of James Andrew, a client of William de la Pole, Earl (later Duke) of Suffolk, who had achieved a certain celebrity some years earlier by falling victim of a factional murder resulting from a dispute with Mowbray retainers over some land in Baylham (Suffolk) in 1434.[56] John Sulyard died on 18 March 1487/8.[57] He left living children by both his wives, and his grandson, Sir William Sulyard became the governor of Lincoln's Inn in 1531–32.

The period during which Cecily had been lovingly working with her youngest son and their respective lawyers over the problem of one of her retainers was also about the time in which the dispute between the Dukes of Clarence and Gloucester was resolved. On 7 February 1473/4, in a letter to the Duke of Milan written in southern France, his servant, Cristoforo da Bolla, reported that:

> The Duke of Gloucester, who by force has taken as his wife the daughter of the late Earl of Warwick who was married to the Prince of Wales, has been constantly preparing for war against the Duke of Clarence. To the latter – in order to retain him – his brother, King Edward promised the earldom of Warwick. He did not want the other [brother] to possess it by the chance of his marriage to the said daughter of that [late] Earl.[58]

This renewed conflict between her two younger sons, who had grown up together in childhood, must have been somewhat distressing for Cecily. But in November 1473 the Paston family 'trust[ed] to God that the ij Dukes of Clarans and Glowcester shall be sette att one by the adward off the Kyng.'[59] Richard, Duke of Gloucester, found himself finally married to Anne Neville some time in 1474.[60] He, his young wife, and his mother-in-law, the dowager Countess of Warwick, then settled in the north of England, at Middleham Castle.

Meanwhile, on 12 March 1473/4 the king confirmed a grant which had been made by his mother at Berkhamsted Castle, about two years earlier

(18 May 1472). This grant had been to her servant, Henry Lassy (Lessy). He was appointed keeper of her park at Brimpsfield, Gloucestershire, and of the neighbouring Buckle Wood.[61] Henry Lassy was probably a relative (maybe the father) of Richard Lessy, who was to serve as the dean of Cecily's chapel at the end of her life, and subsequently as the executor of her last will (see below, Chapter 14).

On 11 May 1474, Cecily Neville had granted to her servant, Henry Lessy, her manor of Purbright (Pirbright) in Surrey. However, Edward IV had enclosed much of the land as a park, so that Lessy had made very little from this gift. Thus on 20 June 1481 the king compensated Lessy by granting him income from the manor of Worpesdon (Worplesdon) in the same county.[62]

Meanwhile, for Cecily, religious faith was now a significant part of her private life. It seems that by this time she had already developed a deep interest in the Benedictine Order and its religious life. On 10 August 1475, Margaret Paston informed her son, Sir John Paston, that the Duchess of York and all her household were in Norfolk, at St Benet's Abbey, Holme, 'and purpose to abide there stille, til the Kynge come from be yonde the see, and lenger if she like the eyre ther, as it is seide.'[63] Cecily appears to have had further connections with St Benet's Abbey later.

Ironically, in spite of the considerable number of children that she had produced, Cecily's own immediate family was now, once again, decreasing in size. On 14 January 1475/6 her eldest daughter, Anne of York, Duchess of Exeter, died and was buried in the north transept of St George's Chapel, Windsor. Her remains were interred not far from the spot where her eldest surviving brother, Edward IV, planned to have his own tomb later.

Cecily had now been reinstated within the royal prayers, though she now found herself mixed up there with the Widvilles. On 21 May 1476 a licence was granted for the founding of a fraternity or guild at Stony Stratford. They were to pray for the good of the king, of Elizabeth Widville, and of Cecily Neville, and for the souls of Richard, Duke of York; of Edmund, Earl of Rutland; of Jacquette, Duchess of Bedford; and of Earl Rivers.[64] Elizabeth Widville's mother had died about four years earlier, on 30 May 1472.

At Berkhamsted Castle, on 29 May 1476 (confirmed 30 July 1476), Cecily Neville granted her servant, John Felde, esquire, the keeping of her park at Standon (Hertfordshire).[65] Two months later saw the royal reburial of her long dead husband, Richard, Duke of York, and of her late second son, Edmund, Earl of Rutland, at the collegiate church of Fotheringhay. However, it seems that Cecily herself did not attend that event, despite the ironic fact that Elizabeth Widville was present, as was Margaret, Countess of Richmond, Cecily's

Beaufort cousin and the mother of the exile who would later seize the English throne for himself under the title of King Henry VII.

Following his victory at the battle of Towton, Edward IV had caused the head of his father, the Duke of York to be taken down from the walls of York (see above, Chapter 10). It was then:

> buried with his trunk, and the corpse of his Son Edward [*sic* Edmund] Earl of Rutland, at Ponfract, from whence their bones, by the said king's command, were with great solemnity afterwards removed, and interred at Fotheringay. In order to which, upon the 22d of July, 1466 [*sic* 1476] , the said bones were put into a chariot covered with black velvet, richly wrapped in cloth of gold and royal habit, at whose feet stood a white angel bearing a crown of gold, to signify that of right he was king. The chariot had seven horses, trapp'd to the ground, and cover'd with black, charged with escocheons of the said prince's arms; every horse carried a man, and upon the foremost rode Sir John Skipwith, who bore the prince's banner display'd. The Bishops and Abbots went two or three miles before, to prepare the churches for the reception of the prince, *in pontificalibus*.
>
> Richard, Duke of Gloucester follow'd next after the corpse, accompanied with a number of nobles, the officers of arms being also present. In this equipage they parted from Ponfract, and that night rested at Doncaster, where they were received by the Convent of Cordeliers, in grey habit. From whence by easie journeys to Blithe, to Toxford in the Clay, to Newark, to Grantham, to Stamford, and from thence on Monday the 29th of July, to Fotheringhay, where they arrived betwixt two and three of the clock in the afternoon, where the bodies were received by several Bishops and Abbots *in pontificalibus*, and supported by twelve servants of the defunct prince.
>
> At the entry of the churchyard was the King, accompanied by several Dukes, Earls, and Barons, all in mourning, who proceeded into the heart of Fotheringhay church, near to the high altar, where there was a herse covered with black, furnished with a great number of banners, bannneretts and pencils, and under the said herse were the bones of the said prince and his son Edmond. The Queen and her two daughters were present, also in black, attended by several Ladies and Gentlewomen. *Item*, over the image was a cloth of majesty, of black sarcenet, with the figure of our Lord, sitting on a rainbow, beaten in gold, having on every corner a scocheon of the arms of France and

> England quarterly, with a vallans about the herse also of black sarcenet, fringed half a yard deep, and beaten with three angels of gold holding the arms within a garter, in every part above the herse.
>
> Upon the 30th July several masses were said, and then at the offertory of the mass of requiem, the King offered for the said Prince his father; and the Queen and her two daughters and the Countess of Richmond offered afterwards; then Norroy king of arms offered the Prince's coat of arms; March king of arms, the target; Ireland king of arms, the sword; Windsor Herald of arms of England and Ravendon Herald of Scotland offered the helmet; and Mr. de Ferrys, the harness and courser.[66]

Cecily's whereabouts at the time of her husband's reinterment at Fotheringhay is unknown. Curiously, it also appears that the Duke of Clarence did not attend the reinterment of his father and brother. Possibly both of them preferred not to share the ceremony with Elizabeth Widville.

Shortly afterwards, however, in the autumn of 1476, it appears that Cecily was once again living at Baynard's Castle in London. On Tuesday 22 October 1476, Elizabeth Stonor wrote to her husband, William Stonor (son of an illegitimate half-sister of John de la Pole, 2nd Duke of Suffolk) an account of her recent meetings in London with his aunt by marriage, Elizabeth of York, Duchess of Suffolk. This had also led to a meeting with Elizabeth's mother, Cecily, Duchess of York, presumably at Baynard's Castle. Elizabeth Stonor then goes on to explain how the Duchess of Suffolk took her mother to the royal manor house at Greenwich for a meeting with Edward IV and Elizabeth Widville. Other sources confirm that the king was resident at Greenwich from 16 October in that year, and that he remained there until about 15 December.[67]

> I have be with my Lady of Southfolke [Elizabeth of York] as on Thursday last [17 October] was, and wayted uppon hyr to my lady the Kynges Modyr and hyrse by hyr commaundment. And also on Satyrday last [19 October] was I wayted uppon hyr [Elizabeth of York] thedyr ageyne, and allso ffro thens she wayted uppon my lady hyr Modyr, and browght hyr [from Baynard's Castle?] to Grenwyche to the Kyngis good grace and the quenyse: and ther I sawe the metyng betwyne the Kynge and my ladye his modyr. And trewly me thowght it was a very good syght.[68]

This account has been interpreted by some historians as implying that meetings between Edward and his mother were, by this time, rather rare. According to that interpretation, it has been suggested that the Duchess of Suffolk may have been trying to restore the relationship between her mother and her brother. Given Cecily's recent absence from the reburial of her late husband and her son, Edmund – an absence which she apparently shared with George, Duke of Clarence – it does seem possible that she no longer felt close to Edward. However, the real picture in respect of the evidence of the Stonor letter is not absolutely clear. That family's surviving letters by no means suggest that meetings occurred frequently between members of the Stonor family and their royal relative by marriage, Elizabeth of York, Duchess of Suffolk. The only other mention of the Duchess of Suffolk in the letters is merely a passing reference, in a letter which probably dates from 1471.[69] Thus Elizabeth Stonor's letter of October 1476 might simply have been expressing her excitement and interest at her own two recent meetings with her namesake, the Duchess, and with other members of the royal family.

Llanthony Priory.

However, it does seem that Edward IV may now have been focussing his thoughts once again on the prospect of his mother's death. On 20 May 1477, he granted to the Augustinian Priory of Llanthony the future right to acquire wood from Buckholt in Gloucestershire after the death of Cecily Neville (who then held the manor of Brimpsfield – see below).[70] Almost certainly the relationship between the king and his mother was now once again being acutely disturbed by a new conflict between George, Duke of Clarence and his elder brother. And this conflict was greatly exacerbated by the very hostile attitude to George of Elizabeth Widville.

The subsequent execution of the Duke of Clarence 'rose of a foolish prophesie, which was, that, after K. Edward, one should reign, whose first letter of his name should be a G. Wherewith the king and queene were sore troubled, and began to conceiue a greeuous grudge against this duke, and could not be in quiet till they had brought him to his end.'[71] The earliest surviving reference to the prophecy of G dates from about 1490. At about that time the existence of the prophecy, and its connection with the fate of the Duke of Clarence, were recorded by John Rous as follows:

> Because there was a prophecy that after E., that is, after Edward the fourth, G would be king – and because of its ambiguity – George Duke of Clarence (who was between the two brothers, King Edward and King Richard) on account of being Duke George, was put to death.[72]

It seems likely that the prophecy was produced by two Oxford academic astronomers and astrologers, Dr John Stacy and Thomas Blake,[73] and that it was then published in London and Westminster in the spring of 1477 by Thomas Burdet, a member of George's entourage who had formally worked for the Boteler family of Sudeley (to which Eleanor Talbot had belonged by her first marriage).

It has often been assumed that the case which was put forward in Burdet's lost pro-Clarence political poems was aimed against Edward IV himself, on the basis of the French story of the king's own bastardy. However, no evidence exists in that respect, and against it we have the report of the fact that, in that same year, Elizabeth Widville became very worried about the legality of her own royal marriage, and the future of her royal children. As the Italian diplomat and spy, Domenico Mancini, reported a few years later, she then (in 1477)

> remembered the insults to her family and the calumnies with which she was reproached, namely that according to established usage she

> was not the legitimate wife of the king. Thus she concluded that her offspring by the king would never come to the throne unless the duke of Clarence were removed.[74]

This implies that by 1477 Elizabeth knew or feared that her brother-in-law had become aware of Edward IV's bigamy with her and his earlier marriage to Eleanor Talbot. Clearly, rather than to dethrone Edward IV himself, the aim of the published prophecy must have been to finally oust Elizabeth Widville and her children from their royal status and to reinstate George, Duke of Clarence as heir presumptive to the English throne. After all, the reported prophecy did not say that Edward IV himself should not be King of England (which it would have said if it was focussing on the myth of his bastardy). Instead, it stated that 'after Edward the fourth' (who was therefore recognised as the rightfully reigning monarch), 'G would be king.' Thus the claim which was put forward can only have been that George was the rightful *heir* not the rightful *king*.[75]

Thomas Burdet and his prophet Stacy were tried and executed,[76] and Edward IV had Bishop Stillington arrested, as well as his brother, presumably because he and Elizabeth Widville thought that the Bishop may already have revealed his role in the Talbot marriage to George (just as he later did in 1483 to the royal council). However, Stillington was subsequently released and pardoned. So presumably he convinced Edward IV that he had not revealed the royal secret. Thus, if George had heard of the Talbot marriage, it must have been via some other source. One possible source might have been Burdet (a former servant of the Boteler family). But, if she had indeed contested the Widville marriage with Edward in 1464, another possible source might have been Edward's and George's own mother, Cecily!

Cecily's son, Richard, Duke of Gloucester (later Richard III), was subsequently well aware of the fact that the person really responsible for George's arrest and execution was Elizabeth Widville. In 1483, when he was king, Richard wrote, in his instructions to the Bishop of Enachden (his envoy to James, eighth Earl of Desmond, in Ireland)

> the said bisshop shall ... shewe that albe it the fadre of the said erle, the king than being of yong age, was extorciously slayne and murdred by colour of the lawes within Ireland *by certain persons than havyng the governaunce and rule there*, ayenst alle manhode, reason, and good conscience; yet, notwithstanding that *the semblable chaunce was and hapned sithen within this royaume of Eingland, as wele of his brother the duc of Clarence as other his nigh kynnesmen and gret frendes*.[77]

This linked the execution of James' father, Thomas, the previous (seventh) Earl of Desmond in 1468, with that of George. Significantly, Elizabeth Widville was believed to have brought about the execution of the Earl of Desmond because he had contested the validity of her marriage to Edward IV.[78]

Since the Duke of Gloucester was well aware of the role played by Elizabeth Widville in George's arrest and execution, presumably his mother must also have known that. It is therefore interesting to note that reportedly it was Cecily who was responsible for the unusual way in which George was finally put to death. Initially he had been sentenced to the normal death of a traitor, namely, hanging, drawing and quartering. However, according to a surviving French report (*circa* 1490) of what took place, the initial sentence was subsequently commuted, thanks to the urgent pleading of George's mother, Cecily Neville, who, even if she could not save the life of her middle son, took firm action to save him from a disgraceful public execution.[79]

> In the said year 77 [1477/78] it came about in the kingdom of England that, because King Edward learned that one of his brothers, who was the Duke of Clarence, intended to cross the sea into Flanders to give aid and assistance to his sister, Duchess in Burgundy, widow of the said deceased last duke, this made King Edward arrest his brother and imprison him in the Tower of London, where he was detained as a prisoner for quite a long time while the said King Edward assembled his council, by whose deliberations he [Clarence] was condemned to be led from the said Tower of London, being dragged on his buttocks to the gibbet of the said city of London, and there to be cut open and his entrails thrown into a fire, and then his neck should be cut and his body made into four quarters. But afterwards, by the great prayer and request of the mother of the said Edward and Clarence, his sentence was changed and moderated, so that in the month of February of the said year, Clarence being a prisoner in the Tower of London was taken and brought out of his said prison, and after he had been confessed, was thrust alive in a cask of Malmsey opened at one end, his head downwards, and there he remained until he had given up the ghost, and then he was pulled out and his neck was cut, and afterwards he was shrouded and borne to burial in [BLANK] with his wife, sometime daughter of that Earl of Warwick who died at the battle of Coventry [*sic* for Tewkesbury] with the Prince of Wales, son of the sainted Lancastrian King Henry [VI] of England.[80]

George's execution took place privately on Wednesday 18 February 1477/8.[81] Cecily was obviously in the London area at about that time, because a month earlier, on Wednesday 14 January, she had attended the splendid marriage of the younger son of Edward IV (Richard of Shrewsbury) to Lady Anne Mowbray, the great granddaughter of her elder sister, Catherine Neville. That marriage had taken place in St Stephen's Chapel at the Palace of Westminster. 'The king and queen were there, with both their sons, and their daughters, Elizabeth, Mary and Cecily. With them, too, was Anne's great great aunt, Cecily, Duchess of York, the king's mother, "queen of right", as she was called.'[82] It is interesting that Cecily's presence at that marriage was recorded, given that she seems to have absented herself from other important royal events, such as the reburial of her husband and her son Edmund. Presumably she attended on this occasion because she was well aware of the fact that George had been imprisoned at the Tower of London for about the last six months (though he had not yet been tried or sentenced) and she was deeply concerned about what would happen to him. In other words, the situation may well have been manipulated in her own and her family interests by Elizabeth Widville.

Parliament was opened at Westminster the day after the marriage, and George then found himself attainted and sentenced to death. Cecily presumably wished, if at all possible, to prevent the killing of her middle son. Unfortunately, in the end that seems to have been way beyond her power, thanks to the determined role played by Elizabeth Widville. However, Cecily must have been very anxious to ensure that at least her middle son was not subjected to hanging, drawing and quartering. Maybe she visited George in prison and discussed the manner of his coming death with him. However, there is no evidence to prove that. Another possibility is that she discussed with Edward IV what would be a respectable way for him to carry out the royal execution of his own brother.

Interestingly, there is the possibility that, earlier, Edward may have executed another royal relative, namely Henry Holland, Duke of Exeter. He was the king's cousin in terms of blood. However, he was also the king's brother by marriage, since he was the husband of Edward IV's eldest sister, Anne of York. The Duke of Exeter drowned in 1475. Possibly he had been put to death in that manner on the orders of Edward IV.[83] At that time, drowning seems to have been seen as a merciful way in which to put someone to death. In medieval Scotland it was the means of execution which was reserved for women 'because it was a less violent death. ... Although drowning was generally reserved for females, being the least brutal form of death penalty, at times a male was executed in this way *as a matter of favour*, for instance in 1526 a man convicted of theft and sacrilege was ordered to be drowned *"by the queen's special grace"*'.[84]

Thus Edward IV himself may have thought that drowning would be a less violent and more genteel form of execution than the gruesome and bloody practice of beheading. Since – possibly against his own will – he now felt himself forced to put George to death, he may have preferred not to spill his brother's royal blood. That idea was supported in the nineteenth century by the historian James Gairdner, who then wrote 'I think it is clear that Edward's feelings were severely tried, and that, while he consented to sanction his brother's death, he shrank from inflicting on him the shame of a public execution, which, in fact, would have reflected on the whole family. He therefore preferred a secret assassination.'[85]

Mancini, writing five years later, in November 1483, confirmed both the responsibility of Elizabeth Widville for the execution (see above), and the unusual manner in which it was carried out. 'The mode of execution preferred in this case was that he should die by being plunged into a jar of sweet wine.'[86] Moreover, it certainly seems that Edward IV regretted his brother's death after the execution. A letter written by his royal councillor, Dr Thomas Langton on 20 February 1477/8 reveals that the king had 'assignyd certen Lords to go with the body of the Dukys of Clarence to Teuxbury, where he shall be beryid' because 'the Kyng intendis to do right worshipfully for his sowle.'[87] It is possible that one of the appointed lords was Edward's and George's youngest brother, Richard, Duke of Gloucester. As for Cecily, she must by now have deeply regretted the state of relationships which her family of children had now reached.

On 22 April 1478 Edward IV granted to his mother, to his brother, Richard, to his daughter, Elizabeth of York, and to his kinsman, Lord Hastings, the joint right to nominate a priest to the next vacancy at the chapel of St Stephen in the Palace of Westminster.[88] Meanwhile, Cecily was by no means immobile or stationary. For example in the summer of 1480 she was once again up in Norfolk, staying at the Benedictine Abbey of St Benet at Holme, not far from Norwich.

At that abbey, on 14 June, she appointed Richard More and Henry Lessy as the keepers of her manor and two parks at Stratfield Mortimer, to the south west of Reading. More was one of the marshalls of the king's hall, and Lessy is described on this occasion as one of the sewers of the king's chamber.[89] Their appointment by Cecily was later confirmed by her son, King Edward IV, on 9 November 1480.[90]

The claim has hitherto been made that in 1480 Cecily became a Benedictine nun. As penned by Halsted in the early nineteenth century, that claim reads as follows:

St Benet's Abbey, Holme, Norfolk (engraving from Dugdale's Monasticon Anglicanum).

The fact of the Lady Cecily having enrolled herself sister of the order of St. Benedict in the year 1480 is proved beyond dispute by the MS. details preserved in the Cottonian library, but it is equally certain from other documents, that she did not retire altogether from the world or lead a life of seclusion in any religious house belonging to the order whose vows she had embraced.

It appears from the Paston Letters (vol. iv.) that during the middle ages it was customary for persons growing in years to procure by purchase or gift a retreat in some holy society; where, abandoning worldly matters, the piously disposed might pass the remainder of their days in prayer and supplication; but this connection with religious houses did not imply always the adopting formally a conventual life or becoming an inmate of those monastic establishments in whose "merits, prayers, and good works," the new member of their fraternity

> shared. Margaret, Countess of Richmond and Derby, for example, mother of King Henry VII., and the contemporary of Cecily, Duchess of York, was enrolled a member of five devout societies; but although she abstained from that period, as far as was compatible with her exalted station, from all worldly pleasures and occupations, yet it is well known that she never became an inmate of any religious house. A recluse in her own dwelling she certainly was, for she never quitted the retirement she had voluntarily embraced, excepting when a sense of duty required a temporary sojourn in the metropolis; and in all likelihood the same devotional feelings, qualified by reservations insurmountable in her remarkable position, influenced the Duchess of York, when she professed herself a member of the Benedictine Sister- hood.
>
> That she never removed from her castle at Berkhampstead excepting for brief intervals, is clear, because she expired within its walls; and the severity of her life there in declining years is made known by the rules and regulations, which have descended to this present day, and which attest that she considered Berkhampstead as her home throughout the varied changes of her troubled life, and that her occasional residence at Baynard's Castle, arose inure from the necessity of the measure with reference to others, than from any reprehensible indulgence in those ambitious feelings which influenced her actions at an earlier period of life.[91]

Halsted's statement is misleading in some respects. Firstly, as we have seen, Cecily was by no means exclusively resident at Berkamsted Castle in 1480. As we shall see shortly, it appears that she spent a good deal of 1483 at her London home. Also, she did not, in reality, ever become a nun. That statement is a misinterpretation based on a lack of understanding of how religious orders work. Actually, Cecily became a Benedictine *oblate*. This means that she remained a lay person. However, she was associated with the Benedictine order, and promised to join that order in daily prayer and other respects.[92] An oblate in respect of a monastic order (of monks) is similar to a tertiary in respect of a mendicant order (of friars). In the fifteenth century a female oblate may well have worn what looked like a religious habit in her day to day life.

The link of an oblate has to be to a specific abbey, or religious house, and in the case of Cecily Neville it therefore seems possible that the Benedictine link which she made may have been with the Abbey of St Benet at Holme in Norfolk, where she had stayed on various occasions. She had been staying there

A fifteenth-century woman wearing a religious-style habit (engraving from The Myroure of Oure Ladye).

in June 1480, and that may have been the occasion upon which she made her promises to the Benedictine community as an oblate.

Further details in respect of Cecily's religious devotion and how deep that was will be explored later (see below, Chapter 14). However, it is clear that, in spite of her religious commitment she was by no means completely cut off from the world. For example, her amicable relationship with her Clare steward, Lord Howard, was obviously maintained well beyond her commitment to the Benedictine Order. A record survives telling us that on 14 February 1481/2 'my Lord [Howard] gaf my Lady [the Kinges Moder] iij yerdes and di. white russet, that cost x corounes and di..'[93] Of course, the three and a half yards of coarse material might possibly have been required as part of the religious habit which Cecily would generally now have been wearing. By the time when he gave her this fabric, Cecily was in her mid sixties. As for John Howard, although his date of birth is not precisely recorded, probably he was also about sixty years old.

Cecily is also mentioned in Howard's surviving accounts on 16 May 1482. Lord Howard had then been settling accounts with his local lawyer, James Hobart (or Hobard).[94] Howard had thought that he owed money to Hobart. However, it emerged that, in addition to his own earlier payments, Hobart had also received £12 'of my Lady the kynges moder, for my Lordes fee.'[95]

Meanwhile, on 11 November 1480 Cecily had become the godmother to yet another of her Widville granddaughters, little Bridget of York, who was then baptised at Eltham. Was this perhaps an attempt to establish amity within the royal family? The other godmother was Elizabeth of York, the baby's eldest sister, and another of Cecily's goddaughters. As for the godfather, he was the Bishop of Winchester.[96]

By the later autumn of 1480 Cecily was living at her Castle of Berkhamsted. There, on 27 November 1480, she appointed Roger Capes as keeper of her park at Bremmesfeld (Brimpsfield) in Gloucestershire, and also of her neighbouring woodland of Buchold (Buckholt). The appointment was for the life of Capes, even if Cecily herself should predecease him. It was confirmed by the king on 15 May 1481.[97] And on 29 November 1480, at the instance of the king's mother, a license was granted for the foundation of a fraternity, or guild, at Thaxsted in Essex. Amongst other things, at the local church of St John the Baptist the fraternity was to have prayers offered for the good estate of Edward IV, Elizabeth Widville, and Cecily Neville.[98] That format for the commissioning of royal prayers now seems to have been the norm. For example, on 30 March 1481 Sir Thomas St Leger, the widower of Cecily's eldest daughter, Anne of York, Duchess of Exeter, was licensed to found a chantry for his late royal wife at St George's Chapel, Windsor. Prayers were to be offered there for the good estate of Edward IV, Elizabeth Widville and Cecily Neville among others.[99]

However, Cecily was still part of the world, and figured in its business in various ways. On 12 June 1482 a reward was given to Henry Lessy (Lassy) for his long service to Cecily, Duchess of York.[100] And on 12 February 1482/3 Sir Ralph Assheton (also known as Sir Ralph de Ashton) of the village of Fryton, Ryedale, Yorkshire, a former sheriff of York, was summoned for having failed to answer in court a case against him in respect of debts he was said to owe. These included a total of £60 owed to Cecily Neville. Assheton had served as the High Sheriff of Yorkshire about ten years earlier, from 1471 to 1473.[101] On 17 February 1482/3 Cecily Neville appointed Sir Giles Daubeney as constable of her castle at Bridgewater in Somerset, and also as steward of her Bridgewater manor. This was confirmed by Edward IV three days later.[102] Also, the king was still taking care of his mother in various ways. Thus, from income from the port of Southampton from 28 July year 21 [1481] to the feast of St Michael [29 September] year 22 [1482] of the reign of Edward IV, 'my lady the kynges moder' was paid £358 3s. 7d. as 'part of payment of hire yerly annuite' (which totalled £689 6s. 8d).[103]

Chapter 13

The Accession of Richard III

A physical suggestion in stone of the significance in Cecily Neville's life of Baynard's Castle in London survived until the Great Fire of that city in 1666. It was her coat of arms:

> Impaled with the Duke's, ensigned with a Coronet, and supported with Two Angels, standing upon as many Roses within the Rays of the Sun, [they] were carved in a Nich, upon the South-East Pillar of St Bennet's Steeple, near Paul's Wharf, according to the ensuing Figure, which I caused to be delineated before the late Conflagration of London, Anno 1666.[1]

Cecily's Arms as formerly displayed near Paul's Wharf (17th century engraving).

It seems that probably Cecily was in London, and at Baynard's Castle, in March and April 1483, when her son, King Edward IV lost his health. It was just after Easter 1483, perhaps on Monday 31 March, that Edward fell ill. 'A tall man and very fat though not to the point of deformity, [he] allowed the damp cold to strike his vitals, when one day he was taken in a small boat with those whom he had bidden to go fishing and watched their sport too eagerly. He there contracted the illness from which he never recovered.'[2]

It seems that rumours of the king's health problem circulated in the capital in early April. A surviving note written by a middle-class Londoner called George Cely may well have been written at that time, because it speculates about the possible death of the king. However, it also contains a mass of wild rumours. Unfortunately, based upon no real evidence, previous historians have tended to assume, for no good reason, that it was written later, and refers to the possible death of the next king, Edward V.[3]

On about 2 April Edward IV seems to have dispatched a letter to his mother's steward, Lord Howard, at the latter's Suffolk home, Tendring Hall, Stoke by Nayland. Howard received the king's letter on Friday 4 April.[4] No record of its contents survives, but maybe Edward was asking Howard to come to London. Howard did not depart at once, but when he did leave his home, three days later, he travelled more quickly than usual. Possibly by that time he had already heard rumours that his sovereign had died. 'On vij day of Aprill my Lord set off for London',[5] spending that night just south of Colchester, at Easthorpe. The next day he hurried on, only briefly pausing at Romford for refreshments. Lord Howard reached London the day after his departure, on Tuesday 8 April, probably in the evening.[6]

There is no surviving evidence to show whether or not messages had also been sent by the king elsewhere – for example, to his own brother, Richard, in the north of England, or to his 'brother-in-law' and his eldest son at Ludlow Castle. It is claimed that, at about the time when he contacted Lord Howard, the king also added codicils to his will, and sought to reconcile the quarreling factions of his friend, Lord Hastings, and his stepson, the Marquess of Dorset.[7] However, no such codicils survive, so there is no certainty as to what (if anything) may have been added to Edward IV's will during the last days of his life. As for the quarrel between Hastings and Dorset, that may well have been related to the fact that each of those two men was involved in an affair with Elizabeth Lambert (Mistress Shore). Ironically, she is also popularly reputed to have been a mistress of the king himself. In reality, however, not one single shred of contemporary evidence survives to prove that a relationship existed between Edward IV and 'Mistress Shore'.[8] Indeed, at this stage of his life the king seems to have been extremely uxorious, and was apparently dominated in more or less every way by Elizabeth Widville.

Cecily lost her eldest surviving son early in April 1483, though the precise date of his death is uncertain. It is usually claimed that Edward died on 9 April 1483,[9] and that is definitely the date upon which the news of his death was made public.[10] However, according to the contemporary York Records it seems that he must have died earlier, either on Tuesday 1 April or on Saturday 5 April (depending on whether his York Requiem Mass was celebrated on the 7th or the 3rd day after his decease).[11] As for Domenico Mancini's account (which was also written in 1483, but about six months after the event), this also claims that Edward IV died earlier – citing Monday 7 April as his death date.[12] Ironically, a *c*.1509 addition to the *Anlaby Cartulary* implies that Edward died *later*, on Tuesday 15 April.[13] However, there is no contemporary evidence to support that view.

The confusion about Edward IV's genuine death date, which seems to have been ignored by previous writers, raises the possibility that, at the time, and for political reasons, the news of his demise may well have been concealed for a day or two by his dominant consort, Elizabeth Widville. She was desperate to ensure that her son, Edward, Prince of Wales, should become king. As her earlier campaign for the execution of the king's middle brother, George Duke of Clarence, clearly shows, she was all too well aware of the fact that in various quarters questions had already been raised about the validity of her royal marriage. Hence she and her family now desperately attempted to stage a coup and to seize power.

Presumably the king's mother must have heard the news that her son was ill. But whether she herself ever saw her sick son is not known. Nor is there any evidence to show when she received the news of his death. However, it seems that she must have been aware of the fact that on the morning of Thursday 10 April her son's body was carried to St Stephen's Chapel within the Palace of Westminster. There it was to lie in state for a week. Immediately after the body had arrived, a requiem mass for the dead king was celebrated in that royal chapel by the Bishop of Chichester.

Meanwhile, someone else – presumably Elizabeth Widville – had made the decision to inter Edward IV in the location which he himself had chosen, at St George's Chapel, Windsor, on Friday 19 April.[14] The royal burial date could very easily have been delayed somewhat, as Henry VIII's was later.[15] However, it seems that, in the case of Edward IV, a prompt interment was considered desirable. The main purpose behind that was presumably to speed up the coronation of Elizabeth Widville's elder royal son. But one other effect which the speedy burial produced was the fact that there was insufficient time for news of the arrangements to be sent to Middleham Castle in Yorkshire. There the senior living prince of the blood royal – Edward's surviving younger brother, the Duke of Gloucester – then resided. It seems that those responsible for the 1483 royal funeral arrangements felt that Gloucester's presence at his brother's interment was unimportant, and not required. It also suggests that Cecily Neville cannot have been consulted regarding the funeral arrangements.

On Wednesday 16 April, the king's body was solemnly processed from St Stephen's Chapel to Westminster Abbey. Cecily's steward, Lord Howard walked in front of the coffin, bearing the king's personal banner.[16] In Westminster Abbey, the body was placed on a great hearse before the high altar, surrounded by candles. There the Archbishop of York celebrated the funeral mass, at which the chief mourner (in the absence of the Duke of Gloucester) was the dead sovereign's next nearest living adult male relative, his nephew, the Earl of Lincoln.[17] The appropriate Hours of the Office for the Dead were probably also celebrated, and the solemnities continued into the night. In the early hours of the following morning[18] the funeral procession reformed and, began to bear the corpse to Windsor, where Edward's remains were interred on Saturday 19 April.

Meanwhile in London a convocation of the clergy had opened. At that assembly prayers were offered for the new king, Edward V, and for Elizabeth Widville, the Queen Mother. However, no other members of the royal family were mentioned. Reference both to the Duke of Gloucester and to his mother, the dowager Duchess of York was omitted.[19]

Arrangements had now been made to bring the late king's eldest son from Ludlow Castle to Westminster, and to crown him early in May. Meanwhile, the Duke of Gloucester was still in the north of England. He appears to have received no official notification of his brother's death from Elizabeth Widville. But by about 20 April the news of Edward IV's death had definitely reached him. His source for this information was Edward IV's chamberlain, Lord Hastings, who apparently felt disturbed about what was going on in London.[20] The Crowland chronicler attributes this decision on Hastings' part to the fact that 'he was afraid that if supreme power fell into the hands of the queen's relatives they would then sharply avenge the alleged injuries done to them by that lord [for] much ill-will … had long existed between Lord Hastings and them.'[21] When he heard that his brother had died, the Duke of Gloucester set off for York. There he exacted oaths of fealty to his nephew, King Edward V, from the city magistrates.[22] He seems to have left York, heading south, on St George's Day (Wednesday 23 April).[23] Although he had apparently received no messages from Elizabeth Widville, 'Gloucester also wrote the most pleasant letters to console the queen', offering fealty to his nephew as England's new king.[24]

It seems that Cecily's only surviving son probably timed his journey from north to south to fit in with the programme which was planned by Elizabeth Widville's brother, Lord Rivers, for transporting the new boy king to London. Thus Gloucester briefly paused on the way at Pontefract, reaching Nottingham on 26 April, and Northampton on Tuesday 29 April.[25] He also seems to have timed his arrival at Northampton to meet his cousin, Henry Stafford, Duke of Buckingham, who appears to have been in touch with him.[26]

Meanwhile the political situation in London, which appears to have disturbed Lord Hastings, now revealed clear manipulation on the part of Elizabeth Widville and her faction, which was obviously intended to insult and oust those whom she did not consider her friends. For example, Cecily Neville's Suffolk steward, who had now held a baronial title for a dozen years, suddenly found his peerage ignored, and heard himself insultingly referred to merely as 'Sir John Howard.'[27] Of course, Elizabeth Widville had long seen him as a potential rival of her younger son, Richard of Shrewsbury, Duke of York and Norfolk, in respect of the Mowbray inheritance. Moreover, Howard had close connections with Elizabeth Talbot, Duchess of Norfolk, and probably also with her late sister, Eleanor.[28] Similarly the Duke of Gloucester, who was also the Lord Admiral of England, was not only never officially informed of his elder brother's death, but was also now effectively displaced as England's marine commander by Elizabeth's brother, Edward Widville in respect of dealing with potential French attacks.[29] When Elizabeth Widville was thus insulting and ousting the Duke of Gloucester and Lord Howard, it seems quite likely that she may also have been ignoring and ousting Cecily herself, whose middle son, George, Duke of Clarence, she had earlier had put to death for the sake of her own political interests.

But on Wednesday 30 April, at Stony Stratford, Cecily's son, Richard, Duke of Gloucester, assumed the protectorship of Elizabeth Widville's son, Edward V. That night or the following night, when she heard the news, Elizabeth Widville fled into sanctuary at Westminster Abbey, together with her brother Lionel, Bishop of Salisbury, her son the Marquess of Dorset, her daughters by Edward IV and her youngest surviving son, Richard of Shrewsbury.[30]

On Sunday 4 May Gloucester, together with his cousin, the Duke of Buckingham, and his nephew, King Edward V, entered London. The new young king was lodged at the the Bishop of London's palace.[31] But it seems that Gloucester joined his mother at Baynard's Castle. Cecily must have been pleased to see him. Not only was he now her only surviving son, but also he bore a strong physical resemblance to his late father, her husband, the Duke of York.[32]

Three days later, on Wednesday 7 May,

> the executors of Edward IV assembled at Baynard's Castle, the London house of Cecily, duchess of York, mother of the late king, and the archbishop [of Canterbury] then and there took over all Edward IV's seals, Great, Privy and Signet.[33]

Obviously there was no reason why the executors should have met at that venue if the late king's mother, and her surviving son, who was now the Lord Protector of the Realm, had not been residing there on that date.

For about four weeks, preparations continued for the coronation of the son of Edward IV and Elizabeth Widville. But on 9 June, Bishop Stillington of Bath and Wells appears to have shocked a council meeting by announcing that, in his view, Edward V could not be crowned because he was illegitimate, since his father had been legally married to Eleanor Talbot. The bishop's evidence must have been quite specific, since he himself had secretly married Edward IV to Eleanor Talbot, about three years before the late king's second secret marriage to Elizabeth Woodville (at a time when Eleanor was still alive).[34] And the news must have leaked out quickly, because that same day Simon Stallworthe wrote a letter to Sir William Stonor, in which he reported that there was now 'gret besyness ageyns the Coronacione'.[35] Since Cecily Neville may have argued with Edward IV in 1464 that he was legally committed to Eleanor (see above, Chapter 9), if her son the Duke of Gloucester discussed the matter with his mother at Baynard's Castle on the evening of 9 June, presumably she would have supported the case against her grandson which the Bishop of Bath and Wells had now made public. Indeed, it might even have been Cecily who had now persuaded the bishop to make a public statement in respect of the Talbot marriage.

In this complex new situation, on the next two days (10 and 11 June) Gloucester requested the support of northern troops. On 22 June sermons were given out at Pauls Cross which publicly raised the issue of the bastardy of Edward V and his siblings.[36] As a result, it became clear to the population of London that:

> the only survivor of the royal stock was Richard, duke of Gloucester, who was legally entitled to the crown, and could bear its responsibilities thanks to his proficiency. His previous career and blameless morals

> would be a sure guarantee of his good government. Although he would refuse such a burden, he might yet change his mind if he were asked by the peers. On hearing this the lords consulted their own safety, warned by the example of Hastings, and perceiving the alliance of the two dukes, whose power, supported by a multitude of troops, would be difficult and hazardous to resist. Whereas they saw themselves surrounded and in the hands of the dukes, and therefore they determined to declare Richard their king and ask him to undertake the burden of office. On the following day [25 June 1483] all the lords forgathered at the house of Richard's mother, wither he had purposely betaken himself, that these events might not take place in the Tower where the young king was confined. There the whole business was transacted, the oaths of allegiance given, and other indispensible acts duly performed.[37]

Amazingly, perhaps, from his own point of view, but apparently with the full support of his mother, who might even have been behind the plan, Richard, Duke of Gloucester had now become King Richard III.

On Friday 27 June 1483, the new sovereign appointed John, Bishop of Lincoln, as chancellor. This was done at his mother's London house.[38] In fact Baynard's Castle seems to have remained Richard's base and headquarters until the start of July.[39] This appears to support the view that Cecily Neville must have been firmly backing Richard's accession. Also, as we shall see, Richard's subsequent relationship with his mother appears to have remained cordial.[40]

Cecily Neville appears to have played no specific role at the coronation of her son, Richard III, and her daughter-in-law and great niece, Anne of Warwick, on 6 July 1483. However, she must have attended their coronation. In the same way, in twentieth century England, Queen Alexandra, Queen Mary and Queen Elizabeth attended the coronations of their respective children, George V, George VI and Elizabeth II, but those Queen Mothers played no formal role of any kind in the coronation ceremonies. They simply sat and watched. Richard and Anne had both been living at Cecily's London home, Baynard's Castle, on 26 June, when Richard was offered the crown, and they remained resident there until 4 July – presumably with Cecily. It was on 4 July that the royal couple moved to the Tower of London, because that was normally the traditional starting place from which English sovereigns travelled to their coronations.

The rules of the Wardrobe Accounts for the coronation of a queen consort state clearly that 'all duchessys, countesses, baronessis with other lades and gentilwomen have had robez and leverys at the seide coronacion.'[41] Since Cecily was a duchess it would be logical to deduce that in July 1483 she would have been one of the robe recipients in respect of the coronation of her daughter-in-law. The fact that she was a *dowager* duchess does nothing to remove her from the list, because Eleanor Talbot's sister (and Anne Mowbray's mother) Elizabeth Talbot, the dowager Duchess of Norfolk, is known to have received the material required for coronation robes and two gowns for Richard and Anne's coronation.[42]

Indeed, a much older dowager Duchess of Norfolk – Cecily's elder sister, Catherine Neville – also received the robes required. The relevant extracts from the Wardrobe Accounts read:

> To the Duchesse of Norfolk, the elder, wydowe, for her liveree of clothing ayenst the saide moost noble coronation of oure saide souveraine Lady the Quene: xiiij yerdes scarlet
>
> To the Duchesse of Norfolk, the yonger, wydowe, for her liveree of clothing ayenst the said moost noble coronation of oure saide souveraine Lady the Quene: xiiij yerdes scarlet
>
> ...
>
> To the Duchesse of Norfolk, thelder, wydow, a longe gowne made of vj yerdes of blue velvet and purfiled with vj yerdes of white cloth of gold. And a long gowne maade of vj yerdes j quarter of purpul velvet and purfiled with vj yerdes of crymysyn clothe of gold.
>
> To the Duchesse of Norfolk, the yonger, wydowe, a longe gowne made of vj yerdes and a quarter of blue velvet and purfiled with vj yerdes and a quarter of crymysyn cloth of gold. And a long gowne made of vj yerdes of crymysyne velvet and purfiled with vj yerdes of white clothe of gold.[43]

Since we have clear evidence that dowager Duchesses – including Cecily Neville's elder sister – were provided with robes for them to attend the coronation, and since the list of named ladies who were provided with the necessary fabric also includes Cecily's daughter, Elizabeth, Duchess of Suffolk – and Cecily's cousin Margaret Beaufort, Countess of Richmond (mother of the future King Henry VII) – it cannot be possible that Cecily Neville did not attend the coronation of July 1483.

Significantly, however, those people whose robes are not mentioned in the wardrobe lists include the king himself and his consort. Presumably this is because in the case of the scarlet robe fabric all the named recipients were apparently simply being sent the necessary material. They themselves were presumably then responsible for having it rapidly made up into the required robe. But of course, Richard and Anne would not have been sent fabric by the Great Warbrobe. Instead, the Wardrobe itself would have prepared their robes for them. And the same may well have been the case in respect of the king's mother, Cecily Neville.

After the coronation King Richard and Queen Anne spent about a week at Greenwich. They then set off on a royal tour. They travelled first to Windsor Castle, then on to Reading, where they stayed on the night of Monday 21 July, and apparently visited the shrine of Our Lady of Caversham. Cecily's Suffolk steward, John Howard, who had been elevated to the rank of Duke of Norfolk a few weeks previously, on 28 June, travelled with them as far as Caversham. It is not clear whether Cecily herself remained in London or set off to some other home, such as Berkhamsted Castle.

On 22 July the new Duke of Norfolk left the royal tour and found himself sent rapidly back to London by Richard III. It appears that following the royal couple's departure there had been a plot of some kind in London, and John Howard was now required to sort it out. The plot might possibly have been an attempt by Richard's cousin, and apparent (but disloyal) supporter, the Duke of Buckingham, to extract the sons of Edward IV and Elizabeth Widville from the Tower of London.[44] Buckingham went on to stage a rebellion - which bears his name - against Richard III. Initially, that rebellion seems to have aimed at the restoration of King Edward V, so logically either Buckingham, or whoever else it was who lay behind the support for young Edward , would have needed that boy in his hands.

Richard III seems subsequently to have had no idea of what became of the two sons of Edward IV and Elizabeth Widville, which suggests that they had somehow been extracted from his custody. Apparently John Howard carried out a trial of those arrested in respect of the London plot. The trial seems to have been held at Crosby's Place in Bishopsgate, a London residence formerly rented by Richard as Duke of Gloucester. Richard III issued a warrant on Tuesday 29 July at Minster Lovell, in respect of the prisoners detained for their recent involvement in some 'enterprise.' And although no details of the alleged crime are specified in his warrant, other sources prove that there had been unauthorised attempts both to extract the late King Edward IV's daughters from sanctuary at Westminster and also to remove his sons from the Tower of London.[45]

After dealing with the arrests made in respect of the London plotting, Howard then went on to play a wonderful role for King Richard in the defeat of Buckingham's rebellion. As a result, Buckingham himself was captured and executed. Where Cecily was during these troubled months from July to November 1483 is not on record. However, she can hardly have been sad to hear the news of the execution of the Duke of Buckingham, even though he was the grandson of her sister, Anne Neville, because not only had he been disloyal to Richard III, but he was also the official who had carried out the execution of her middle son, George, Duke of Clarence, in 1477/8.

When Buckingham's rebellion had been dealt with, on 4 December 1483 Richard III licensed the foundation of a chantry at the Church of the Blessed Virgin Mary at Rykall (Riccall) in Yorkshire.[46] Prayers were to be offered there for the good estate of King Richard, Queen Anne, and Edward of Middleham, Prince of Wales while they lived, and for their souls after death. Prayers were also to be offered for the souls of the king's parents. In the surviving documentation, no specific mention is included of prayers for the good estate of Cecily Neville during her lifetime. However, the normal procedure would have been that, if her soul was to be prayed for after death, during her lifetime, prayers would be offered for her good estate, so presumably that was the intention.

Significantly, four days later, on 8 December 1483, Richard III awarded an annuity of 20 marks per annum to a lady who had served both him and his mother. It was a woman named Joan who had been married, first to John Malpas esquire, and then to Sir John Peysmersh, but both husbands were now deceased.[47] The annuity was to reward her for her services to the king when he was young, and to his mother, Cecily, Duchess of York. It replaced an earlier award, which had been made by his late brother, King Edward IV.

On 9 February 1483/4, Richard III also confirmed the late Edward IV's earlier grants to his mother of various manors, lands and rents to cover her jointure, together with the grants of Berkhamsted and King's Langley in Hertfordshire.[48] Richard also granted his mother the right to export bales of wool via London, Sandwich and Southampton, in an attempt to recompense her for the fact that Edward IV's notional grants to her of a total of £689 6s. 8d. a year had never actually been paid.[49]

On 3 June 1484 Richard III wrote to his mother from Pontefract Castle:

> Madam, I recommaunde me to you as hertely as is to me possible, beseching you in my most humble and effectuouse wise of youre daly blessing to my synguler comfort & defence in my need. And madam I hertely beseche you that I may often here from you to my comfort.

> And suche newes as bene here my servaunt Thomas Bryane, this berere, shall shew you, to whome please it you yeve credence unto. And madam I beseche you to be good & gracious lady to my lord, my Chambreleyn, to be your officer in Wilshire in such as Colingbourne had. I trust he shall therein do you good service, and that it please you that by this berere I may understande youre pleasure in this behalve. And I pray God sende you th'accomplishemnent of youre noble desires. Written at Pountfreit the iij[de] day of Juyne, with the hand of
> Youre most humble son
> Ricardus Rex [50]

The precise meaning of Richard's request to 'often here from' his mother is unclear. It could imply that he would like her to contact him more frequently. However, it may also mean that he already hears from her regularly, very much enjoys it, and wishes such contact to continue, even increasing in its frequency. That might well explain why he now solicits Cecily's 'daly blessing.'

Richard also confirmed two other grants to his mother made by Edward IV:

Of the proffites of Stanclyff … [to] Cecile duchesse of York	£100
The same duchesse of the fee ferme of Chestre	£4 17s. 4d.[51]

And on 9 May 1485, just over three months before the end of his brief reign, Richard III licensed the foundation of a chantry chapel in the church of St John the Baptist at Marldon in Devon, with the provision that prayers should be offered there for the good estate of the king and of his mother, and that after their deaths their souls should be prayed for in the chantry.[52] It is significant that by this time only two members of the royal family (the king and his mother) were mentioned in this religious foundation. And on Tuesday 17 May 1485, Richard paid a visit to his mother at Berkhamsted Castle.[53] This was the final occasion on which Cecily saw and spent time with her last surviving son.

Chapter 14

The Reign of Henry VII

The following record survives to offer a picture of how Cecily's day went in the closing years of her life, during the reign of her granddaughter's husband, King Henry VII.

A compendous recytacion compiled of the order, rules, and constructione of the house of the Righte Excellent Princesse Cecill, late mother unto the Right Noble Prince, King Edward the Fourthe.

Me semeth yt is requisyte to understand the order of her owne person, concerninge God and the worlde.

She useth to arise at seven of the clocke, and hath readye her Chapleyne to saye with her mattins of the daye, and mattins of our lady; and when she is fully readye she hath a lowe masse in her chamber, and after masse she takethe somethinge to recreate nature; and soe goeth to the Chappell hearinge the devine service, and two lowe masses ; from thence to dynner ; duringe the tyme whereof she hath a lecture of holy matter, either Hilton of contemplative and active life, Bonaventure de infancia, Salvatoris legenda aurea, St. Maude, St. Katherin of Sonys, or the Revelacions of St. Bridgett.

After dinner she giveth audyence to all such as hath any matter to shewe unto her by the space of one hower; and then sleepeth one quarter of an hower, and after she hath slepte, she contynueth in prayer unto the first peale of evensonge: then she drinketh wyne or ale at her pleasure. Forthwith her Chapleyne is ready to saye with her both evensonges; and after the last peale she goeth to the Chappell, and heareth evensonge by note; from thence to supper, and in the tyme of supper she recyteth the lecture that was had at dynner to those that be in her presence.

After supper she disposeth herself to be famyliare with her gentlewomen, to the secac'on of honest myrthe; and one howre before her goeing to bed, she taketh a cuppe of wyne, and after that goeth to her pryvie closette, and taketh her leave of God for all nighte,

> makinge ende of her prayers for that daye: and by eighte of the clocke is in bedde. I truft to our lordes mercy that this noble Princesse thus devideth the howers to his highe pleasure.[1]

This account makes it clear that Cecily was following daily the religious life of a Benedictine oblate. Waking at 7 a.m., she began by saying morning prayer of the day and morning prayer of the Blessed Virgin Mary, together with her chaplain. This was followed by a low mass in her chamber, followed by breakfast. Then she would attend the hour of prayer and masses in her chapel. She would then eat her midday meal, during which religious works would be read to her. In the afternoon she would receive people in audience, rest for a while, and have a drink. After that she would attend evening prayer in her chapel, then have supper and chat with her women attendants. She would then say the final office of prayers for the day (presumably compline), and go to bed at 8 p.m.

It also offers an intriguing list of books which Cecily studied, or had read to her, on a regular daily basis. The books listed are as follows:

Hilton, *Of Contemplative and Active Life.*

This presumably refers to Walter Hilton's *The Epistle on the Mixed Life*. This is a book which offered guidance in respect of Christian meditation to devout laymen and laywomen. Unlike some other writers,[2] Hilton advised them not to give up their active lives in order to become contemplatives, but to combine the two forms of life. Walter Hilton (*c.*1343–24 March 1396) was an Augustinian Canon and a mystic. He was probably educated at the University of Cambridge, and subsequently served within the diocese of Ely.

Bonaventure de infancia.

This appears to refer to St Bonaventura's *De Infancia Salvatoris* (*The Infancy of Our Saviour*), which presumably comprised just a part of the fuller original text produced by St Bonaventure (Latin and Italian *Bonaventura*). That work was a text with the title *Speculum Vitæ Christi* (*A Mirror of the Life of Christ*).[3] The original text was in Latin, though by the 1490s translated versions had been produced – and copies had been printed by Caxton.

St Bonaventura was a Bishop who was later made a Doctor of the Church. A member of the Franciscan order, Bonaventura was born in central Italy in 1221 and died in 1274. His real first name was John, but he reportedly received the name *Bonaventura* from St Francis of Assisi, who, on seeing him as a child, prayed for his recovery from a dangerous illness, and when the prayer appeared to be working, cried out *O buona ventura!* ('Oh, good fortune!')

Cecily Neville's apparent focus on the childhood section of St Bonaventura's work may suggest that children had a special significance for her. She may also have felt a connection to St Bonaventura because in 1265 he had been appointed Archbishop of York – a role later held by one of her Neville nephews, and a title which partially paralleled Cecily's own title as Duchess of York. Her interest in him may also have stemmed partly from the fact that she and her husband had previously had a Franciscan friar as one of their chaplains, not to mention the fact that her youngest son, Richard III, lay buried in a Franciscan Priory Church.

Salvatoris legenda aurea.

The *Legenda Aurea* (Golden Legend) now forms part of what is generally known as the Apocryphal New Testament. It comprises *The Gospel of Pseudo-Matthew*, or the *Liber de Infancia* (*Book of Childhood*). This includes a detailed life-story for the Virgin Mary, beginning with her miraculous birth to Anna and Joachim (after having been announced to Anna by an angel), and the story of her growing up. It then goes on to Mary's own miraculous pregnancy and the birth and upbringing of her son, Jesus.[4] It also reveals the wider family in which Jesus grew up, including the sons and daughters of St Joseph.

Although this book was never formally included in the New Testament, there is no clear record of any official church decision which ruled it out. Moreover, medieval iconography shows that elements of its story, including the identity of the Virgin Mary's parents, and the account of her young life, were widely accepted and believed. Significantly, such elements appear to have been depicted in the new, stone-built shrine chapel, constructed around the timber Holy House at Walsingham in the 1450s:

> During the last [= 19th] century remains of some alabaster carvings were found among the stone work in a barn at East Barsham [just over a mile from Walsingham priory]. They represented Our Lady as a child, being taught to read by her mother, St. Anne. It is not unlikely that in the arcading of the chapel was a series of carvings representing the whole of Mary's life.[5]

The broken alabaster carving of St Anne teaching the Virgin to read was photographed by the author at East Barsham Church in the 1980s (see plate 21 B). Unfortunately it subsequently seems to have been stolen from the church. But possibly it had originally been commissioned by Cecily and her husband for the new shrine chapel at Walsingham Priory (see above, Chapter 6). Also, the fact that Cecily read the *Salvatoris legenda aurea* emphasises once again how important family life had felt for her, including her own links with all her children and also their inter-relationships.

St. Maude.

Presumably this was the life story of the German Saint Maud, or Mathilda (895–968). She was the daughter of a Count (Earl) and as a result of her marriage she became a queen. Thus her life was in many ways parallel to that of Cecily herself. Maud (or Mathilda) also had sons. However, she lost her husband, and her own life was then ruined by the conduct of some of her sons. Eventually, however, her sons repented and restored to their mother everything that had been taken from her. She then became a great giver of alms, and a great sponsor of religious life.[6] Once again it sounds as though this book may have seemed particularly significant to Cecily because the story of St Maud (Mathilda) so strongly echoed and reflected her own life experiences.

St Katherin of Sonys (St Catherine of Siena).

St Catherine of Siena (1347–1380) was a tertiary of the Dominican Order (which was similar to Cecily's own role as an oblate of the Benedictine Order). In some ways her life reflected Cecily's, so it could possibly have been Catherine's life story which Cecily read. However, it is more probable that she studied a book written by St Catherine herself. If so, the most likely work is *The Dialogue of Divine Providence*, which was written by St Catherine in 1377–1378. This work comprises conversation between a soul rising up to God, and God himself.

The Revelacions of St Bridgett.

St Bridget of Sweden (1303–1373), was the founder of the Bridgettine Order. The daughter of a knight, she was related to the Swedish royal family. She bore her husband a number of children. But following the death of her husband, she became devoted to religious life. She then had visions, and produced extensive revelations in written form. This presumably was what Cecily Neville read and studied.

Incidentally, since Cecily read *The Revelations of St Bridget*, and since one of her granddaughters and goddaughters was named after this saint, and later became a nun, it seems likely that when she, and her children, made the sign of the cross, they would probably have done so in the same way as modern Catholics: namely, up, down, left shoulder, right shoulder. Eastern (Orthodox) Christians make the sign of the cross slightly differently (up, down, right shoulder, left shoulder), and the surviving instructions of Pope Innocent III (1198–1216) and other early medieval sources appear to show that western (Catholic) Christians once did the same.[7] However, *The Miroure of Oure Ladye*, an early sixteenth-century book, which set out the practices of the Sisters of the Bridgettine Monastery of Sion at Isleworth, ordered that the cross sign should be made in the manner employed by modern Catholics:

> in thys blyssynge ye begynne with youre honde at the hedde downewarde. & then to the lyfte syde. and after to the righte syde. in token and beleue that oure lorde Iesu cryste came downe from the hed. that is from the father in to erthe. by his holy incarnacion. & from the erthe to the lyfte side that is hel. by his bytter passion. & from thense unto his fathers ryghte syde by his glorious ascencion.[8]

In addition to the details of her diet, and of the books studied by the elderly Cecily Neville, the source on her daily life in her final years also offers information in respect of how her household was run:

> The rules of the House. [9]
>
> Upon eatynge dayes at dynner by eleven of the clocke, a first dynner in the tyme of highe masse, for carvers, cupbearers, sewers, and offycers.
>
> Upon fastinge dayes by xii of the clocke, and a later dynner for carvers and for wayters.
>
> At supper upon eatinge dayes for carvers and offycers, at foure of the clocke; my lady and the housholde at five of the clocke, at supper.
>
> When my lady is served of the seconde course, at dynner, at supper, the chamber is rewarded and the hall with breade and ale, after the discretyon of the usher. Rewardes from the kytchin is there none, savinge to ladyes and gentlewomen; to the heade offycers if they be present; to the Deane of the Chappell, to the Almoner, to the gentlemen ushers, to the carvers, cupbearers, and sewers, to the Cofferer, to the Clerke of the Kytchin, and to the Marshall.
>
> There is none that dyneth in their offyces, savinge onely the cookes, the scullery, the sawcerye, the porters, the baker if they be occupyed with bakeinge.
>
> Uppon sondaye, tuesdaye, and thursdaye, the houshoulde at dynner is served with boyled beefe and mutton, and one roste; at supper leyched beefe and mutton roste.

Uppon mondaye and wensdaye at dynner, one boyled beefe and mutton; at supper, ut supra.

Upon fastinge dayes, salte fyshe, and two dishes of fresh fishe; if there come a principall feaste, it is served like unto the feaste honorablye.

If monday or wensdaye be hollidaye, then is the houshold served with one roste, as in other dayes.

Upon satterdaye at dynner, saltfyfhe, one freshfishe, and butter; at supper saltfishe and egges.

Wyne daylie to the heade offycers when they be presente, to the ladyes and gentlewomen, to the Deane of the Chappell, to the Almoner, to the gentlemen-ushers, to the Cofferer, to the Clerke of the Kytchin, and to the Marshall.

Upon frydaye is made paymente for all manner of freshe cates; at every moneth ende is made paymente for all manner other things; on every quarter ende the chappell is payde of their wages.

At every halfe yeare the wages is payde to the houshoulde; and livery clothe once a yeare. Payment of fees out of the houshoulde is made once a yeare.

Proclamacion is made foure times a yeare about Berkhamsted in market townes, to understande whether the purveyors, cators, and other, make true paymente of my ladyes money or not; and also to understande by the same whether my ladyes servantes make true payment for theyre owne debts or not; and if any defaulte be founde, a remedy to be had forthwith for a recompence.

Breakfastes be there none, savinge onely the head officers when they be present; to the ladyes and gentlewomen, to the Deane and to the Chappell, to the Almoner, to the gentlemen ushers, to the Cofferer, to the Clerke of the Kitchin, and to the Marshall.

All other offycers that must be at the brevement, have their breakfaste together in the Compting-house, after the breavementes be made.

The remaynes of every offyce be taken at every monethes ende, to understande whether the Offycers be in arrearadge or not.

Lyvery of bread, ale, and fyre, and candle, is assigned to the heade offycers if they be presente; to the ladyes and gentlewomen as many as be marryed; to the Deane and to the Chappell; to the Almoner, to the chapleynes, to the gentlemen ushers, to the cofferers, to the Clerke of the Kitchin, to the Marshall, and to all

> the gentlemen witin the house, if they lye not in the towne; that is to saye, whole lyverie of all such thinges as is above fpecyfied, from the feafte of allhallowe unto the feaste of the purifycation of our ladye; and after the purificatyon, hall lyverie of fyres and candles unto good frydaye; for then expireth the the tyme of fyre and candle alsoe.
>
> To all sicke men is given a lybertye to have all such thinges as may be to theire ease; if he be a gentleman and wil be at his owne dyett, he hath for his boarde weekelye xvid. and ixd. for his servant, and nothing out of the house.
>
> If any man fall impotente, he hath styll the same wages that he had when he might doe best service, duringe my ladyes lyfe; and xvid. for his boarde weekelye, and ixd. for his servante. If he be a yeoman xiid. a groome or a page ten pence.

This account shows that Cecily's household was actually not exceptionally religious. Nothing is said specifically about Friday food because Friday was a 'fasting day' – meaning not literal fasting, but abstinence. On Friday every household in the Christian world had to abstain from meat and eat fish. Evidence which survives in his own household accounts confirms that Cecily's late Suffolk steward, John Howard, and his family and retainers had always maintained Fridays as meatless days throughout the year, in accordance with the church's ancient tradition.

However, some fifteenth-century households also avoided eating meat on Wednesdays and Saturdays. It is clear from Cecily's surviving account that in the case of her household, fish was provided instead of meat on Saturdays. However, on Wednesdays meat (boiled beef and mutton) was eaten in her household. By comparison, John Howard's household had been slightly less religious in this respect than Cecily's. For them Saturday abstinence from eating meat was carried out during the penitentials season of Advent. But at other times of the year, the Howard household apparently saw no reason why it should not consume meat on Saturdays.[10]

Yet the early fifteenth-century accounts of Dame Alice de Bryene, of Acton Hall Suffolk, show that, in the case of the Bryene household, abstinence from meat was consistently observed on Wednesdays, Fridays and Saturdays throughout the year.[11] Thus, in respect of diet, Dame Alice de Bryene must have been slightly more religious than Cecily. At the same time, as we have seen, Cecily in turn seems to have been slightly more religious than John Howard.

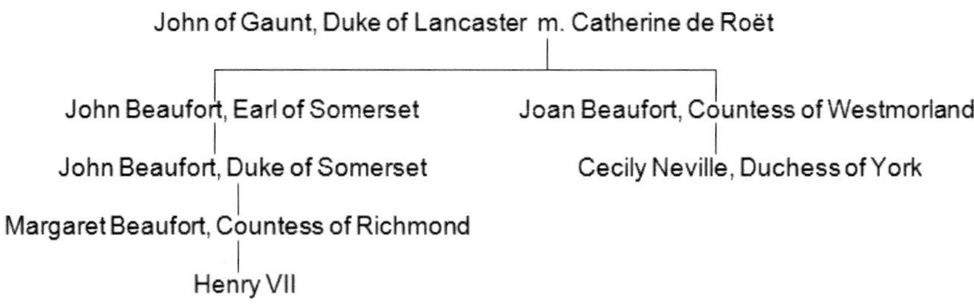

Cecily's Relationship to Henry VII

The context in which Cecily found herself living after August 1485 was that of the usurpation of her cousin twice-removed, Henry VII, who had ousted and killed her last surviving son, King Richard III. 'The Chronicle of King Edward IV' which comprises pages 5–30 of *The Chronicles of the White Rose of York*, and which had previously been published by Hearne 'at the end of his Edition of Sprott's Chronicle',[12] offers an interesting statement in respect of that new king and his regime. The writer of 'The Chronicle of King Edward IV' is unnamed, but he was apparently either a relative or a member of the household of Thomas Howard, 2nd Duke of Norfolk. Thus his text must have been written after 1514, when Thomas Howard was restored to the ducal title which had been held by his father before the death of Richard III.

It is interesting to note that, in this chronicle, the writer 'finds great fault with the falsification made by the Lancastrian Chroniclers, who, on the accession of Henry VII, sought favour in the eyes of the King by blackening the rival family.'[13] It is very important to recognise the fact that this was known at that time to be the case. Unfortunately that point often seems to have been overlooked. Presumably it means that the people living at the time – including Cecily Neville herself – must have been well aware of what was going on as the recent history was rewritten by the new government. Similarly, Elizabeth Talbot, dowager Duchess of Norfolk, was apparently well aware of the fact that Henry VII was determined that her late sister, Eleanor, 'maie be for ever out of remembraunce and allso forgott',[14] and she did her best to ensure that accurate records of Eleanor did survive.[15]

Nevertheless, Henry VII did not personally attack Cecily herself. On 11 February 1485/6 he granted her a licence to export some wool annually without any payment of customs until the king provided her with some other source of income. This was done on account of the fact that she was not currently obtaining an annual income of £689 6s. 8d. which Edward IV had granted her in the first year of his reign.[16] Moreover, on 17 June 1486 Henry VII confirmed the grant to Cecily of manors and other estates made to her by Edward IV on 1 June 1461.[17] (See above, Chapter 9, and Appendix 1).

However, Henry knew that Cecily would not be around for ever. Probably he also knew that she was not really his friend. At all events, from the autumn of 1486 onwards he seems to have concentrated mainly on the fact that her span of days was probably approaching its end. Whereas Cecily held for life the Castle and the honour of Clare in Suffolk, with its additional appurtenances in other counties (all of which was due to revert to the king when she died), on 28 November 1486, Henry VII decreed that upon Cecily's death his supporter, the Earl of Oxford, should become the steward of this honour on his behalf.[18]

As for Henry VII, his own status was by no means certain at that time. By November 1486 he was aware of the fact that Cecily's younger surviving daughter, Margaret of York, had the alleged son of the late Duke of Clarence staying with her at her Mechelen palace, and that she was supporting that boy's claim to the English throne. Two months later Margaret and the boy in question were joined by Richard III's great friend, Francis, Viscount Lovell, and about a month after that, Cecily Neville's senior living grandson, John de la Pole, Earl of Lincoln, also joined 'King Edward VI' in Mechelen. Thus the spring and summer of 1487 were very worrying times for Henry VII. And although no evidence survives to show that Cecily actively supported the attempt to oust him, Henry must have viewed her and all the living members of the house of York with suspicion until he managed to defeat the Yorkist claim at the battle of Stoke in June 1487.

Meanwhile, Henry had married the girl whom he had officially re-designated as the heiress of the house of York. But owing to pregnancy and other reasons it was only in October 1487 that Cecily's granddaughter and elder goddaughter, Elizabeth of York, found herself officially crowned as Henry VII's queen consort at Westminster Abbey. 'On Friday, the 23rd, the Queen left Greenwich by water for her coronation … accompanied by the Countess of Richmond, her mother-in-law, and by an extensive retinue of peers and peeresses.'[19] However the presence of her grandmother and godmother, Cecily Neville, is not recorded.

For her actual coronation ceremony, Elizabeth was accompanied by 'her sister Cecily, her aunt the Duchess of Bedford [Catherine Widville, sister of Elizabeth Widville], the Duchesses of Norfolk [which one?] and Suffolk [Elizabeth of York senior, sister of Edward IV], [and] the Countess of Oxford [Margaret Neville, sister of Warwick the Kingmaker', and cousin of Edward IV].'[20] The identity of 'the Duchess of Norfolk' who attended the young queen on this occasion is rather mysterious and intriguing. Does the title refer to Elizabeth Talbot (Mowbray), sister of Eleanor Talbot (whom Henry VII was now carefully writing out of history), and widow of the last Mowbray Duke of Norfolk? Or does it refer to Margaret Chedworth, the widow of Cecily's Suffolk steward, John Howard, who had been most recent holder of the dukedom of Norfolk, but who had been killed at Bosworth and subsequently attainted? At all events, it is interesting that on this grand ceremonial occasion Elizabeth of York junior was accompanied by various significant relatives. However, once again her grandmother and godmother, Cecily Neville, was apparently not included.

On 21 January 1487/8 Henry VII approved Cecily's grant for life to Ralph Verney esquire, of the keepership of her parks and lordships of Berkhamsted and Kings Langley, Hertfordshire.[21] But on 30 April 1488 Henry VII granted to his servant and knight of the body, Roger Cotton, the reversion of the stewardship of Cecily's lordships of Huchyn [Hitchin] and Ansty [Anstey], Herts., and Sowfrith [South Frith], Kent, together with the office of keeper of her parks of Soufrith [South Frith] and Henden, Kent, which Cecily had granted for life to one of her own servants.[22]

On 20 November 1488 Henry VII granted to either Sir Thomas Grey / Gray (who currently held the post which he had been given by Cecily herself) or to his own servant John Proctor – whichever of them survived longest – the keepership of Cecily's parks at Thackstede [Thaxsted], Essex.[23] But on 1 December 1488 Henry VII – evidently thinking once again of when Cecily would pass away – granted to his servant, John Knolles, the reversion of keepership of Cecily's park of Mersshewode Vale [Marshwood], Dorset, when the Duchess of York should die.[24]

Likewise, on 4 September 1489 Henry VII confirmed Cecily's grant to Sir William Hastings and / or to her priest, Richard Leissy the right of presentation to the deanery of Stoke by Clare. However, when Cecily died he noted that the right of presentation would revert to the king himself, and when that happened he would grant it to Archbishop John Morton, Richard, Bishop of Exeter, Sir Giles, Lord Dawbeney, Richard Leissy and Elizabeth Cousyne.[25]

In the reign of her grandson-in-law and cousin twice removed, Cecily was apparently not included in prayers for the royal family. For example, on 2 March 1491/2 the king's aunt, Margaret St John, Abbess of Shaftesbury, Dorset, was granted a licence to found a chantry, which was to pray for the good estate of the king, his wife, Elizabeth of York, his mother, Margaret, Countess of Richmond, and for the souls of the Abbess's parents, Sir Oliver St John and Margaret Beauchamp, Duchess of Somerset.[26]

On 1 February 1491/2 numerous lands held by Cecily were granted by Henry VII to pass on her death to her granddaughter (and his wife),

Elizabeth of York.[27] As for Cecily's household, it is clear that Henry did not automatically trust all her servants. Significantly, on Saturday 31 January 1494/5 'a preest called M. Lessy, Stewarde vnto the Duches of Yorke [was] … atteynted of misprision, and so commytted vnto the Tower.'[28] Ironically Lessy was subsequently to help Cecily achieve her will in spite of the fact that, had he known about one of her bequests, Henry VII would almost certainly have tried to prevent it (see below, Chapter 15). The arrest of Lessy was accompanied by the arrest – but subsequent pardon – of Thomas Cressener, one of Cecily's living Suffolk relatives.[29] About sixth months later, 'this yere [1495], in the moneth of Jun, dyed the Duchesse of York.'[30]

Chapter 15

Cecily's Bequests, and what they Reveal

WILL OF CECILY DUCHESS OF YORK, 1495.[1]

In the name of allmyglity God, the blessed Trinite, fader and son and the holigost, trusting in the meanes and mediacions of oure blessed Lady Moder, of oure most blessed Saviour Jh'u Crist, and by the intercession of holy Saint John Baptist, and all the saintes of heven: I, Cecille, wife unto the right noble prince Richard late Duke of Yorke, fader unto the most cristen prince my Lord and son King Edward the iiijth, the first day of Aprill the yere of our Lord M.cccc.lxxxxv. after the computacion of the Church of Englond, of hole mynde and body, loving therfore be it to Jh'u, make and ordeigne my testament in fourme and manor ensuyng. Furst, I bequeath and surrendour my soule in to the mercifull handes of allmyghty God my maker, and in to protecion of the blessed virgin our lady Saint Mary, and suffrage of Saint John Baptist, and of all other saintes of heven. Also my body to be buried beside the body of my moost entierly best beloved Lord and housbond, fader unto my said lorde and son, and in his tumbe within the collegiate church of Fodringhay,[2] if myn executours by the sufferaunce of the King finde goode sufficient therto; and elles at the Kinges pleasure. And I will that after my deceasse all ray dettes sufficiently appering and proved be paid, thanking oure Lord at this tyme of making of this my testament to the knolege of my conscience I am not muche in dett; and if it happen, as I trust to God it shalnot, that there be not found sufficient money aswell to pay my dettes as to enture my body, than in advoiding such charges as myght growe for the same, the whiche God defende, I lymytte and assigne all such parcelles of [p. 2] plate as belongith to my chapell, pantry, cellour, ewry, and squillcry, to the perfourmyng of the same, as apperith in the inventary, except such plate as I have bequeithed. Also I geve and bequeith to the Kinges noble grace all such money as is owing to me of the customes, and two cuppes of gold. Also I geve and bequeith to the Quene a crosse croslette of diamantes, a sawter with claspes of silver and guilte enameled covered with grene clothe of golde, and a pix with the fleshe of Saint Cristofer. Also I bequeith to my lady the Kinges moder[3] a portuos with claspes of gold covered with blacke cloth of golde. Also I geve to my lord Prince a bedde of arres of the Whele of Fortune and testour of the same, a counterpoint of arras, and a tappett of arres with the pope. Also I geve to my lord Henry Duke of Yorke[4] three tappettes of arres, oon of them of the life of Saint John Baptist, another of Mary Maudeleyn, and the thirde of the passion of our Lord and Saint George. And if my body be buried at Fodringhay in the colege there with my most entierly best beloved lord and housbond, than I geve to the said colege a square canapie of crymeson clothe of gold with iiij. staves, twoo auter clothes of crymeson clothe of gold, twoo copes of crymeson clothe of gold, a chesibull and twoo tenucles of crymyson clothe of gold, with iij. abes,[5] twoo auter clothes of crymeson damaske browdered, a chesibiill, twoo tenucles, and iij. copes of blewe velwett brodered, with iij. abes, thre masse bokes, thre grayles, and vij. processioners. Also I geve to the colege of Stoke Clare a chesibull and twoo tenucles of playn crymyson cloth of gold with iij. abes, twoo auter clothes, a chesibull, twoo tenucles, and fyve coopes of white damaske browdered, with iij. abes, twoo awter clothes of crymeson velwett upon the velwete (sic), a vestement of crymeson playne velvet, iiij. antiphoners, iiij. grayles, and sixe processioners. Also I geve to the house of Sion two of the best coopes of crymy- son clothe of gold. Also I geve to my doughter Brigitte[6] the boke of Legenda Aurea in velem, a boke of the life of Saint Kateryn of [p. 3] Sene, a boke of Saint Matilde. Also I geve to my doughter Cecill a portuous with claspes silver and gilte covered with purple velvet, and a grete portuous without note. Also I geve to my doughter Anne the largest bedde of bawdekyn, withe countrepoint of the same, the barge with bailies, tilde, and ores belonging to the same. Also I geve to my doughter Kateryn a traves of blewe satten. Also I geve to my doughter of Suifolke[7] the chare with the coveryng, all the quoshons, horses, and harneys belonging to the same, and all my palfreys. Also I geve to my son of Suifolke[8] a clothe of estate and iij. quoschons of purpull damaske cloth of gold. Also I geve to my son Humfrey[9] two awter clothes of blewe damaske brawdered and a vestyment of crymeson satten for Jh'us masse. Also I geve to my son William[10] a traves of white sarcenet, twoo beddes of downe, and twoo bolsters to the same. Also I geve to my doughter Anne,[11] priores of Sion, a boke of Bonaventure and Hilton in the same in Englishe, and a boke of the

Revelacions of Saint Burgitte. Also I woll that all my plate not bequeithed be sold, and the money thereof be putte to the use of my burying, that is to sey, in dis- charging of suche costes and expensis as shalbe for carying of my body from the castell of Barkehampstede unto the colege of Fodringhey. And if any of the said plate be lefte unexpended I woll the said colege have it. Also I geve to the colege of saint Antonies in London an antiphoner with the ruelles of musik in the later ynd. Also I geve unto Master Richard Lessy all suche money as is owing unto me by obligations what soever they be, and also all such money as is owing unto me by the Shirfe of Yorkeshire, to helpe to bere his [p. 4] charges which he has to pay to the Kinges grace, trusting he shall the rather nyghe the said dettes by the help and socour of his said grace. Also I geve to Master William Croxston a chesibull, stoles, and fanons of blake velwett, with an abe. Also I geve to Master Richard Henmershe a chesibill, stoles, and fanons of crymyson damaske, with an abe; and a chesibill, stoles and fanons of crymeson saten, with an abe. Also I geve to Sir John More a frontell of purpull cloth of gold,[12] a legend boke, and a colett boke. Also I give to Sir Eandall Brantingham a chesibill, stoles, and fanons of white damaske, orfreys of crymson velvet, with an abe, the better of bothe. Also I geve to Sir William Grave a chesibill, stoles, and fanons of white damaske, orfreys of crymeson velvett, with an abe; a masse-boke that servith for the closett, a prymour with claspes silver and gilt, covered with blewe velvett, and a sawter that servith for the closett covered with white ledder. Also I geve to Sir John Blotte a gospell boke, a pis till covered with ledder, and a case for a corporax of grene playne velvett. Also I geve to Sir Thomas Clerk a chesibill, twoo tenucles, stoles, fanons, of rede bawdeken, with iij. abes. Also I geve to Sir William Tiler twoo coopes of rede bawdekyn. Also I geve to Robert Claver iij. copes of white damaske brawdered, and a gowne of the Duchie[13] facion of playne blake velvett furred with ermyns. Also I geve to John Bury twoo old copes of crymysyn satten cloth of gold, a frontell of white bawdekyn, twoo curteyns of rede sarcenett fringed, twoo curteyns of whit sarcenet fringed, a feder bed, a bolstour to the same, the best of feders, and two whit spervers of lynyn. Also I geve to John Poule twoo auter clothes, a chesibull, twoo tenucles, stoles, and fanons of white bawdekyn, with iij. abes; a short gowne of purple playne velvett furred with ermyns, the better of ij. and a kirtill of damaske with andelettes of silver and gilt furred. Also I geve to John Smyth twoo auter clothes, a chesibill, twoo tenucles, stoles, and fanons of blew bawdekyn, with iij. abes. Also I geve to John Bury twoo copes of crymysyn clothe of gold that servith for Son- [p. 5] days. Also I geve to John Walter a case for corporax of purple playne velvett, twoo cases for corporax of blewe bawdekyn, twoo auter clothes, a chesibill of rede and grene bawdekyn, a canapie of white sarcenett, iij. abes for children, and iiij. pair of parrours of white bawdekyn, twoo pair parrours of crymsyn velvett, twoo pair parrours of rede bawdekyn, a housling towell that servith for my selfe, twoo corteyns of blewe sarcenett fringed, a sudory of crymysyn and white, the egges blak, a crose cloth and a cloth of Saint John Baptist of sarcenett painted, a long lantorn, a dext standing doble, twoo grete stondardes and ij. litill cofers. Also I geve to John Peitwynne twoo vestimentes of white damaske, a white bedde of lynnyn, a federbedde and a bolstour, and a short gowne of purple playne velvet furred with sabilles. Also I geve to Thomas Lentall six auter clothes of white sarcenett, with crosses of crymsyn velvet. Also I geve to John Long iij. peces of bawdekyn of the lengur sorte. Also I geve to Sir [John] Verney knighte and Margarett his wife[14] a crosse [of] silver and guilte and berall, and in the same a pece of the holy crosse and other diverse reliques. Also I geve to Dame Jane Pesemershe, widue, myne Inne that is called the George in Grauntham, during terme of her life; and after her decesse I woll that the reversion therof be unto the college of Fodringhay for evermore, to find a prest to pray for my Lord my housbond and me. Also I geve to Nicholas Talbott and Jane his wife a spone of gold with a sharp diamount in the ende, a dymysent of gold with a collumbine and a diamont in the same, a guirdill of blewe tissue harnessed with gold, a guirdill of gold with a bokull and a pendaunt and iiij. barres of gold, a hoke of gold with iij. roses, a pomeamber of gold garnesshed with a diamont, sex rubies and sex perles, and the surnap and towell to the same. Also I geve to Richard Boyvile and Gresild his wife my charrett and the horses with the harnes that belongith therunto, a gowne with a dymy trayn of purpull saten furred with ermyns, a shorte gowne of purple saten furred with jennetes, a kirtill of white damaske with aunde- [p. 6] lettes silver and gilte, a spone of gold, a dymysynt of gold with a columbjne garnesshed with a diamant, a saphour, an amatist, and viij. perles, a pomeamber of gold enameled, a litell boxe with a cover of gold and a diamant in the toppe. Also I geve to Richard Brocas and Jane his wife a long gown of purpull velvett upon velvet furred with ermyns, a greate Agnus of gold with the Trinite, Saint Erasmus, and the Salutacion of our Lady; an Agnus of gold with our Lady and Saint Barbara ; a litell goblett with a cover silver and part guild; a pair of bedes of white amber gauded with vj. grete stones of gold, part aneled, with a pair of bedes of x. stones of gold and V. of corall; a cofor with a rounde lidde bonde with iron, which the said Jane hath in her keping, and all other thinges that she hath in charge of keping. Also I geve to Anne Pinchbeke all other myne Agnus unbequeithed, that is to sey, ten of the Trinite, a litell malmesey pott with a cover silver and parte guilte, a possenett with a cover of silver, a short gowne of playne russett velvett furred with sabilles, a short gowne of playne blewe velvett furred with sabilles, a short gowne of purple playn velvet furred with grey, a tester, a siler, and a countrepoint of bawdekyn, the lesser of ij. Also I geve to Jane Lessy a dymysent of gold with a roos, garnisshed with twoo rubies, a guirdell of purple tissue with a broken bokull, and a broken pendaunt silver and guilte, a guirdill of white riband with twoo claspes of gold with a columbyne, a guirdell of blewe riband with a bokell and a pendaunt of gold, a litell pair of bedes of white amber gaudied with vij. stones of gold, an haliwater stope with a strynkkill silver and gilte, and a laier silver and part guilte. Also I geve to John Metcalfe and Alice his wife all the ringes that I have, except such as hang by my bedes and Agnus, and also except my signet, a litell boxe of golde with a cover of golde, a pair of bedes of Ixj. rounde stones of golde gaudied with sex square stones of golde enemeled, with a crosse of golde, twoo other stones, and a scalop shele of geete honging by. Also I geve to Anne Lownde a litell bokull and a litell pendaunt of golde for a guirdill, a litell guirdell of golde and silke with a bokill and a pendaunt of golde, a guirdell of white riband with aggelettes of golde enameled, a hoke [p. 7] of golde playne, a broken hoke of golde enameled, and a litell rounde bottumed basyn of silver. Also I geve to the house of Assherugge a cheslbull and ij. tenucles of crymysyn damaske embrawdered, with thre abes. Also I geve to the house of Saint Margaretes twoo auter clothes with a crucifix and a vestiment of grete velvet. Also I geve to the parish church of Stoundon a coope of blewe bawdekyn, the orffreys embrawdered. Also I geve to the parishe church of Much Barkehampstede a coope of blewe bawdekyn, the orffreys embrawdered. Also I geve to the parish church of Compton by sides Guilford a corporax case of blake cloth of gold and iiij. auter clothes of white sarcenett embrawdered with garters. Also I geve to Alisaunder Cressener my best bedde of downe and a bolster to the same. Also I geve to Sir Henry Haidon knyght a tablett and a cristall garnesshed with ix. stones and xxvij. perles, lacking a stone and iij. perles. Also I geve to Gervase Cressy a long gown of playn blewe velvet furred with sabilles. Also I geve to Edward Delahay twoo gownes of musterdevilers furred with mynckes, and iiijli of money. Also I geve to Thomas Manory a short gowne of crymesyn playn velvet lyned, purfilled with blake velvet, and iiijli in money. Also I geve to John Broune all such stuf as belongith to the kechyn in his keping at my place at Baynardcastell in London, and iiijli in money. Also I geve to William Whitington a short gown of russett cloth furred with matrons and calabour wombes, a kirtill of purpull silke chamblett with awndelettes silver and gilte, all such floures of brawdery werke and the cofer that they be kept in, and xls. in money. Also I geve to all other gentilmen that be daily a waiting in my houshold with Mr. Richard Cressy and Robert, Lichingham everich of theime iiijli in money. Also I geve to every yoman that be daily ad waiting in my houshold with John Otley xls. in money. Also I geve to every grome of myne xxvjs. viijd. in money. And to every page of myne xiijs. iiijd. in money. Also I geve to Robert Harison xls. in money and all the gootes. And if ther be no money founde in my cofers to perfourme this my will and bequest, than I will that myne executours, that is to sey the reverend fider in God Master Olyver King bisshop of [p. 8] Bath, Sir Reignolde Bray knight, Sir Thomas Lovell, councellours to the Kinges grace, Master William Pikinham doctour in degrees dean of the colege of Stoke Clare, Master William Felde master of the colege of Fodringhey, and Master Richard Lessy dean of my chapell, havyng God in reverence and drede, unto whome I geve full power and auctorite to execute this my will and testament, make money of such goodes as I have not geven and bequeithed, and with the same to content my dettes and perfourme this my will and testament. And the foresaid reverend fader in God, Sir Rignold Bray knyght. Sir Thomas Lovell knyght. Master William Pikenham, and Master William Felde, to be rewarded of suche thinges as shalbe delivered unto theme by my commaundement by the hondes of Sir Henry Haidon knyght stieward of my houshold and Master Richard Lessy, humbly beseching the Kinges habundant grace in whome is my singuler trust to name such supervisour as shalbe willing and favorabull diligently to se that this my present testament and will be perfittely executed and perfourmyd, gevyng full power also to my said executours to levey and receyve all my dettes due and owing unto me at the day of my dethe, as well of my receyvours as of all other officers, except such dettes as I have geven and bequeathed unto Master Richard Lessy aforesaid, as is above specified in this present will and testament. And if that Master Richard Lessy cannot recover such money as I have geven to hym of the Shirffes of Yorkeshire and of my obligacions, than I will he be recompensed of the revenues of my landes to the sume of v C. marcs at the leest. In wittenesse herof I have setto my signet and signemanuell at my castell of Berkehamstede the last day of May the yere of our Lord abovesaid, being present Master Richard Lessy, Sir William Grant my confessour, Richard Brocas clerc of my kechyn, and Gervays Cressy.

Proved at "Lamehithe" the 27th day of August, a.d. 1495, and commission granted to Master Richard Lessy the executor in the said will mentioned to administer, &c. &c.

The list of Royal Family beneficiaries named in the will includes Cecily's cousin, Lady Margaret Beaufort, Countess of Richmond & Derby. Of Cecily's own children only one is mentioned, Elizabeth of York, Duchess of Suffolk. This is because all the others were already dead except for Margaret of York, Duchess of Burgundy. As for Margaret, she was deeply distrusted by the new English regime, which characterised her as the 'diabolicall duches'. It would therefore probably have been difficult for Cecily to leave anything to that daughter by name in her will. However, in difficult situations – as in the case of the Abbey of St John at Colchester – Cecily appears to have found

Signature of Cecily, Duchess of York.

ways of having bequests made secretly (see below). It is therefore possible that she did so in the case of her daughter, Margaret. Cecily's bequest to Richard Boyvile and his wife may possibly have been significant in this respect (see below, Appendix 2). Also it is reported that 'in the years after her husband's death, Cecily's other daughter, Elizabeth, Duchess of Suffolk, paid a visit to her younger sister in the Low Countries.'[15] Since the Duke of Suffolk died in 1492, Elizabeth's visit to Margaret could well have taken place after the death of their mother in 1495. So maybe Elizabeth carried with her a last gift from Cecily to Margaret.

Of Cecily's grandchildren and their spouses those mentioned in the will are King Henry VII, Queen Elizabeth of York, Bridget of York (nun), Cecily of York (Viscountess Welles), Anne of York (wife of Thomas Howard), K(C)atherine of York (Countess of Devon), Edmund de la Pole (Duke of Suffolk), Humphrey de la Pole, William Stourton, and Anne de la Pole (nun). Cecily also mentions her two great grandsons: Arthur, Prince of Wales, and Henry, Duke of York (Henry VIII).

However, her following grandchildren are not mentioned in her will:

Anne St Leger, Baroness de Ros
Edward of Clarence, Earl of Warwick
Margaret of Clarence, Countess of Salisbury
Richard III's bastard children, John and Catherine
Sons of Edward IV (Edward V; Richard of Shrewsbury; 'the Lord Bastard'; Arthur Wayte)
Sir William de la Pole
Richard de la Pole
Catherine de la Pole, Baroness Stourton

The significance (if any) of these omissions is by no means clear. Some people might suppose that Edward IV's sons by Elizabeth Widville were omitted because Cecily thought they were dead. However, they could equally well have been omitted because although their grandmother knew that one or more of them was alive, she did not wish to attract them and their whereabouts to the attention of Henry VII and his government. Alternatively, she herself may have been unaware of the true situation in respect of them. Moreover, the fact that some – but not all – of the children of Elizabeth, Duchess of Suffolk, were included is perplexing. And it is completely unclear why the daughter of Anne, Duchess of Exeter, and the two children of George, Duke of Clarence, should have been omitted from their grandmother's will.

The first living person mentioned in the will is the reigning monarch, Henry VII, husband of Cecily's granddaughter, Elizabeth of York. Cecily bequeaths 'to the Kinges noble grace all such money as is owing to me of the customes, and two cuppes of gold.' The manner in which she refers to Henry is politically correct, but not effusive. And in terms of her bequest, she is giving back to the king her income from customs – which would presumably have reverted to him and his government in any case. Apart from that she simply leaves him two gold cups. No details are supplied of the items in question, so although they may have been of value in monetary terms it does not sound as if they were significant possessions of the Duchess.

Her bequest to her granddaughter, the queen, is much more specific – and possibly significant – in terms of the items given. It comprises three religious items: a small diamond cross, a psalter, and a reliquary containing 'the fleshe of Saint Cristofer'.

The third person mentioned is Cecily's first cousin once removed: the woman who had supplanted her in 1485 as England's rightful queen and as the mother of the reigning monarch. Lady Margaret Beaufort's position in relation to Henry VII closely paralleled Cecily's role from 1461 to 1485, and both Cecily and Margaret may have been conscious of that similarity. Cecily's relationship with Margaret has been guessed at by previous writers, but the only solid piece of evidence we have is the fact that, when she wrote her last will, Cecily bequeathed 'to my lady the Kinges moder a portuos with claspes of gold covered with blacke cloth of golde'. It is possibly significant that nothing affectionate or respectful is said in the will about this legatee.

A 1455 source confirms that a fifteenth-century 'portuos' was a book which contained 'lessons, chapiters, sawter [psalter] and ympnes [hymns]'.[16] In other words, a portuos was a Book of Hours. By the time when Cecily was approaching her death, we know that Margaret was following a somewhat similar path to her cousin in respect of her religious life. Indeed one previous writer has proposed that Margaret may have been using Cecily as a model.[17] However, a religious life for an elderly widow was quite normal in the fifteenth century. Thus, a claim that some relationship must have existed between Cecily and her cousin may well be going too far. So why did Cecily leave Margaret a Book of Hours?

Although the book in question cannot be identified for certain, it is a curious fact that a surviving prayer book does still exist which was once owned by Margaret Beaufort (who inscribed her name in it). Moreover, intriguingly, the prayer book in question is known to have belonged previously to a key member of the house of York. It is the well-known *Hours of Richard III*.[18] Thus it could well be that the prayer book mentioned in Cecily's will as her bequest to

Margaret Beaufort was actually the Book of Hours which had once been owned – and regularly used – by Cecily's youngest son.

As it survives today, Richard III's Book of Hours was rebound in leather, with two brass clasps, in the sixteenth century.[19] Thus, in its present form, it does not now precisely match Cecily's physical description of a prayer book bound in black cloth of gold with gold claps, as specified in her will. Also, it cannot be proved for certain that Richard's Book of Hours was subsequently owned by his mother. However, it is certainly possible that, after Richard's death at Bosworth, the Duchess had treasured his prayer book.

Earlier writers have suggested that Richard III's Book of Hours must have been part of the loot which was found after the battle of Bosworth in the king's tent.[20] But there is, in fact, no clear evidence for this. It is equally possible that Richard may have given the prayer book to his mother before Bosworth – perhaps when she aided him at Baynard's Castle, in the difficult summer of 1483 (see above), or possibly on his last recorded visit to her at Berkhamsted, on Tuesday 17 May 1485.[21] Moreover, even if the Book of Hours really was found in Richard's tent after the battle of August 1485, that would by no means preclude the possibility that it had then been given to his mother.

If the prayer book which Cecily subsequently left to her cousin, Margaret Beaufort, really was the Book of Hours of Richard III, obviously that would raise a highly intriguing question as to what kind of message that bequest was supposed to convey. Of course, in drafting her legacies, Cecily was being politically correct. Obviously she wanted to ensure that her dying wishes were carried out. Thus Richard III is nowhere mentioned in his mother's will. But if she left his Book of Hours to the mother of his usurper that would strongly suggest that Richard remained important in Cecily's memory and that she did not love those who had seized power from him. If Margaret Beaufort later used Richard's prayer book, she would, of course have regularly been reminded, in the context of her own religious life, of that king whose throne her own son had snatched away from him, and whose reputation she and Henry had since done their best to blacken.

In arranging her bequests, Cecily Neville seems to have taken care to ensure that she said nothing in her will which could provoke the anger of the reigning monarch. However, she nevertheless left legacies to several people who seem to have had close relationships with her youngest son, King Richard III – though without ever referring to that connection. (See below, Appendix 2.)

She also arranged for a legacy to a religious house which had backed the Yorkist cause, even at dangerous times. However, she did this by writing nothing to that effect in her will, but by giving secret instructions to her executor – a man who had himself remained a Yorkist, even after the defeat of August 1485. Presumably this was, once again, a careful manoeuvre which she made for political reasons.

The result is that, while Cecily made no mention in her will of St John's Abbey in Colchester, Richard Lessy, her executor and the dean of her Chapel, stipulated in *his* subsequent will of February 1498:

> In primis I owe to the hous of saynte Johannes sayntuare in Colchester for my Ladies dettis – whom god pardonn – xxj li the which summe I will be made and spent to the bieng of v chales to be geven to the saide hous of colchestre to praie for my Ladie and for me as procuratoure of this benifete so that the chalesis be Clerely worth xxj li. Beside the facioun the which my will is: to paie for of my owne coste and charge.[22]

It appears that Lessy was acting upon secret instructions, which must have been given him privately by Cecily. It is also highly significant that Lessy, in his honouring of Cecily's bequest, specifically refers to the house as 'St John's *sanctuary*'. He is clearly alluding to the fact that the important mitred Benedictine Abbey of St John's possessed the most impressive rights of chartered sanctuary, identical to those enjoyed by Westminster Abbey (see below).

St John's Abbey, Colchester (redrawn from a medieval manuscript).

The history of St John's Abbey had been rather interesting throughout the political machinations of the fifteenth century. (For the list of fifteenth-century Abbots of Colchester, see below: Appendix 3.) In the early years of the fifteenth century, Abbot Geoffrey Story had favoured the cause of King Richard II. When that legitimate king was deposed by his cousin, Henry of Lancaster, Abbot Story found himself involved in the plot to restore Richard to the throne. Actually the king was probably already dead. Nevertheless, Abbot Story backed a pretender – the deposed king's chaplain, Richard Maudeleyn – who reportedly closely resembled Richard. As a result of the abbot's involvement in this Ricardian plot, St John's Abbey subsequently found itself sequestered by the Lancastrian usurper, Henry IV, and committed to the custody of the archbishop of Canterbury. A full investigation of the abbey's political involvement then followed. Finally Abbot Story was pardoned. However, it emerged that other members of the Colchester Benedictine community had also been implicated in the plot.

Subsequently the abbey continued to harbour anti-Lancastrian sentiments throughout the 15th century. By the 1460s it was closely linked with Cecily Neville's friend, Suffolk neighbour, and steward of Clare, Sir John Howard (later Lord Howard and Duke of Norfolk). Howard exerted some influence during the abbatial election which followed the death of Abbot Ardeley in 1464. Thus he secured the election of Abbot John Canon. Canon's abbacy was short (he died in 1468). But Howard probably then also supported the election of Abbot Stansted. At all events, the 'Kingmaker' Earl of Warwick, when he transferred his own political support to the house of Lancaster, evidently distrusted Abbot Stansted, who was not summoned to the House of Lords of the Parliament of 1470–71 (though he attended subsequent parliaments of the restored Edward IV).[23]

Moreover, John Howard himself took sanctuary at St John's Abbey during the brief Lancastrian restoration of 1470–71. He did this because Colchester Abbey was such a safe place of refuge. It was when Edward IV was forced to flee into exile in the Low Countries, that Howard, claimed sanctuary at the Colchester abbey, together with one of Lord Hastings' brothers.[24] Subsequently, in April 1471, Howard re-emerged, to proclaim in the eastern counties the restoration of Edward IV as King of England.[25]

Other distinguished visitors to the abbey during the first part of the reign of Edward IV are likely to have included the king's teenaged younger brother, Richard Duke of Gloucester (the future Richard III).[26] After the deaths of Richard III and John Howard (then, Duke of Norfolk) at the Battle of Bosworth in 1485, Richard's friend, Francis, Viscount Lovell and other prominent

Yorkists once again took sanctuary at the abbey in Colchester. It was from that location that they then attempted to foment rebellion against the new king, Henry VII. It has also been suggested (on the basis of no solid evidence) that Richard of Shrewsbury, Duke of York, the younger of the two sons of Edward IV and Elizabeth Woodville (popularly known as 'the princes in the Tower') may have been given shelter at the abbey after the accession of Henry VII, with his identity concealed in order to protect him.[27]

It was probably because the pro-Yorkist sympathies of Colchester Abbey were maintained into the 'Tudor' period, that Henry VII, like his predecessor, the Lancastrian usurper, Henry IV, apparently regarded the abbey with suspicion. And that probably explains why Cecily Neville – who obviously remembered the abbey with gratitude and affection – made carefully concealed and secretive provision for her bequest to St John's.

Henry VII probably stayed at the abbey, when he came to Colchester, to correct the town's political leanings and political records.[28] Certainly his daughter-in-law, Catherine of Aragon (the first wife of Henry VIII) stayed at the abbey in 1515. Later, when Henry VIII discarded Catherine, and embarked on the 'Dissolution of the Monasteries', St John's Abbey, remembering, perhaps, its earlier political status, was one of only a tiny handful of religious houses that offered resistance to that king.

It is the specific sanctuary status of Colchester Abbey which explains why it acted as the refuge and place of safety for key supporters of the house of York in troubled times. 'There were two types of sanctuary in medieval England'. Any church could offer some degree of protection, but 'some abbeys and minsters had special rites of sanctuary … anyone who took refuge in such a sanctuary could remain there with impunity for life.'[29] Colchester Abbey had originally been granted such extraordinary rights of sanctuary in 1109,[30] but these rights seem later to have been contested. Therefore, in the fifteenth century, Abbot William Ardeley (Abbot of Colchester, 1432–1464) appealed to Henry VI for the rights of sanctuary of his Colchester Abbey to be confirmed. Abbot Ardeley's request for this royal support was made on the grounds that during Henry VI's incapacity, the community at St John's had expended much time and effort in praying for his recovery. On 13 May 1453 the king had obliged.[31] Moreover, he defined the geographical extent of the sanctuary very precisely. The protected area extended throughout the entire abbey precinct.

Chapter 16

Cecily's DNA and her Dental Record

About nine years after the battle of Bosworth, in the summer of 1494, King Henry VII commissioned the creation of a fitting tomb for Richard III at the Franciscan Priory in Leicester. Sir Reynold Bray and Sir Thomas Lovell, were put in charge of this project. Although both men were loyal followers of Henry VII, Richard III's mother, appears to have considered them both to be trustworthy, because in April–May 1495 she named them amongst the executors of her will (see above). The writing of the will took place within a year of the two men being given responsibility for her son's tomb, at precisely the time when the work for Richard III was being done. Since Cecily wished to ensure that she herself would be appropriately buried and commemorated beside her late husband at Fotheringhay, she was presumably aware that Bray and Lovell were carrying out the creation of a respectful tomb for her youngest son. They could therefore be trusted in such matters.

The only record of possible expenditure for the tomb which was originally created for Cecily at Fotheringhay was 100 marks (roughly £66). This amount would have been quite similar to what appears to have been paid by Henry VII for the 1494/5 monument to her son, King Richard III, at Leicester.[1] Such a sum would have been sufficient to pay for the creation of a good quality alabaster monument of the period.[2] Whatever the tomb was like, it was presumably created – and Cecily was interred – somewhere in the choir of the College Church at Fotheringhay. The provision for spending 100 marks for Cecily's tomb was made in the 1498 will of her chapel dean and executor, Richard Lessy. He requested that 'if therbe spared of my dette c marcs than I wille that the saide c marcs be bestowed and spente upon my ladies tombe at Fodrynghey by the discrecion of the master there and of my executores.'[3]

An alabaster tomb of the late fifteenth century may have resembled the roughly contemporary tomb of Cecily's daughter, Elizabeth of York and her husband, John de la Pole, the Duke and Duchess of Suffolk, in the College Church at Wingfield (see plate 33). Such a tomb would normally have lasted satisfactorily within the church building (only suffering from possible later graffiti from choristers). However, the problem arose when Cecily's great grandson, Henry VIII, terminated his Yorkist ancestral collegiate foundation at Fotheringhay as part of his religious reforms. The choir of the church then lost its roof, and became exposed to the elements. In that situation an alabaster monument would suffer from precipitation and frost. Half a century later, when Elizabeth I was in the area, she found that the tombs of her Yorkist ancestors at Fotheringhay were in a state of decay. She therefore ordered the bodies to be reburied in the surviving nave of the church, and provided with new monuments:

> The Bones of the Duke of York, and of his Son the earl of Rutland, with the Body of Dutchess Cecilie lapp'd in Lead, being removed out of Fotheringhay Church-yard (for the Chancel in the Choir, where they were first laid, in that Fury of knocking Churches and Sacred Monuments in the Head, was also fell'd to the Ground) were buried in the Church, by the Commandment of Queen Elizabeth, and a mean Monument of Plaister, wrought with the Trowel erected over them, very unbefitting to Great Princes.
>
> Mr Creuso, a Gentleman, who dwelt in the College at the sametime, told my Author, That their Coffins being open'd, their Bodies appear'd very plainly to be discover'd, and withal, that the Dutchess Cecilie had about her Neck, hanging on a Silk-Riband, a Pardon from Rome, which penn'd in a fine Roman Hand, was as fair and fresh to be read, as if it had been written but the Day before.[4]

Only two of Cecily's children outlived their mother. They were Elizabeth of York, Duchess of Suffolk, and Margaret of York, Duchess of Burgundy. Both of them died in 1503. Elizabeth probably died first of those two, and was buried beside her late husband at Wingfield Church in Suffolk, where her remains still lie undisturbed. As for Margaret, she died on 23 November 1503 at her palace in Mechelen. She was buried, at her own request, in the Franciscan priory Church in Mechelen, just beyond the nave, in the entrance to the choir. Curiously, it now appears from this that Margaret must have known exactly where her brother, Richard III, had been buried at the Franciscan Priory in Leicester, and that she chose to be interred in an identical position. In Margaret's case, however, she was buried honourably in a splendid tomb.

Sadly, about half a century later her burial place was wrecked by English troops, sent to the Low Countries by Margaret's great niece, Queen Elizabeth I. As a result Margaret's tomb site became lost – again, just like that of Richard III. During the twentieth century, archaeological work on the priory site in Mechelen discovered three sets of female remains which appeared to belong to women of roughly the correct age. Therefore in 2003, at a five-hundreth anniversary commemoration of Margaret's death in Mechelen, the present writer was asked by Belgian colleagues how the identity of the remains could be established. I suggested DNA, and my Belgian colleagues requested me to work on that.

Thus it was that my search for the mtDNA of Cecily Neville and all her children began. Originally it had nothing to do with Richard III, though later its most important outcome was in that direction. All children inherit their mitochondrial DNA only from their mother, and normally unchanged. Thus all Cecily Neville's sons and daughters would have inherited their mtDNA from Cecily, and they would all have been identical in respect of that part of their DNA.

In 2003 I therefore began searching for all-female lines of descent from Cecily via her two elder daughters, Anne and Elizabeth. And eventually, in 2004, I traced a living female line descendant of Anne of York, Duchess of Exeter, who was then living in Canada. Feeling somewhat nervous, I made contact with the lady in question, whose married name was Joy Ibsen. Fortunately, she was fascinated to hear the story I had to tell her about her ancestry. Therefore she very kindly agreed to give a DNA sample. Also she subsequently gave me permission to publish the results.

In July 2004, in part of the friendly correspondence which grew up between us, Joy wrote to me that 'we are off shortly to Vancouver Island to dog-sit for our daughter at her seaside house. Our sons are flying in from Toronto and England for a small family reunion and I plan to surprise them with all your startling revelations about my family tree, the DNA etc. They are aware of the Pitt and Frere ancestors but not of their mother's descent in the female line from Cecily Neville, Duchess of York. They'll have to start showing me due respect!'[5]

The mtDNA haplogroup which Joy's sample revealed was compared by Professor Cassiman of the Catholic University of Leuven with the three sets of female remains which had been found at the Franciscan Priory site in Mechelen. Sadly it proved not to match any of them. So I published these findings in Belgium, with the conclusion that if Joy's mtDNA really was that of Cecily Neville and her children, then none of the discovered Belgian bones could belong to Margaret of York. In other words Margaret's body was still missing.

Sadly, Joy Ibsen died of cancer in 2008. Thus she did not live to see how her mtDNA subsequently proved to precisely match that of the Richard III bones which Philippa Langley and I, through the LOOKING FOR RICHARD PROJECT, subsequently had found at the Leicester Greyfriars site in 2012. Yet, as a result of that, it is now absolutely certain that Joy was a direct descendant of Cecily Neville. Thanks to Joy we now know that Cecily Neville had one of the rarer European types of mitochondrial DNA: haplogroup J, inherited through her mother, Joan Beaufort, and her grandmother, Catherine de Roët, from a female line ancestor who may have been living about 10,000 years ago, in the region of modern Syria.[6]

There is also another curious modern scientific element to the story of Cecily Neville. In the twentieth century a hypothesis was presented that she and at least one of her siblings must have inherited and transmitted hypodontia. The sibling who, by implication, appears to be thought to have shared the genes for congenitally missing teeth with Cecily, was her elder sister, Catherine Neville, Duchess of Norfolk. However, the physical remains of neither sister (nor indeed of any of the other Neville siblings) have actually been examined, so no precise evidence has ever been available in this respect. As a result, the allegation has never really been anything more than a hypothesis. And the present writer recently showed that evidence on which it was based is in fact highly questionable.

One of the elements upon which the theory was based was the fact that the remains of Catherine Neville's great granddaughter, Anne Mowbray, were examined in 1965, and that her teeth showed clear signs of hypodontia. The relevant report in respect of Anne Mowbray's dental evidence, written by M.A. Rushton, was published in the *British Dental Journal*.[7] It states that Anne had:

> congenital absence of upper and lower permanent second molars on the left. There is no sign of these tooth germs or of any relevant disturbance of the bone structure, so that it is clear that the teeth could never have been present. There is no indication of third molars and it is rather probable that these also would have been lacking.[8]

Rushton felt that the congenital absence of those particular teeth was unusual. He also put forward the view that congenital absence of teeth is normally a hereditary trait, though it may not be present in the same format in all the members of a family.[9] The implication was that Anne Mowbray must have shared the trait of congenitally absent teeth with some of her relatives in one of her family lines.

Of course, based solely on the evidence of Anne Mowbray's remains, it is impossible to predict whether her hypodontia – assuming that it really was inherited – came to her from her father, John Mowbray, 4th Duke of Norfolk, or from her mother, Elizabeth Talbot. Unfortunately the body of neither of Anne's parents has been found or examined. However, the present writer has advanced tentative evidence from the possible remains of one of Anne's close Talbot relatives, together with documentary evidence relating to a Talbot ancestor. The bones in question were found at the White Friars' site in Norwich, and they may well be the bones of Anne's maternal aunt, Eleanor Talbot. As for the documentary evidence, that relates to Anne's maternal grandfather, John Talbot, first Earl of Shrewsbury. The Norwich bones show one congenitally missing premolar. As for the remains of John Talbot, they were identified on the battlefield where he had been killed on the basis of a missing molar. The evidence in question therefore appears to suggest that hypodontia may have been a feature of the Talbot family in the fifteenth century. If so, presumably the likely source for Anne Mowbray's hypodontia would have been her maternal line.

Earlier, however, given that nothing had then been published in respect of either Anne's Mowbray ancestors or her Talbot ancestors, Rushton (albeit with a degree of reservation), followed by other writers (who seemed to feel much more certain of what they were claiming) assumed that Anne had inherited her hypodontia via her father. As a result, the suggestion emerged that Anne Mowbray had actually inherited her congenitally missing molars from her father's father's mother – and Cecily's sister – Catherine Neville.

The reason for that assumption was the fact that the congenitally missing teeth of Anne's skull were compared with the alleged missing teeth of two skulls of unknown gender, dating from an unknown period, which had been found at the Tower of London in 1674, during rebuilding work there. Those Tower of London bones were ultimately reinterred at Westminster Abbey on the authority of King Charles II. The reason for that reburial was that they were assumed to be the remains of the two sons of Edward IV and Elizabeth Widville who are commonly known as 'the princes in the Tower.' In reality, of course, the identity of those bones has never been proved. In the present context they will therefore be referred to as *Tower of London 1* and *2* respectively – hereinafter abbreviated to TL1 and TL2. The term TL1 refers to the skull of the individual (boy or girl) who died at the more advanced age, while TL2 will be used to refer to the skull of the younger individual.

As in the case of Anne Mowbray, the skull of TL1 revealed congenitally missing teeth. The missing teeth in question were the upper second premolars on both sides and the lower wisdom teeth on both sides. Compared with the very unusual dental anomalies of Lady Anne Mowbray, the absence of teeth displayed by TL1 is not so unusual. In fact the present writer shares with TL1 the congenital absence of both of the lower wisdom teeth!

A further claim was made that TL2 also had one congenitally missing tooth. However, Rushton argued that 'this cannot be considered proved beyond doubt since the tooth could have been lost early.'[10] The missing tooth of TL2 was the lower right deciduous last molar. The absence of that tooth is said to be quite a common phenomenon.

Nevertheless, on the basis of the congenitally missing teeth of TL1 and the alleged congenitally missing tooth of TL2, the claim was put forward that TL1 and TL2 must have been related to one another – and also to Anne Mowbray. Anne was the second cousin once removed of Richard of Shrewsbury, Duke of York, to whom she was married as a child in 1477/8. On that basis it has therefore been asserted that TL1 is Edward V and TL2 is Richard, Duke of York.[11]

Anne Mowbray was related to the two sons of Edward IV and Elizabeth Widville in various ways. But their closest connection was via their shared Neville descent. That was the relationship which Pope Sixtus IV alluded to when, at the request of King Edward IV, he granted a dispensation for Anne to marry Richard.[12] Anne's Neville descent was from her great grandmother, Catherine Neville. As for Edward and Richard, they were of Neville descent via their father's mother, Catherine's younger sister, Cecily. It has therefore been implicitly assumed that hypodontia must have been a feature of the Neville family – a feature inherited by Cecily, Catherine, and their descendents.

However, one strange fact – picked up by no one but the present writer – has recently produced intriguing new evidence (or rather the absence of any evidence) in respect of the alleged Neville hypodontia.[13] In terms of teeth, the remains of King Richard III, which were rediscovered in Leicester in 2012 (see above) raise doubts about the claims which were made previously in respect of the dental evidence of TL1 and TL2. If the two individuals represented by those skulls really were the sons of Edward IV and Elizabeth Widville, that

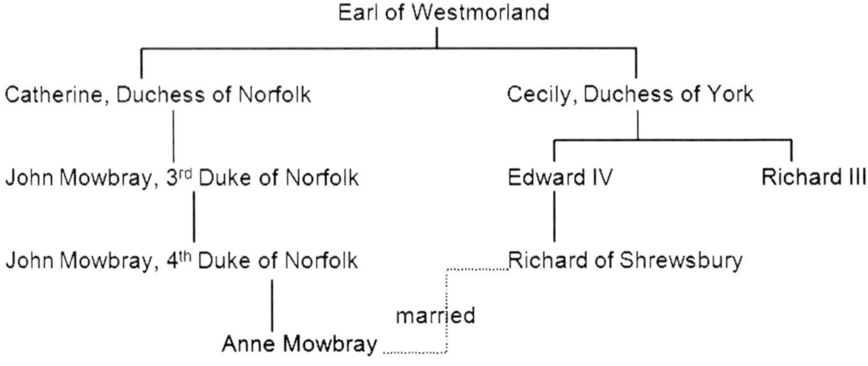

The relationship of Edward IV's sons to Anne Mowbray and to Richard III

would mean that they were also Richard III's nephews. Indeed, the so-called 'princes in the Tower' were much more closely related to Richard III than they were to Anne Mowbray.

Nevertheless, as reported by Rai in the *British Dental Journal* the skull of Richard III reveals no evidence of hypodontia (see plate 36). Although Rai's article contains some errors in terms of history,[14] his dental evidence shows very clearly that during his lifetime King Richard had a complete set of normal adult teeth. Logically that could be seen as implying that no blood relationship exists between Richard III and TL1 and TL2. In other words, based on the latest evidence in respect of teeth, the bones which now lie in an urn in the Henry VII Chapel at Westminster seem unlikely to be the remains of Richard III's nephews.

It therefore seems to be the case that, in spite of earlier assumptions in this direction, there is not a shred of evidence for believing that the Neville family suffered from hypodontia. The logical deduction would therefore now be that probably neither Catherine Neville, Duchess of Norfolk, nor Cecily Neville, Duchess of York, would have shown any sign of congenitally missing teeth.

Appendix 1

Alphabetical List of the Manors granted by Edward IV to his mother in 1461

Where possible the spelling of the names has been modernised. However, the places are listed under their fifteenth-century counties (the boundaries of which have sometimes now been changed). Place names which are underlined have not been identified. The list includes some other properties and sources of income.

Berkshire

Newbury (plus the borough)
Wokefield,
Stratfield Mortimer

Buckinghamshire

Bourton
Nash (see below, Whaddon)
Salden
Steeple Claydon
Wendover
Whaddon Nash (with the chase of Whaddon)

Cambridgeshire

income from rent in Bottisham

Dorset

Crichel ?[1]
Gussage ?[2]
Marshwood

Pimperne
Portland (Isle)
Steeple
Tarrant Gunville
Wareham
Weymouth (town)
Wyke
    Plus the hundreds of
    Haselor
    Roborough
    Rushmore
Plus a tenement called 'Helwell' (Hollywell?).

Essex

Bardfield Saling ?[3]
Claret Hall
Latchley's Farm ?[4]
Layham (⅓rd)
Thaxsted
Wood Hall

Gloucestershire

Bordesley
Bisley
Brimpsfield
Charlton
Doughton
Lechlade
Miserden
Winstone

Hampshire

Hook Mortimer
King's Worthy ?[5]
    Plus annual income from the fee farm of the town of Andover.

Herefordshire

Marcle
Moreton ?[6]

Hertfordshire

Anstey
Hitchin (manor and lordship)
Standon
Popsale

Huntingdonshire

Fees, leets and courts of Woolley[7] and Grandison[8]

Kent

Deptford
Erith
Kingsdown
Shillingheld
South Frith
Strood
Swanscombe
Tonge

Lincolnshire

Deeping
Grantham
Keelby
Stamford (manor, castle & town)
Plus revenue from the fee farm of West Deeping.

London

An inn or tenement called 'Baynards Castle'
Plus annual income from customs paid in the port of London.

Norfolk

The manors and lordships of
Bircham
Great Walsingham
Little Walsingham

Northamptonshire

Fotheringhay (castle and manor)
Nassington
Upton
Yarwell

Oxfordshire

Finmere[9]

Somerset

Bridgwater (castle & borough)
Haygrove
Milverton
Odcombe
Plus annual income from the forests of Exmore, Rachiche and Mendip, on the borders of Somerset and Devon.

Suffolk

Clare (borough, castle, manor, lordship and honour)
Erbury Place
Hunden
Sudbury (town)

Surrey

Pirbright
Shere (Guildford)
Drayton[10]

Sussex

Revenue from the fee farm of the city of Chichester.

Wiltshire

Chelworth
Compton
Cricklade (town / borough)
Easton
Highworth (hundred & borough)
Sevenhampton
Somerford Keynes
Tockenham
Winterbourne
Old Wotton (manor and lordship, with the borough of Wotton)[11]

Worcestershire

Bromsgrove
Clifton
Kings Norton
Oddingley
Plus revenue from the fee farm of the town of Wyche.

Yorkshire

Annual income from the county, including revenue from the customs paid on wool and hides at the port of Kingston upon Hull

Appendix 2

Members of the Entourage of Cecily Neville

All the people named here were connected in various ways with Cecily Neville. Those labelled **[W]** are mentioned in Cecily's will. Other significant links are labelled as follows:

B	=	involved with the Duke of Buckingham against Richard III
H	=	involved with Lord Hastings against Richard III
H7	=	connected with Henry VII
M	=	connected with Margaret, Duchess of Burgundy
R3	=	connected with Richard III / Duke of Gloucester
RE	=	supporter of 'Richard of England / Perkin Warbeck'
RY	=	connected with Richard, Duke of York (Cecily's husband)
–	=	nothing certain is known about them

Individuals are listed in alphabetical order, under surname.

Banys: Thomas, chaplain

On 27 May 1463, when she wrote to the mayor of Folkestone concerning provision for him, Thomas Banys was Cecily Neville's chaplain.

Blotte: Sir John, priest [W; –]

Cecily left him a Gospel book, a pistill [Epistle? – possibly a section of the New Testament of the Bible] covered with leather, and a plain green velvet case for a corporal (the square linen cloth which is placed upon the altar during the celebration of mass).

Boyvile [Boyvyle]: Richard, esquire, and Gresild [Gresilda / Griselda] his wife [M; R3; W]

There are earlier fifteenth-century records of men with the surname 'Boyvyle' in Leicestershire and the county of Rutland, in London, and also in Calais, but none of them bore the name Richard.[1] However, the link of William Boyvyle with Calais may be relevant, because on 14 September 1480, Edward IV made a grant to 'Richard Boyvyle, esquire, and Gresilda, his wife, for his good service to the king's sister, the duchess of Burgundy.'[2] Probably this service had been rendered in connection with the three-month state visit to England of the dowager Duchess of Burgundy, which had taken place that summer.

On 20 April 1484 King Richard III confirmed the earlier grant by Edward IV to Richard and Griselda Boyvyle (of Barford, Northants) of an income of £20 a year from 'the demesnes of Preston and Uppyngham co. Rutland … during the minority of Edward, son of Isabel Nevill, late wife of George duke of Clarence deceased.'[3] Later, in her will, Cecily Neville does not imply that the Boyvyle couple had ever been in direct service to her, so it is possible that she too was grateful for what they had done in 1480 for her daughter, Margaret. She left them her carriage, together with its horses and their harness, and a number of good quality items of clothing and jewellery.

Brantingham: Sir Randall, priest [W;–]

Cecily Neville left him a set of mass vestments: an alb, maniples and stoles of white damask with red velvet orphreys, together with a chasuble.

Bray: Sir R(e)ignold, knight [R3; H7; W]

Reynold Bray [of Woking, Surrey, d. 1503] received a general pardon from Richard III,[4] but apparently supported the claim to the throne of Henry VII. Henry commissioned him to work with Thomas Lovell on the royal tomb for Richard III (1494–95), and he later worked on Henry VII's new chapel at Westminster.

Brocas: Richard, and Jane his wife [R3?; W]

Richard was clerk of Cecily's kitchen. Jane was his wife. They may possibly have been relatives of 'Sir Herry brokas Chapellain within the manoire of Eltham [who] hathe x markes yere for his Salary of thissues of the said manoire' from King Richard III.[5]

Broune: John [W; –]

John may have been Cecily's cook at Baynard's Castle in London.

Bury: John (de), priest [R3; W]

'Brother John Bury clerk, the king's orator' was awarded an annual income of £10 from the customs and subsidies of the port of Southampton by King Richard III on 17 December 1484. This was a payment for Richard's earlier grant to him of 'the custody of the king's chapel of St George within the Tower at Southampton' where John Bury himself or another suitable person was to celebrate 'divine service for the good estate of the king, his consort Anne queen of England, prince Edward his son, and for their souls after their deaths.'[6] The record of this appointment in the Patent Rolls refers to the recipient as 'the king's orator brother John *de* Bury.' This form of his name, including the words 'de' means that he might possibly have been a Scotsman called, 'John de Bury', whom Edward IV had authorised to dwell in England on 22 May 1481.[7]

Catesby: John, lawyer; knight [E4; H7; R3]

A cousin of William Catesby, 'of Hooberne, Beds; d. 1487.'[8] He was a member of Cecily's 'learned council', and was appointed by her to act in the John Prince case. He was a member of parliament in the reign of Edward IV, and also formed part of the parliament of 1484 which issued the act known as *titulus regius* for Richard III.[9] In 1483 he received coronation livery as a justice for the coronation of Richard III, who appointed him one of the guardians of 'Edward Son & heire of John late Erle of Wilteshire.'[10] In the reign of Richard III he also had 'the keping of the palois of Westmynster.'[11] After the battle of Bosworth he was reappointed justice by Henry VII, but he died in 1486, leaving eight sons and two daughters, and asking to be buried at the Abbey of St James, Northampton.[12]

Caux: Anne de [E4; R3; RY]

Anne probably came from the Norman region known as the *Pays de Caux*, to the north of Rouen, around the ports of Le Havre and Dieppe. This coastal region of Normandy was presumably the geographic point of origin both of Edward IV's nurse, Anne – and of her surname. She was employed at Rouen by the Duke and Duchess of York, as nurse to their children. In 1474 she was awarded an annual pension of £20 by one of the babies in question – King Edward IV.[13] Obviously Anne had accompanied the York children back to England, and had then remained resident in that foreign country. Probably she had also served the younger children. At least, she was clearly known to Richard

III, who continued (or renewed) her pension in January 1483/4.[14] She may have predeceased her employer, the Duchess of York, because the name Caux is not mentioned in the latter's will. However, Cecily did make bequests to two women bearing the name Anne: Anne Lownde and Anne Pinchbeke, and the connection between these two Annes and the Duchess of York is not traceable. It is therefore conceivable that Anne de Caux may have married an Englishman after 1484 and changed her surname. Jane Malpas (the other nurse whom we know that Cecily employed for her younger children) is known to have married more than once (see below).

Claver: Robert, priest [R3?; W; –]

He might possibly have been a relative of Alice Claver, silkwoman, who supplied the Great Wardrobe, and who contributed material for Richard III's coronation.[15]

Clay [Cley]; Sir John [E4; RY]

There were two John Clay [Cley]s in Yorkist service: a father and a son. John Cley the elder was attainted in 1459 for participating in the rebellion of Richard, Duke of York against King Henry VI.[16] On 23 December 1459 the land, goods and chattels held by the elder John Cley esquire at Cheshunt in Hertfordshire were confiscated and granted to Elizabeth Say.[17]

'Master John Clay' was one of the messengers who bore a request from the Earl of March to Christopher Hanson in October 1460 for the Duchess of York and her three youngest children to stay for a while at the Paston house in Southwark. It seems probable that this 'Master John Clay' was not John Clay esquire (who was probably then out of England with the Duke of York) – but was his son, whose name was also John.

More details of the family are given by Edward IV in a record dating from 22 December 1461, which restored to 'John Clay, king's knight, Joan his wife, and John his son' the reversion of their manor in Cheshunt whenever Edward IV's godmother, Elizabeth Say, passed away. In the meantime, Edward IV granted the family an annual income from some other property.[18]

It appears from this record of the restoration of the family estate that John Clay esquire must have been knighted at Edward IV's coronation. At some uncertain date Sir John Cley then became Cecily Neville's chamberlain. His tenure of that office is mentioned in a letter from Margaret Paston to her husband, John Paston, proposing the marriage of their daughter to Cley's eighteen-year-old son.[19] Gairdner suggests that this letter dates from November 1463. By 10 February 1463/4, Sir John Clay was the sheriff of Essex.[20] But on 2 April 1465 his death was recorded by Edward IV in a grant to his widow, his son and another executor of the dead knight's will.[21]

In 1471 a John Clay / Cley fought on the Yorkist side at the battle of Tewkesbury and was then knighted by Edward IV.[22] Presumably this was the younger John Cley (son). His coat of arms is said to have depicted three lions facing another lion and engaging in a quarrel.[23]

Clerk: Sir Thomas, clerk of the chancery [W]

On 1 August 1483 John Benet, citizen and grocer of London, gave all his goods and chattels in the city of London 'to Thomas Clerk, one of the six chancery clerks'.[24] Similar gifts came to him from another London citizen on 1 October 1484.[25]

Cley – see Clay

Cressener: Alisaunder [Alexander], esquire [R3; W]

Alexander Cressener was Cecily's nephew, the son of her half-sister Margaret Neville by the latter's second husband, William Cressener of Suffolk. On 24 May 1483 Alexander Cressener was one of the co-recipients of a Suffolk manor. His fellow recipients included Sir Thomas Howard, John Tymperley, John Sulyard and James Hobart.[26] Alexander was knighted by Richard III at his coronation.[27]

Cressy [Cressi]: Gervays [Gervaise], esquire [R3; W]

On 5 February 1483/4, King Richard III ordered the sheriff of Bedford and Buckingham to pay £6 13s. 4d. annually to 'the king's liege, Gervaise Cressi esquire' for the rest of his life.[28] Cressy was present when Cecily's will was signed.

Cressy: Mr. Richard [W]

According to the text of her will he was at daily work in Cecily's household in her last days.

Croxston [Croxton?]: Master William, priest [W; –]

On 10 October 1483 John Prentys of Essex made gifts to various people of the same county, including a William Croxton of Ramsden Bellhouse, near Billericay,[29] but it is not certain that he was the individual mentioned in Cecily's will.

Daubeney: Sir Giles, later 1st Baron, 1451–1508 [B]

Giles was the son and heir of William Daubeny of Southpederton, Somerset. His father died before April 1461, leaving Giles still a minor.[30] He had come of age by August 1473.[31] Shortly afterwards he began receiving royal commissions.[32] In 1475 he accompanied Edward IV to France,[33] and he appears to have been regarded as a loyal servant of Edward IV. In respect of the county of Somerset he served on commissions with Robert Stillington, Bishop of Bath and Wells, with George, Duke of Clarence, and with Richard, Duke of Gloucester.[34] In April 1478 Sir Giles Daubeney was commissioned by the king to enquire into the West Country possessions held by the recently attainted and executed George, Duke of Clarence.[35] In March 1478/9 he received a grant from Edward IV in gratitude for money he had given the king. By this time he was a Knight of the Body.[36] He received his commission from the Duchess of York in February 1482/3, as constable of her Castle of Bridgewater, Somerset.[37] He was again commissioned by Edward V, and by Richard III in April and in August 1483 in respect of the county of Somerset ,[38] And he attended Richard III's coronation. However he then took part in Buckingham's Rebellion, and when it failed he fled to the self-styled Earl of Richmond in Brittany. Throughout the rest of the reign of Richard III, he was officially declared a traitor.[39] His position was restored and promoted by Henry VII after the battle of Bosworth. He then became the first Baron Daubeney and was appointed Lieutenant of Calais. Later he was made Lord Chamberlain. He was buried in Westminster Abbey.

Delahay: Edward [R3?; W; –]

Possibly related to Thomas Delahay, who was a servant of Richard III.[40]

Felde: John, esquire

Cecily's servant and park keeper (Herts). On 12 December 1473 Henry Frowyk esquire of South Mimms in Hertfordshire released his rights to properties and income in that county to 'John Felde the younger' and others.[41] A similar gift to John Felde the younger was made by Richard Baseley on 3 April 1476 in the Canterbury region of Kent.[42] John Felde the elder, alderman of London, must have died in 1476 or 1477, for on 30 October 1477 a pardon of outlawry was issued in respect of Richard Salkeld's failure to answer the 'plea that he render £60 to John Felde, son of John Felde, and Agnes his wife, executors of the will of John Felde' senior.[43] In November 1483 the release of rights in a manor and other property in Hertfordshire to John Felde the younger and others received an exemplification.[44]

Felde: Master William [W]

Master of the college of Fotheringhay, William Felde had earlier been described as the 'chantour of Fodrynghey' in the 1479 'will of Anne, wife of Sir Robert Wingeffeld and daughter of Sir Robert Harlyng'.[45]

Grant: Sir William [W]

Cecily's confessor at the end of her life, and present when her will was signed.

Grave: Sir William, priest [W, –]

Gray / Grey: Sir Thomas [R3]

Keeper of Cecily's parks at Thaxsted, Essex, he was probably the Sir Thomas Grey of Croydon, Cambridgeshire (d. *c.*1495). Croydon is about twenty-five miles from Thaxsted. Richard III granted him an annuity of £40.[46]

Gylmyn [Gilmyn]: Richard, esquire

Cecily's park keeper, possibly in Norfolk. On 19 August 1476 William Cokkys, citizen and skinner of London gaves his goods and chattels in the city of London to Richard Gilmyn, serjeant at arms, and others.[47]

Gylmyn: John

Yeoman of Cecily's chamber, and park keeper for her in Norfolk.

Haidon – see Haydon

Harison: Robert [H7; W]

Robert Harrison was a servant of Henry VII.[48]

Hastings: Sir William

Granted the right of presentation to the deanery of Stoke by Clare by Cecily.

Haydon [Haidon / Heydon]: Sir Henry, knight, (d. 1504), [E4; H7; R3?; W]

Sir Henry Haydon was the steward of Cecily's household when she made her will. He was a Norfolk man by birth, the son of John Haydon of Baconsthorpe (d.1479), and of his wife, Eleanor Winter. Henry himself became the husband of Anne Boleyn (the great-aunt of the subsequent queen of the same name).[49] A lawyer by training, Henry was a loyal Yorkist supporter in Norfolk during the reigns of Edward IV, Edward V and Richard III, but he never received a knighthood during the Yorkist period.

In May 1476, when his father would still have been alive, the young Henry appears to have had some kind of connection with his namesake, the young Henry, Duke of Buckingham.[50] But in 1476 and 1478 he was an associate of Cecily Neville's nephew, George, the new Lord Bergavenny,[51] who had succeeded to his father's title in 1476. In February and March 1477/8 Henry Haydon received a commission of the peace and other commissions in respect of the counties of Norfolk and Suffolk. Those named with him on those occasions included Sir Thomas Howard (later 2nd Duke of Norfolk), the lawyers John Sulyard and James Hobart, and others.[52] On 5 November 1480 he received a license for the alienation of certain property in Norfolk, together with Anthony Widville, Earl Rivers and others.[53] On 12 November 1482 he was commissioned – again with Earl Rivers and others – to examine a dispute in Norfolk.[54] On 27 April 1483 he was commissioned in the name of Edward V, together with Earl Rivers, Sir Thomas Howard, John Paston, James Hobart and others, to assess subsidies granted to the new king in Norfolk.[55] In August 1483 he received a similar commission from Richard III.[56] On 1 May 1484, together with the Dukes of Norfolk and Suffolk, and others, he received a commission of array in respect of Norfolk.[57] The same occurred again on 8 December 1484.[58]

His long-standing connection with John Howard, 1st Duke of Norfolk, and his son, Thomas, would appear to imply that Howard would have called Henry up to support Richard III at the battle of Bosworth. However, the picture in this respect is clouded by the fact that Henry was subsequently knighted at the coronation of Henry VII. He was later one of those appointed to receive Catherine of Aragon when she arrived in England as the new royal bride. On his death, Sir Henry was buried at Norwich Cathedral.

Heydon – see Haydon

Henmershe: Master Richard, priest [W; –]

Holt: Alexander, esquire [R3?]

Alexander Holt was serjeant of Cecily's pantry. His wife was called Katherine. It is possible that Alexander died before 8 March 1483/4, on which date a grant was made by Richard III to 'Katharine Holt, widow.'[59]

Howard: Sir John, Lord, later Duke of Norfolk, *c.*1425–1485 [E4; R3; RY]

Cecily's steward of the honour of Clare, Suffolk. Cousin of her nephew, John Mowbray, 3rd Duke of Norfolk, he was in the service of the Duke of York from the 1450s. Later he served, and was knighted by Edward IV. He also remained in close connection with John Mowbray, 4th Duke of Norfolk, and the latter's wife, Elizabeth Talbot, and appears to have also served other members of Elizabeth's family, including her sister, Eleanor Talbot. In 1483 he appears to have supported the offering of the crown to Richard III (whom he had befriended when Richard was young), and in 1485 he was killed fighting for Richard at Bosworth.[60]

King [Kyng]: Oliver, Bishop of Bath (d. 1503) [E4; H; H7; W]

On 5 May 1477, Richard Forthey esquire of Southampton gave all his goods and chattels to 'Oliver Kyng, one of the clerks of the signet, and Richard Newedyke gentleman.'[61] On 27 February 1479/80 he was appointed parish priest of a Calais church,[62] in June 1480 he was given custody of the king's signet whenever the king's secretary was absent,[63] and in October of that year he was appointed prebend of St George's Chapel, Windsor.[64] However, following the death of Edward IV, on Friday 13 June 1483 Oliver King, who was then secretary to Edward V, was arrested with the Archbishop of York and the Bishop of Ely (Morton) in connection with the plot (and execution) of Lord Hastings. A letter of Simon Stallworth records that they were still imprisoned in the Tower a week later.[65] He was promoted Bishop of Bath and Wells in the reign of Henry VII.

Kyrisshawe: Ralph, esquire

Cecily's park keeper in Dorset, and 'one of the sewers of her chamber.'

Lassy – see Lessy

Lentall: Thomas, priest [W; –]

Lessy [Lassy]: Henry [E4]

Servant of Cecily. Of Bacton [Baketon] in Norfolk. In November 1480 (when he received an appointment as one of the keepers of her manor and parks at Stratfield Mortimer in Berkshire from Cecily Neville – the other keeper being Richard More – see below) Henry was one of the sewers of King Edward IV's chamber.[66] Seven months later he was recompensed by the king for the lack of income from the keepership he had been granted by Cecily, due to the creation of a royal hunting park in the area.[67] He was apparently still alive in May and June 1482, when further corrective grants were made to him by the king.[68] On 12 June 1482 Edward IV referred specifically to the 'long services which he [Henry] is still rendering to the king's mother Cecily duchess of York.'[69] However, it appears that Henry made a will in 1482,[70] so he probably died before Edward IV.

Lessy: Jane [W; –]

Possibly the widow of Henry ? (See above).

Lessy: Richard [RE; R3?; W]

Dean of the chapel to Cecily, and an executor of her will. With a number of other people, Richard Lessy was granted a general pardon by Richard III on

28 November 1483.[71] On that occasion he was described as 'clerk, one of the cubiculars of the pope, *alias* late of London, "gentilman"'.[72] Arthurson has claimed that the granting of this pardon may mean that Lessy had been involved in some way in Buckingham's Rebellion.[73] However, that seems a groundless claim. 'General pardons' were quite standard documents and were not normally associated with rebellions. They were sometimes granted, for example, as a way of clearing a person's record before a new post was taken up. Later, Arthurson suggests that Richard Lessy seems to have been a supporter of 'Richard of England' ['Perkin Warbeck'], citing the fact that he was 'accused of misprison.'[74] It is not clear precisely what that means. (Misprison has various meanings: '*a*: neglect or wrong performance of official duty *b*: concealment of treason or felony by one who is not a participant in the treason or felony *c*: seditious conduct against the government or the courts.'[75]) However, in January 1494/5 Lessy was imprisoned by Henry VII until he paid a fine of £200.[76] It is therefore credible that he had remained a loyal Yorkist supporter to the extent of accepting the claim of 'Richard of England'. Earlier, on 4 September 1489 Cecily's earlier grant (made in the reign of Edward IV) to 'Richard Leissy, clerk' and Lord Hastings, of the right of presentation to the office of Dean at Stoke-by-Clare was confirmed by Henry VII – though Lessy now had to work on it with Archbishop John Morton and others.[77]

Lichingham: Robert, gentleman [W]

He, and all the other gentlemen serving in her household, was left the sum of £4.

Long [Longe]: John [W]

On 16 March 1478/9 a John Longe acted as a witness to gifts made by Constance Browne in the city of London.[78] In November 1479 a man of this name was one of a group licensed to found 'a fraternity or perpetual gild of four wardens and the commonalty of freemen of the mistery of brewers' in London.[79] On 23 March 1480 a John Long received a commission of peace for the county of Wiltshire.[80]

Lovell: Sir Thomas, knight [H7; W]

Richard III granted the lordship of Polstedhalle, Burnham, Norfolk to Thomas and his mother, Agnes,[81] but Thomas supported Henry VII's claim to the throne. Henry VII knighted him for his services against the Yorkist claimant

'King Edward VI', at the battle of Stoke. Later, with Sir Reynold Bray he worked on the royal tomb for Richard III in 1494–95.

Lownde: Anne [R3?; W; –]

Possibly related to Robert Lounde who received payments from Richard III.[82]

Malpas [Peysmersh / Pesemershe]: Joan / Dame Jane [R3; W]

The nurse for Cecily's younger children. On 4 August 1461 Edward IV granted an income of 20 marks a year to 'John Malpas esquire and Joan his wife.'[83] This was in the context of a number of gifts made to those who had served the king's parents. But in the case of John and Joan Malpas no precise reason for the gift was stated. Later, however, on 8 December 1483, Richard III made a replacement grant of 20 marks a year 'for life to Joan late the wife of John Malpas esquire, and afterwards the wife of John Peysmersh, knight, deceased, for her good service to the king in his youth and to his mother the duchess of York.'[84] Richard III also granted money to William Malpas, who might possibly have been a relative (son of Joan's first marriage?).[85] In her will (see above), Cecily left 'to Dame Jane Pesemershe, widue, myne Inne that is called the George in Grauntham, during terme of her life', with provision that the inn should then pass to the College of Fotheringhay. That church was to use the income from the inn to pay for a priest who would pray for the souls of Cecily and her husband – which indicates that Cecily still cared for the Duke of York, although her husband had been dead for twenty-five years.

Manory: Thomas [R3?; W]

On 28 November 1483 'Thomas Manory late of Berkhampstede, "gentilman",' received a general pardon from Richard III. He was one of six men who received a general pardon on this occasion, and the list also included Richard Lessy (see above).[86]

Metcalfe: John and Alice his wife [W; –]

More: Sir John, priest? [E4; W]

Master John More, clerk of the king's closet, was granted custody of the hospital of St Bartholomew at Playden (Rye), Sussex, by Edward IV in 1478.[87]

More: Richard [E4]

Manor and park keeper for Cecily. On 8 November 1480 Cecily Neville's grant to Richard More, one of the marshals of the king's hall (together with Henry Lessy, one of the king's sewers – see above), made at the Abbey of St Benet at Holme in Norfolk on 14 June 1480, was confirmed by Edward IV. The grant gave the two men the keeping of her manor and parks of Stratfield Mortimer in Berkshire.[88]

Otley: John [W; –]

Peitwynne: John, priest [W; –]

He might possibly have been related to Richard Peitvyn who was authorised with others to grant a manor in Somerset by Richard III in November 1484.[89]

Pesemershe [Peysmersh] – see Malpas:

Pikenham [Pykenham]: Master William [W]

Archdeacon of Suffolk; associated with Sir Thomas, son of Lord Howard; with Sir Thomas Montgomery; with Alexander Cressener; with James Hobart and with John Sulyard.[90]

Prince: John (Essex?) [R3]

A servant of Cecily.

Serle: John (Essex)

A park keeper for Cecily. On 17 October 1480 John Serle the younger, 'husbondman', of Elmdon, Essex, the son of William Serle, and executor of the will of Thomas Parker, was cited for failing to appear in answer to a plea for the payment of £40 to John Serle the elder, 'bocher', of Elmdon.[91]

'On 20 January 1474 … John Serle, citizen of London, was appointed [the King's Painter] and it seems likely that Serle retained the office under Richard III to die in the first years of Henry VIII's reign.'[92] He did heraldic paintings for the funerals of Elizabeth of York and Prince Arthur.

Serle: Thomas (Essex)

A park keeper for Cecily. In 1483 a tailor of the same name worked in the Great Wardrobe for 6 days.[93]

Smyth: John, priest [W]

On 11 November 1480 Thomas Lincoln was appointed priest at the parish church of St Giles, Scorthowe, in the diocese of Lincoln in place of John Smyth, who had resigned.[94] This may be the person referred to. But the name is common. For example another John Smythe priest died in 1482.[95]

Talbott: Nicholas and Jane his wife [R3; W]

On 26 November 1481 Nicholas Talbot esquire was one of a number of lawyers appointed to resolve a dispute between tenants of the Prince of Wales, and tenants of the Duke and Duchess of Suffolk.[96]

Nicholas Talbot esq. (d. 1501), 'in the service of [the] duchess of York; brother of Edmund',[97] was given a warrant by Richard III 'to pull downe the pales of the parc of Purbrighte [Pirbright, Surrey]' on 10 January 1484/5.[98]

Tiler: Sir William, priest [W]

Towneshend [Tounesende]: Roger, lawyer

An Eastern Counties lawyer, appointed by Cecily to act in the John Prince case. In October 1477 he was told to take on the grade of serjeant at law on 9 June of the following year.[99] He was a member of parliament in the reign of Edward IV, and also formed part of the parliament of 1484 which issued the act known as *titulus regius* for Richard III.[100]

Verney: Sir [John], knight, and Margaret (*née* Whitingham) his wife (died c.1509) [H7; R3; W]

Margaret Verney was the daughter of Sir Robert Whitingham, a Lancastrian adherent. But she married a committed Yorkist. [101]An earlier published account of the couple has suggested that they did not do well during the Yorkist period.[102] But that does not appear to be the truth (see below).

On 7 April 1479 John Verney was commissioned by Edward IV to investigate certain felonies committed in Dunstable.[103] On 24 January 1482/3 'John Verney esquire and Margaret his wife, niece of the grantor' received all the goods and chattels owned by Richard Whityngham, gentleman, at Northchurch in Hertfordshire.[104] On 13 July 1483, 'the king's servant, John Verney' was appointed keeper of the park at Donyate in Somerset by Richard III on behalf of his nephew, Edward of Clarence, Earl of Warwick.[105] On 1 August 1483 he was commissioned with others to assess incoming subsidies in the county of Buckingham for King Richard III.[106] On 18 October 1483 he and others received all the goods and chattels of Henry Danvers, citizen and mercer of London.[107] This gift implies that John Verney was probably related to Sir Ralph Verney, a London alderman and former mayor of the staple of Westminster. The following year John Verney acted as a witness in respect of a grant to Thomas Danvers and others.[108] On 1 May and 8 December 1484 he received commissions of array for the same county, together with Francis, Viscount Lovell, and others.[109] On 12 May 1484 John Verney esquire received the manor and lordship of Huish Champflower in Somerset from Richard III as a reward 'for his good service against the rebels.'[110] In May 1485 Verney was serving as escheator in the county of Dorset.[111] However, he seems to have been knighted after the Yorkist period had ended.

The Verneys received from Cecily Neville a reliquary cross of silver gilt, set with beryl, containing a fragment of the Holy Cross and other relics.

Verney: Ralph

Keeper of Cecily's parks and lordships of Berhamsted and Kings Langley, Hertfordshire.

Walker: John

A servant of Cecily, John was the porter at Fotheringhay Castle. He died before 18 November 1478, on which date the king appointed Peter Wraton as his successor.[112]

Walter: John, priest [W; –]

Whitington: William [W; –]

Appendix 3

The Fifteenth-century Abbots of Colchester[1]

1380–1405	Abbot Geoffrey Story *alias* de Sancta Ositha
1405–1418	Abbot Roger Best
1418–1432	Abbot Robert Gryton
1432–1464	Abbot William Ardeley[2]
1464–1468	Abbot John Canon[3]
1468–1497	Abbot Walter Stansted
1497/8–1517	Abbot William Lyndesey *alias* Sprowton

Appendix 4

Lucy Fraser, 'Synopsis of Cicely; or the Rose of Raby. An Historical Novel (1795)'[1]

As part of *The Corvey Project at Sheffield Hallam University*, Lucy Fraser gave a summary of Agnes Musgrave's late eighteenth-century novel, *Cicely; or the Rose of Raby*.

She notes that in the novel Cicely becomes known as 'the Rose of Raby' because of her alleged beauty. Cicely is correctly presented by Musgrave as a daughter of the Earl of Westmorland by his wife, Joan. Her marriage to the Duke of York and her motherhood of Richard III are also presented. However, the book contains a great deal of fantasy. It presents the young Cicely as having been kidnapped with her brother's page, Thomalin, and abducted to Scotland. Later she is said to have been shipped to France, where she became a prisoner of the Duke of Orleans, who fell in love with her. However, Cicely herself is said to have been in love with her companion, the page, Thomalin, who rescued her, and whom she then married. With Thomalin, Cicely escaped from France into Spain. Their marriage was kept secret, but Thomalin produced a son by Cicely. Unfortunately, however, Thomalin was then murdered by the angry Duke of Orleans.

Cicely finally manages to get back to England, where she marries the Duke of York. That couple :

> have a number of children together and, although Cicely never truly loves him, they have a relatively happy marriage.
>
> For the first time since leaving Spain, Cicely sees the son she had to Thomalin, who has successfully claimed the title of Count d'Aranjeus. However as tension grows between the House of Lancaster and the House of York and war breaks out, Cicely's husband, one of her sons, Edmund, and the Count d'Aranjeus all die in a battle.
>
> Cicely's sad history concludes with the account of the changing situation on the throne of England, with another of Cicely's sons becoming King Richard III.[2]

Richard ('the dark designing Gloucester') was earlier accused of 'working upon the pride of Edward [to bring about] … the fall of the unsuspecting Clarence',[3] and his mother is represented in the novel as not regretting Richard's death at Bosworth.

Incidentally, Musgrave did not employ in her book the phrase 'War of the Roses.' That was only invented early in the following century. However, in the novel Cicely was told in a prophetic vision that she would live 'til I saw the white rose twined around the red.'[4] Musgrave also spoke of how the Duke of York's chief squire 'wore in triumph the white rose, which all who adhered to the Duke wore: – soon after, the red rose was assumed by the Lancastrians.'[5]

Appendix 5

The allegiance of Cecily's siblings in the 1450s and beyond

Unknown

The allegiance of some of Cecily's siblings and their families is unknown. Her half brother, Ralph Neville (d. 1458) and her half sister, Alice Neville (d. after 1453, married to Sir Gilbert Lancaster), belong in this category.

Political correctness

The allegiance of some members of Cecily's family might best be described as 'political correctness.' In other words they seem to have supported whoever was in power at the time. For example, Cecily's half-brother, John Neville died before 1420. But his sons and grandsons supported Henry VI until 1461. Afterwards they were Yorkists until 1483, but later they supported Henry VII. Likewise, Cecily's half-sister, Philippa Neville (d. after 1453) married Thomas, Lord Dacre (d. 1457/8), who probably supported Henry VI, but in whose service and household the rebel leader known as John Cade had served. Their eldest son, Humphrey Lord Dacre, supported Henry VI until 1461. Afterwards he became a Yorkist. Their grandson, Thomas, Lord Dacre, fought for Richard III at Bosworth. But later he supported Henry VII.

Yorkist

Five of Cecily's siblings seem to have been Yorkist.

One of her half sisters Margaret Neville (d. 1463) married as her second husband William Cressener of Sudbury, Suffolk, who was not a major political figure, but who lived in an area which was generally Yorkist in its support. Moreover, Margaret chose to be buried at Clare Priory (next to Cecily's Suffolk castle). Margaret's son by her first husband: Henry, 4th Lord Scrope of Bolton (d. 1459), and his son and heir, John, 5th Lord Scrope of Bolton (1437–1498), both seem to have been firmly Yorkist. The 5th Lord Scrope fought for Richard III at Bosworth, and later supported the Dublin Yorkist King 'Edward VI'.

Four of Cecily's brothers were firm Yorkists:
Richard Neville, Earl of Salisbury (1400–1460)
William Neville, Lord Fauconberg, Earl of Kent (*c*.1405–1463)
George Neville, Lord Latimer (*c*.1407–1469 but he became insane *c*.1450)
Edward Neville, Lord Bergavenny (*c*.1412–1476 who in 1448 married as his second wife Catherine Howard the sister of Sir John, Lord Howard, later first Duke of Norfolk)

Also the family of Cecily's elder sister, Catherine Neville, Duchess of Norfolk (*c*.1397–1483), seems predominantly to have been Yorkist. Catherine's third husband (married *c*.1443), John Beaumont, Viscount Beaumont, was killed fighting on the Lancastrian side at the battle of Northampton in 1460. But her fourth husband (married 1465) Sir John Woodville (d. 1469) was presumably a Yorkist. As for Catherine's son, John Mowbray, 3rd Duke of Norfolk, and her grandson John Mowbray, 4th Duke of Norfolk, they were firm Yorkists.

Lancastrian

Two of Cecily's sisters seem to have belonged to families which were essentially Lancastrian. Eleanor Neville (*c*.1398–1472) married as her second husband, Henry Percy, second Earl of Northumberland who was killed fighting for Henry VI at the first battle of St Albans in 1455. Ironically, his father and grandfather had initially opposed the Lancastrian usurpation. But several of his sons by Eleanor died fighting for Henry VI. The couple's grandson was initially a Yorkist, but later supported Henry VII.

Anne Neville (*c*.1414–1480) married as her first husband Humphrey Stafford, Duke of Buckingham, who was killed on the Lancastrian side at the battle of Northampton in 1460. Her second husband (married by November 1467), Walter Blount, Lord Mountjoy (d. 1474), was a Yorkist. But Anne's son Humphrey, Earl of Stafford, married his cousin, Margaret, a daughter of Edmund Beaufort, Duke of Somerset, and seems to have been Lancastrian. Her grandson, Henry, 2nd Duke of Buckingham, was brought up as a Yorkist. But under Edward IV he carried out the execution of Cecily's son, George, Duke of Clarence. In 1483 he initially appeared to support Richard, Duke of Gloucester (Richard III), but subsequently he led Buckingham's Rebellion against Richard. As part of his rebellion he may possibly have taken possession of the so-called 'princes in the Tower'.

Appendix 6

Where Cecily appears to have been living or staying on specific dates

Hatfield, Herts., August 1439
Hatfield, Herts., February 1440/1
Hatfield, Herts., May/June 1441
Rouen, Normandy, July 1441–October 1445
Fotheringhay Castle, 7 July 1447
Neyte, Westminster, 7 November 1448
Dublin Castle, Ireland, June 1449
Dublin Castle, Ireland, 21 October 1449
Trim Castle, Ireland, end of 1449–September 1450
Baynard's Castle, London, 6 October 1450
Bury St Edmunds, Suffolk, 16 October 1450
Walsingham, Norfolk, October 1450
Baynard's Castle, London, April 1451
Warwick Castle, Warks., September 1451
Ludlow Castle, Shropshire, December 1451
Fotheringhay, 2 October 1452
Sandal Castle, Yorks., 19 August 1454
Sandal Castle, Yorks., May–June 1456
Caister Castle, Norfolk, October(?) 1456
Ludlow Castle, Shropshire, October 1459
Coventry, Warks., December 1459
Penshurst Place, Kent, January 1459/60–July 1460
Fastolf Place, Southwark, September 1460
Hertford, Herts., September 1460
Baynard's Castle, London, October 1460
Baynard's Castle, London, April 1461
Palace of Westminster, November 1461
Canterbury, Kent August 1462
Baynard's Castle, London, 27 May 1463
Clare Castle, Suffolk, 8 October 1463

Clare Castle, Suffolk, June 1465
Westminster 11 February 1466
Clare Castle, Suffolk, July 1467
Kennington, Kent, May 1468
Canterbury, Kent, 14 June 1469
Baynard's Castle, London, March 1469/70
Baynard's Castle, London, April 1471
Berkhamsted Castle, Herts., 18 May 1472
Berkhamsted Castle, Herts., 25 June 1473
Berkhamsted Castle, Herts., 13 December 1473
Berkhamsted Castle, Herts., 15 March [1474?]
St Benet's Abbey, Holme, Norfolk, 10 August 1475
Berkhamsted Castle, Herts., 29 May 1476
Baynard's Castle, London, 17–19 October 1476
St Benet's Abbey, Holme, Norfolk, 14 June 1480[1]
Berkhamsted Castle, Herts., 27 November 1480
Baynard's Castle, London, June–July 1483
Berkhamsted Castle, Herts., June 1495

Acknowledgements

I should like to thank Eleri Pipien and Claire Hopkins for commissioning me to write a study of Cecily Neville. My thanks also go to all those people who have helped me in various ways in preparing this book, including the staff at the Essex and Norwich Libraries, Dr. Lynsey Darby, Archivist of the College of Arms, Olga Hughes, Marie Barnfield, Mark Goacher, Valerie Quinlivan and Dave Perry. Any errors which remain in the finished work are, of course, my responsibility.

Endnotes

Introduction – confronting the problems

1. A. Licence, *Cecily Neville Mother of Kings*, Stroud 2014; 2015, p. 11 (my emphasis).
2. *Royal Commission on Historical Manuscripts: Fifth Report*, 2 vols., London 1876, vol. 1, p. 590.
3. A. Licence, *Cecily Neville*, p. 13.
4. http://www.le.ac.uk/richardiii/science/genealogy.html (consulted October 2016).
5. F. & C. Rol. Hudleston, ART. IX. 'Medieval glass in Penrith Church.' Read at Penrith, 4 September 1951. The footnotes of the original article are here enclosed within the text in square brackets, and italicised. http://archaeologydataservice.ac.uk/archiveDS/archiveDownload?t=arch-2055-1/dissemination/pdf/Article_Level_Pdf/tcwaas/002/1951/vol51/tcwaas_002_1951_vol51_0012.pdf (consulted November 2017).

Chapter 1: Cecily's Family Background

1. Licence, *Cecily Neville*, p. 17.
2. *ODNB*, C. Harper-Bill, 'Cecily, duchess of York'.
3. '1415. … In this year Cecily, wife of Richard, Duke of York, daughter of the Earl of Westmorland, was born on the 3rd May'. J. Stevenson, ed., *Letters and Papers illustrative of the wars of the English in France during the Reign of Henry the Sixth, King of England*, vol. 2, part 2, London 1864, p. 759. Stevenson's text is taken from the College of Arms, Arundel MS 48, f. 124v. I am grateful to the Archivist, Dr. Lynsey Darby, for allowing me to check that original source.
4. *ODNB*, Harper-Bill, 'Cecily, duchess of York'.
5. J. Ashdown-Hill, 'The Red Rose of Lancaster?', *Ricardian*, vol. 10, no. 133, June 1996, pp. 406–420 (p. 406), citing Scott's novel, *Anne of Geierstein*, which referred to 'the wars of the white and red roses'.
6. A. Musgrave, *Cicely, or the Rose of Raby*, 4 volumes, vol. 1, London 1795, p. 19.
7. *ODNB*, A. Tuck, 'Neville, Ralph first earl of Westmorland'.

8. J. Ashdown-Hill, *The Secret Queen*, Stroud 2016, p. 98.
9. *ODNB*, C. Harper-Bill, 'Beaufort, Joan'.
10. 13 January 1395/6, in Lincoln Cathedral.
11. *ODNB*, Harper-Bill, 'Beaufort, Joan'.
12. *ODNB*, Harper-Bill, 'Beaufort, Joan', citing BL, Cotton MS Vespasian F.xiii.
13. Ralph's behaviour in this respect was not a unique example of such conduct in the case of twice-married fathers. Later a similar course seems to have been followed by John Talbot, first Earl of Shrewsbury.
14. C. Halsted, *Richard III*, London 1844, 2 volumes, vol. 1, Appendix P (pp. 424–25), citing *Blore's Monumental Remains*, part iii.
15. For example, under https://en.wikipedia.org/wiki/Ralph_Neville,_1st_Earl_of_Westmorland (consulted October 2016).
16. One of three conspirators in the Southampton Plot against Henry V in 1415. He had eight or nine children by Alice. In 1412 he married his twelve-year-old son and heir, Thomas Grey, to Isabel (later Countess of Essex), the three-year-old daughter of Richard Earl of Cambridge.
17. Richard Despencer, Baron Burghersh.
18. 1332–40, Sir Ingram de Umfraville: http://wappenwiki.org/index.php/Balliol_Roll (consulted January 2017).
19. Sable, a leopard's head (or face) argent, jessant a fleur-de-lis or: https://www.houseofnames.com/mauley-family-crest (consulted January 2017).
20. That is the claim made by Catherine Reynolds in D. Bates & A. Curry, eds, *England and Normandy in the Middle Ages*, London 1994, p. 302. I am grateful to Joanna Laynesmith for drawing that publication to my attention. For the alleged Grey arms see https://en.wikipedia.org/wiki/Henry_de_Grey (consulted January 2017).
21. https://en.wikipedia.org/wiki/Thomas_Grey_(of_Heaton) (consulted January 2017).
22. Bates & Curry, eds, *England and Normandy in the Middle Ages*, London 1994, p. 302.

Chapter 2: Cecily's Childhood and Marriage

1. P.A. Johnson, *Duke Richard of York 1411–1460*, Oxford 1988, p. 1 and fn. 1.
2. J. L. Kirby, *Calendar of Inquisitions Post Mortem ... volume 20. 1-5 Henry V [1413–1418]*, British History Online 1995 http://www.history.ac.uk/cipm-20-part-iv (consulted December 2016), no. 390.
3. http://www.history.ac.uk/cipm-20-part-iv (consulted December 2016), no. 391.
4. http://www.history.ac.uk/cipm-20-part-iv (consulted December 2016), nos. 469; 472.

5. Halsted, *Richard III*, vol. 1, Appendix 0 (pp. 420-24), citing *Paston Letters*, vol. i, p. 86; Sandford, *Geneal Hist.*, book iv, p. 294; *Anglo. Spec.*, p. 773.
6. *CPR*, 1374–1377, p. 354.
7. *CPR*, 1374–1377, pp. 474–75.
8. 'The ix. yeer of king Richard, he held a parlement at Westmynstre, and there he made ij. dukis, a markeys, and v. erlis. Ffirst, he made ser Edmund of Langley, erl of Cambrige, his vncle, duke of York'. J. S. Davies, ed., *An English Chronicle of the Reigns of Richard II, Henry IV, Henry V, and Henry VI*, London 1856, p. 4.
9. Halsted, *Richard III*, vol. 1, Appendix 0 (pp. 420–24).
10. *Ibid.*
11. On 1 November 1387 Richard II granted Berkhamsted Castle for a year to Robert de Vere, Duke of Ireland (*CPR*, 1385–1389, London 1900, p. 366). On 8 October 1388 it was granted to 'the King's brother, John earl of Huntingdon ... for his abode' (*CPR*, 1385–1389, p. 518).
12. *ODNB*, Tuck, 'Neville, Ralph first earl of Westmorland'.
13. *Petitio Johanne Comitissae de Westmoreland super custodia Ricardi Ducis Eborum.* (Pat. 4 Hen. VI. P. 2. M. 15.)
14. *CPR*, 1422–1429, p. 343.
15. http://www.british-history.ac.uk/rymer-foedera/vol10/pp349–368 (consulted September 2016).
16. He was *knighted* at Leicester on 19 May 1426, by John, Duke of Bedford, the younger brother of King Henry V.
17. *Pro Duce Eborum, facto Milite.*
Rex Omnibus, ad quos &c. Salutem.

Monstravit nobis, carissima Consanguinea nostra, Johanna Comitissa Westmerlandiae, qualiter ipsa, ut Executrix Testamenti carissimi Domini & Viri sui Radulphi nuper Comitis Westmerlandiae Defuncti, habet Custodiam & Gubernationem carissimi Consanguinei nostri Ricardi Ducis Eborum, virtute Concessionis nostrae eidem nuper Comiti factae,

Pro cujus quidem Ducis Sustentatione, per avisamentum Concilii nostri, Concessimus eidem nuper Comiti Ducentas Marcas, percipiendas Annuatim, durante Minori Aetate ejusdem Ducis,

De quibus quidem Ducentis Marcis praedictus Dux honorificè, prout convenit Statui suo, sustentari non potest, pro eo quod ipse Miles efficitur, & in Honorem, Aetatem, & Haereditatem crescit, qui Majores Expensas & Custus exquirunt, ad magnum onus dictae Consanguineae nostrae ut dicit,

Nos, praemissa considerantes, de avisamento & assensu Concilii nostri, Concessimus praefatae Consanguineae nostrae Centum Marcas, percipiendas Annuatim pro Sustentatione ipsius Ducis, ultra dictas Ducentas Marcas, durante

Minore Aetate ejusdem Ducis, de Dominiis, Terris, & Tenementis quae fuerunt Edmundi nuper Comitis Marchiae, nunc in manibus nostris ratione Minoris Aetatis ejusdem Ducis existentibus, infra Comitatus Dorsetiae & Suffolciae, per manus Firmariorum vel Occupatorum eorumdem; videlicet,

Unam Medietatem Summae praedictae, per manus Firmariorum Dominiorum, Terrarum, & Tenementorum praedictorum, infra Comitatum Dorsetiae,

Et aliam Medietatem ejusdem Summae, per manus Firmariorum Dominiorum, Terrarum, & Tenementorum praedictorum infra Comitatum Suffolciae,

In cujus &c.

Teste Rege apud Leycestr. vicesimo sexto die Maii.

Per Breve de Privato Sigillo. http://www.british-history.ac.uk/rymer-foedera/vol10/pp349-368 (consulted September 2016); also Halsted, *Richard III*, vol. 1, Appendix K (pp.415–16),citing Rymer's *Foedera*, tome x. p. 358. However, Halsted's quote contains minor errors, omitting sections of the Latin text.

18. B. Wolffe, *Henry VI*, London 1981, p. 37.
19. *ODNB*, G.L. Harriss, 'Humphrey, duke of Gloucester'.
20. Wolffe, *Henry VI*, p. 31.
21. Leicestershire Record Office B. R. II/3/3: R.A. Griffiths, 'Queen Katherine de Valois and a missing statute of the realm', *Law Quarterly Review* , 93 (1977), 257–8.
22. *Katerina regina et mater Henrici sexti … voluit habuisse dominum Edmundum Bewforde comitem de Morten; sed dux Glocestriae et quamplures alii domini renuerunt.* ['Catherine, queen and mother of Henry VI … had wanted to have the lord Edmund Bewford, Count of Mortain; but the Duke of Gloucester and many other lords had refused'.] J. A. Giles, ed., *Incerti scriptoris chronicon Angliae de regnis trium regum Lancastriensium Henrici IV, Henrici V et Henrici VI*, London, 1848, Part Four, p. 17.
23. *ODNB*, G.L. Harriss, 'Eleanor, duchess of Gloucester'.
24. *CPR*, 1429–1436, p. 38.
25. *ODNB*, C. Harper-Bill, Cecily, Duchess of York', versus *ODNB*, J. Watts, 'Richard, third duke of York'. Watts suggests they married in 1424. However, Harper-Bill says they were probably betrothed in the autumn of 1424, but suggests they only married five years later.
26. *CPR*, 1429–1436, p. 35.
27. Sixteen is thought to have been the normal age for the consummation of a marriage in which one (or both) of the contracting partners was a minor: B.J. Harris, *English Aristocratic Women, 1450–1550*, Oxford 2002, p. 45. The conduct of Lord Sudeley in respect of the marriage of Eleanor Talbot to his son

and heir, Sir Thomas Boteler, appears to confirm that this was the normally accepted age – see J. Ashdown-Hill, *The Secret Queen*, Stroud 2016, p. 93.

28. Licence, *Cecily Neville*, p. 62.
29. Licence, *Cecily Neville*, p. 57.
30. J.M. Horne, ed., *Fasti Ecclesiae Anglicanae 1300–1541*, vol. 5, *St Paul's, London*, London 1963, http://www.british-history.ac.uk/fasti-ecclesiae/1300-1541/vol5 (consulted December 2016).
31. J.A. Twemlow, ed., *Calendar of Papal Registers Relating To Great Britain and Ireland: vol. 7, 1417–1431*, London, 1906, http://www.british-history.ac.uk/cal-papal-registers/brit-ie/vol7 (consulted December 2016).
32. 'To the archbishop of York. Mandate to absolve from excommunication incurred, first separating them for a time, and enjoining a salutary penance, and afterwards to dispense to contract anew and remain in the marriage which Richard of York (*de Eboraco*), knight, and Anne of March (*de Marchia*), damsel, of the dioceses of York and Winchester, cousin and kinswoman respectively of king Henry, without consent of their parents and without the customary banns, contracted and caused to be solemnized before the church, not being ignorant that they were related on one side in the fourth and on the other in the second degree of kindred. Offspring past and future is to be declared legitimate. *Romani pontificis'*. 10 Kalends of June [23 May] 1408. http://www.british-history.ac.uk/cal-papal-registers/brit-ie/vol6/pp128-147 (consulted December 2016).
33. http://www.british-history.ac.uk/cal-papal-registers/brit-ie/vol8/pp122-136 (consulted September 2016), pp. 132 and 133, citing f. 246 & f. 257.
34. B. Wolffe, *Henry VI*, London 1981, p. 61.
35. C. Willett & P. Cunnington, *The History of Underclothes*, London 1951, republished New York 1992, p. 23.
36. *Ibid.*
37. *CPR*, 1429–1436, p. 207.
38. *CPR*, 1429–1436, p. 192.
39. *CPR*, 1429–1436, p. 225.
40. *CPR*, 1429–1436, pp. 616, 621, 624, 625, 626, 627.
41. *CPR*, 1429–1436, p. 608.
42. *CPR*, 1429–1436, pp. 614, 616, 624, 627.
43. *CPR*, 1429–1436, p. 533.
44. *CPR*, 1429–1436, p. 535.
45. ODNB, A.J. Pollard, 'Talbot, John, first earl of Shrewsbury'.
46. The address '*Duci Eboracen.*' is added in the margin both in Reg. CCCLIX and in the Barberini and Chigi MSS.

47. http://www.british-history.ac.uk/cal-papal-registers/brit-ie/vol8/pp212-237 (consulted September 2016), p. 228.
48. J. Weever, *Antient Funeral Monuments*, London 1767, p. 474.
49. *ODNB*, J. Watts, 'Pole, William de la, first duke of Suffolk'.
50. J. Gairdner, *The Paston Letters*, Gloucester 1986, vol. 2, p. 50.

Chapter 3: Cecily's List of Children

1. J. Ashdown-Hill, *The Private Life of Edward IV*, Stroud 2016, pp. 115–16.
2. See Ashdown-Hill, *The Private Life of Edward IV*.
3. R. Vaughan, *Charles the Bold*, second edition, Woodbridge 2002, p. 159.
4. *ODNB*, Harper-Bill, 'Cecily, duchess of York'.
5. K.W. Barnardiston, *Clare Priory*, Cambridge 1962, p. 69.
6. *Sequitur generacio illustrissimi principis Ricardi, Ducis Eboraci &c ex serenissima principissa, uxore sua, Caecilia*'. T. Hearne, *Liber Niger Scaccarii nec non Wilhelmi Worcestrii Annales Rerum Anglicarum*, vol. 2, London 1774, p. 525. Hearne's text is a generally accurate published version of the College of Arms, Arundel MS 48, f. 85v.
7. J. Stevenson, ed., *Wilhelmi Wyrcester, Annales*, as published in *Letters and Papers Illustrative of the Wars of the English in France during the Reign of Henry the Sixth, vol, 2, part 2*, London 1864, p. 743. In respect of his list of births of the York children, Stevenson's text is a published version of the College of Arms, Arundel MS 48, f. 125 (r & v), though curiously Stevenson has added approximately six pages of text between the entries on f. 125v of the original manuscript which refer to 1449 and to 1450.
8. Stevenson, ed., *Wilhelmi Wyrcester, Annales*, p. 793.
9. At the manor of the Bishop of Ely – '*in quodam manerio Domini episcopi Eliensis nuccupato* [*sic* in MS] Hatfeld'.
10. This implies knowledge of Edward's elder brother, Henry (Harry), though he is not named.
11. The fact that his death is recorded means this record must date after 1460.
12. Records of arrangements for Elizabeth's baptism show that she must have been born in September.
13. The manor of the Abbot of Westminster.
14. Stevenson / Worcester, p. 762.
15. All correct in terms of a possible date in that calendar year.
16. Stevenson / Worcester, p. 763.
17. Stevenson / Worcester, p. 763.
18. Stevenson / Worcester, p. 763.
19. Stevenson / Worcester, p. 763.

20. Stevenson / Worcester, p. 764.
21. Stevenson / Worcester, p. 765.
22. manor of the Abbot of Westminster, Ebury ('Ey')
23. Stevenson / Worcester, p. 765.
24. Stevenson / Worcester, p. 765.
25. Thomas may have been born – and may have died – at Baynard's Castle, in London (see below, Chapter 6).
26. Stevenson / Worcester, p. 771.
27. Stevenson / Worcester, p. 771.

Chapter 4: Wife and Mother in France

1. Rolls of Parliament 9, Edw. IV, as published in J. Strachey, ed., *Rotuli Parliamentorum ut et Petitiones et Placita in Parliamento*, 1767–77, vol 6, London 1777, rolls 1472–1503, p. 232.
2. Jasper, Earl of Pembroke, is generally guestimated to have been born in about 1432.
3. In a letter 'Written at our towne of Tenbye the xxvth of ffeu'r [1459/60]', Jasper referred to the fact that 'my father yor Kinsman' had been put to death. http://www.theanneboleynfiles.com/guest-article-giveaway-jasper-tudor-debra-bayani/#ixzz4U7PRfSLq (consulted January 2017).
4. 1442 *Natus est Edwardus, filius secundus Ricardi, Ducis Eboraci, & heres, Rex Angliae & Franciae, XXVIII° die Aprilis, hora II post mediam noctem in mane diei Lunae, apud Rothomagum, qui conceptus est in camera proxima capellas palacii de Hatfelde*. T. Hearne, *Liber Niger Scaccarii nec non Wilhelmi Worcestrii Annales Rerum Anglicarum*, vol. 2, London 1774, p. 462.
5. M. Jones, *Bosworth 1485 Psychology of a Battle*, London 2014, p. 81
6. M. Clive, *This Sun of York*, London 1973, p. xxi.
7. Jones, *Bosworth 1485*, p. 83; present author's emphasis.
8. Jones, *Bosworth 1485*, p. 83; present author's emphasis.
9. F. Madden, 'Political Poems of the Reigns of Henry VI and Edward IV', *Archaeologia* vol.29, 1842, pp. 318–347 (pp. 331; 332).
10. Quote from Jones – see above, note 8.
11. Quote from Jones – see above, note 8.
12. C. Weightman, *Margaret of York Duchess of Burgundy 1446–1503*, Gloucester 1989, p. 168, citing H. Ellis, ed., E. Hall, *Chronicle* etc., London 1809, p. 472.
13. *ODNB*, A.J. Pollard, 'Neville, William earl of Kent'. Pollard erroneously cites as his source Davies, ed., *An English Chronicle of the Reigns of Richard II, Henry IV, Henry V, and Henry VI*, p. 91. In actuality, the quote which refers to

'lytelle Fauconbrege, a knyghte of grete reuerence' is to be found on p. 93 of Davies' edition of the *English chronicle*.

14. J. Ashdown-Hill, *The Third Plantagenet*, Stroud 2014, plate 1.
15. J. Laynesmith, 'Yorkist children – lost bones "rediscovered"', *The Ricardian Bulletin*, March 2017, pp. 34–35, citing C.H. Hunter-Blair, ed., *Visitations of the North III A Visitation of the North of England circa 1480–1500*, Surtees Society 144, 1930.
16. C. Ross, *Edward IV*, London 1974, p. 7, and citing *CPR*, 1467–77, p. 439.
17. *CPR*, 1476–1485, p. 411.
18. Ashdown-Hill, *The Private Life of Edward IV*, chapter 3.
19. Scofield, *The Life and Reign of Edward the Fourth* (hereinafter *Ed.IV*), vol. 1, p. 2, citing Rolls of Parliament, V, 471.
20. *Et die Sabbati sequenti dictus dominus Scales, compater dicti comitis Marchiae …*, Stevenson, ed., *Letters and Papers Illustrative of the Wars of the English in France during the Reign of Henry the Sixth King of England*, Vol. 2, part 2, London 1864, p, 773 (William Worcester, *Annales*).
21. Scofield, *Ed.IV*, vol. 1, p. 1.
22. L. Stratford, *Edward the Fourth*, London 1910, pp. 11–12.
23. See above, Chapter 3 – table of Cecily's possible conception dates and the gaps between them.
24. Scofield, *Ed.IV*, vol. 1, p. 1 and not 2.
25. For the recorded dates of birth of Edmund and Elizabeth of York, see the list of York children.
26. http://www.british-history.ac.uk/cal-papal-registers/brit-ie/vol8/pp263-271 (consulted September 2016), p. 269.
27. M. Jones, ed., *Philippe de Commynes Memoires*, Harmondsworth 1972, p. 258.
28. Jones / Commynes, p. 239.
29. J. Stevenson, ed., *Letters and papers illustrative of the Wars of the English in France during the reign of King Henry the Sixth, King of England*, vol. 1, London 1861, pp. 79–82. This is Stevenson's translation. The Duke of York's original letter is in French.
30. *filiam specie et formam praestantem*, Thomas Basin, 1.156, quoted in *ODNB*, Dunn, 'Margaret of Anjou'.
31. *CSP Milan*, *1385–1618*, 18–19, quoted in *ODNB*, Dunn, 'Margaret of Anjou'.
32. *ODNB*, D.E.S. Dunn, 'Margaret of Anjou'.
33. *ODNB*, Dunn, 'Margaret of Anjou'.
34. *ODNB*, Dunn, 'Margaret of Anjou'.
35. *ODNB*, Dunn, 'Margaret of Anjou'.

Chapter 5: Wife and Mother in Ireland

1. *ODNB*, G.L. Harriss, 'Beaufort, Henry'.
2. Henry's father and grandfather had both been dukes of Exeter, but his grandfather had been attainted and the ducal title, which had meanwhile been granted to Thomas Beaufort, was therefore re-created for his father in 1444.
3. *ODNB*, M. Hicks, 'Holland, Henry, second Duke of Exeter' (consulted December 2016).
4. *CPR*, 1446–1452, p. 43.
5. 'there is evidence that his will was being administered by 1449, though its terms remain unknown'. *ODNB*, G.L. Harriss, 'Humphrey, duke of Gloucester'.
6. H. Morley, ed., John Stow, *A Survay of London, … written in the year 1598*, London 1893, p. 93.
7. Morley, ed., Stow, *A Survay of London*, p. 93.
8. *CPR*, 1446–1452, pp. 234–235.
9. In 1448.
10. P. A. Johnson, *Duke Richard of York 1411–1460*, Oxford 1988, p. 70, citing three fifteenth-century sources.
11. The fourth earl was killed, the fifth earl died of the plague.
12. *ODNB*, J. Watts, 'Pole, William de la, first duke of Suffolk'.
13. P.M. Kendall, *Richard the Third* (hereinafter *R3*), London 1955, p. 20.
14. E. Curtis, 'Richard Duke of York as Viceroy of Ireland, 1447–1460; with unpublished materials for his relations with native chiefs', *The Journal of the Royal Society of Antiquaries of Ireland*, Seventh Series, Vol. 2, No. 2 (Dec. 31, 1932), pp. 158–186 (p. 165).
15. J. O'Donovan, ed. and trans., *The Annals of the Kingdom of Ireland by the Four Masters* [*Annála Ríoghachta Éireann*], Dublin 1848–51, Vol. 4, p. 965 . http://www.ucc.ie/celt/published/T100005D/index.html (consulted May 2013).
16. C.Weightman, *Margaret of York Duchess of Burgundy 1446-1503*, Gloucester 1989, p. 13.
17. *CPR* 1476–85, p. 411.
18. *CPR* 1476–85, p. 374.
19. E. Curtis, 'Richard Duke of York as Viceroy of Ireland, 1447–1460; with unpublished materials for his relations with native chiefs', *The Journal of the Royal Society of Antiquaries of Ireland*, Seventh Series, Vol. 2, No.2 (Dec. 31, 1932), pp. 158–186 (p. 172).
20. '*Natus est Dominus Georgius, sextus filius praedicti principis, XXI die Octobris, apud castrum Debline in Hibernia, anno Domini MCCCCXLIX, in meridie diei antedicti, & baptizatus in ecclesia Sancti Salvatoris*', T. Hearne, *Liber*

Niger Scaccarii nec non Wilhelmi Worcestrii Annales Rerum Anglicarum, vol. 2, London 1774, p. 526; see also J. Bohn, ed., *The Chronicles of the White Rose of York*, London 1843, 2nd edition, London 1845, p. 301.

21. 'On 21st of October 1449, the Duke of York's ninth child, George of York, afterwards Duke of Clarence, was born in Dublin Castle, and the Earls of Desmond and Ormonde stood sponsors at the font'. S. Hayman and J. Graves, eds., *Unpublished Geraldine Documents*, Dublin 1870-81, p. 79, cited in J. Ashdown-Hill & A. Carson 'The Execution of the Earl of Desmond', *The Ricardian* 15 (2005), pp. 70–93, (p. 72, n. 7).

Chapter 6: The End of Maternity

1. *ODNB*, Watts, 'de la Pole, William'.
2. *ODNB*, I. M. W. Harvey, 'Cade, John'.
3. *ODNB*, Harvey, 'Cade, John'.
4. *ODNB*, Harvey, 'Cade, John'.
5. *ODNB*, Harvey, 'Cade, John'.
6. *ODNB*, C. Richmond, 'Beaufort, Edmund'.
7. *ODNB*, Watts, 'Richard, third duke of York'.
8. Davies, ed., *English Chronicle*, p. 71.
9. Gairdner, *Paston Letters*, vol. 2, p. 174.
10. *Ibid.*
11. Gairdner, *Paston Letters*, vol. 2, pp. 180–81.
12. Gairdner, *Paston Letters*, vol. 2, p. 179.
13. 'Towards the middle of the 15th century a new development began with an undertaking rarely paralleled in the Middle Ages. This was the planning of the Chapel to protect the original Holy House.' C. Green & A.B. Whittingham, 'Excavations at Walsingham Priory, Norfolk, 1961', *The Archaeological Journal*, vol. 125, 1968, pp. 255–290 (pp. 274–75).
14. Gairdner, *Paston Letters*, vol. 2, p. 184.
15. Her name is often cited as 'Richeldis'. However, that version of her name comes from a medieval *Latin* document relating to the shrine at Walsingham. The only surviving medieval *English* record of her name gives it in the form 'Rychold'.
16. Gairdner, *Paston Letters*, vol. 2, p. 186.
17. M. Barnfield, 'Diriment Impediments, Dispensations and Divorce: Richard III and Matrimony', *Ricardian* 17 (2007), pp. 84–98 (p. 89) citing Bodleian MS Dugdale 15,fol. 75. My underlining. The highlighted phrase means 'and even though George's mother raised the same Isabel from the holy font [i.e. was her godmother]'.

18. Clive, *This Sun of York*, p. xxxvi, citing BM Cotton MS, Vespasian f iii.f.16; Gairdner, *Paston Letters*, vol. 1, p. 148, citing MS Cott., Vespasian F. xiii fol. 35.
19. Johnson, *Duke Richard of York*, p. 110.
20. In Kent the Duke of York held Deptford Strand ('Depfordstrand'), Erith, South-Frith ('Southfrith') and 'Shillingyeld'. J.T. Rosenthal, 'The Estates and Finances of Richard, Duke of York (1411–1460)', *Studies in Medieval and Renaissance History*, vol. 2, 1965, p. 141.
21. A. Crawford, *Letters of Medieval Women*, Stroud 2002, pp. 233–35, citing Rawcliffe, BIHR, 1987, pp. 237–8; Huntingdon Library, California, Battle Abbey MS 937.
22. W.G. Searle, ed., *The Chronicle of John Stone Monk of Christ Church 1415–1471*, Cambridge 1902, p. 87.
23. Gairdner, *Paston Letters*, vol. 1, pp 259–61.
24. Searle, ed., *The Chronicle of John Stone*, p. 87.
25. Gairdner, *Paston Letters*, vol. 1, pp. 263–64.
26. Thomas Hunt was the 16th elected head of the Augustinian Priory at Walsingham. He was in post there from 1437 until 1474.
27. Gairdner, *Paston Letters*, vol. 2, pp. 331–32.
28. Gairdner, *Paston Letters*, vol. 3, p. 2.
29. The dukedom had been abolished following the disgrace and death of William de la Pole in May 1450. The ducal title was only restored by Edward IV in March 1462/3.

Chapter 7: Through the Menopause, into Custody

1. Gairdner, *Paston Letters*, vol. 3, p. 25.
2. Gairdner, *Paston Letters*, vol. 3, p. 31.
3. Gairdner, *Paston Letters*, vol. 3, p. 32. Curiously, HISTORIC ENGLAND states online that the site of the former religious house is now "misleadingly termed 'The Priory'." (https://historicengland.org.uk/listing/the-list/list-entry/1017519 consulted April 2017.) This reveals astonishing ignorance on the part of that official organisation which is supposed to exist to protect England's historic heritage. Of course a Franciscan religious house can perfectly correctly be referred to either as a friary or a priory!
4. '*Ultima iam matris proles fuit Ursula, regis / Que summi voto celesti iungitur agno*'. J Weever, *Antient Funeral Monuments*, London 1767, p. 474. From the Latin text of Friar Osbern Bokenham's poem listing the children of the Duke and Duchess of York.
5. *ODNB*, Watts, 'Richard, third duke of York'.

6. Gairdner, *Paston Letters*, vol. 3, p. 75.
7. Gairdner, *Paston Letters*, vol. 3, p. 86.
8. Gairdner, *Paston Letters*, vol. 3, p. 92.
9. Aristotle, *History of Animals*, 585b, cited in http://menopausesupplement.com/menopause-in-the-ancient-world/ (consulted January 2017).
10. I am grateful to Dave Perry for bringing this claim to my attention.
11. Gairdner, *Paston Letters*, vol, 3, p. 93.
12. Gairdner, *Paston Letters*, vol, 3, p. 110.
13. Gairdner, *Paston Letters*, vol. 3, p. 125.
14. *ODNB*, Watts, 'Richard, third duke of York'.
15. *certa notabilia monilia et jocalia auri cum lapidibus preciosis garnizata, videlicet unum monile ditissimum vocata Anglice* a White Rose *nuper domini ducis Eborum cum magno precioso lapide vocato* a poynted dyamant. Gairdner, *Paston Letters*, vol, 4, p. 233.
16. ... *ou ilz trouverent le duc dYorc, la ducesse sa femme et tous leurs enfans, excepte Edouard comte de La Marche quy estoit demoure a Callaix*. W. & E.L.C.P. Hardy, eds, Waurin, *Recueil des Chroniques et Anchiennes Istories de La Grant Bretaigne, à present nommé Engleterre*, vol. 5, Cambridge 2012, p. 286.
17. *Il prinst congie du duc dYorc, de la ducesse et de leurs enfans, il se mist a chemin, avec luy madame sa mere quy longuement sestoit tenue avec madame dYorc.* Hardy & Hardy, eds, Waurin, *Chroniques*, vol. 5, p. 286.
18. Among those attainted were the Duke of York himself, and his and Cecily's eldest surviving sons the Earl of March and the Earl of Rutland. Also Cecily's relatives, the Earl of Salisbury, his Countess, and their son the Earl of Warwick, and Sir Thomas and Sir John Neville. Other attainted supporters included Lord Powys, Lord Clynton, Sir Thomas Harrington, Sir Thomas Parre, Sir John Conyers, Sir John Wenlock, Sir William Oldhall, Edward Bourchier and his brother, Thomas Vaughan, Thomas Colte, Thomas Clay, John Denham, Thomas Moryng, John Oter, Master Richard Fisher, and Hastings (Gairdner, *Paston Letters*, vol, 3, p. 199). However, the name 'Thomas Clay' in the Paston documents appears to have been an error. It should read 'John Cley' (*CPR*, 1452–1461, p. 572).
19. C.L. Kingsford, ed., *Chronicles of London*, Oxford 1905, p. 170.
20. Gairdner, *Paston Letters*, vol, 3, p. 198.
21. Bohn, ed., *The Chronicles of the White Rose of York*, pp. 5–30: Hearne's edition of 'The Chronicle of King Edward IV' (originally published 1719 'at the end of his Edition of Sprott's Chronicle') pp. 5–6.
22. J. Gairdner, ed., *The Historical Collections of a Citizen of London in the Fifteenth Century*, London 1876, Gregory's Chronicle p. 206.

23. i.e. Margaret (later Duchess of Burgundy), George (later Duke of Clarence), and Richard (later Richard III).
24. *CPR*, 1452–1461, pp. 542–543.
25. Gairdner, Gregory's Chronicle, p. 207.
26. Gairdner, *Paston Letters*, vol, 3, p. 203.

Chapter 8: The Blue Velvet Carriage to Bereavement

1. Gairdner, Gregory's Chronicle, p. 208.
2. 'hys lyvery was white and brewe … i-brawderyd a-bove with fetyrlockys'. Gairdner, Gregory's Chronicle, p. 208.
3. J. Ashdown-Hill, *The Private Life of Edward IV*, Stroud 2016, chapter 6, 1459–1461 – Itinerary.
4. Feast of the Nativity of the BVM – Monday 8 September 1460.
5. Letters missing due to hole in paper.
6. Ditto.
7. 29 September.
8. N. Davis, ed., *Paston Letters and Papers of the Fifteenth Century*, 2 vols., Oxford 1971 & 1976, vol. 2, p. 216; Gairdner, *Paston Letters*, vol, 3, p. 233. The two published versions offer slightly different spellings.
9. For full details on John Cley / Clay, together with the relevant source material, see Appendix 3.
10. M. Kowaleski, review of a Museum of London Archaeological Report, 2011, https://scholarworks.iu.edu/dspace/bitstream/handle/2022/13031/11.02.26.html?sequence=1 (consulted Jan. 2017).
11. Kendall, *R3*, p. 37, citing three contemporary sources.
12. Gairdner, *Paston Letters*, vol, 3, p. 226.
13. W. Hardy & E.L.C.P. Hardy, eds., J. de Wavrin, *Recueil des Chroniques et Anchienne Istories de la Grant Bretaigne, à Present Nommé Engleterre,* Vol. 5, 1891, reprinted Cambridge 2012, p. 318.
14. Gairdner, *Paston Letters*, vol, 3, p. 239 and note 1.
15. *ODNB*, Watts, Richard, third duke of York.
16. Ashdown-Hill, *The Private Life of Edward IV*, chapter 6, 1459–1461 – Itinerary.
17. Kingsford, ed., *Chronicles of London*, p. 174.
18. '*le roy Edouard avoit deux jennes frères, lun eagie de neuf ans et lautre de huit ans*', Hardy / Wavrin, p. 357.
19. 'Milan: 1461', Calendar of State Papers and Manuscripts in the Archives and Collections of Milan: 1385-1618 (1912), pp. 37-106. http://www.british-history.ac.uk/report.aspx?compid=92248 (consulted January 2017).

20. 'Milan: 1461', Calendar of State Papers and Manuscripts in the Archives and Collections of Milan: 1385-1618 (1912), pp. 37–106. http://www.british-history.ac.uk/report.aspx?compid=92248 (consulted January 2017).

Chapter 9: The First Reign of Edward IV

1. *CPR*, 1452–1461, p. 287.
2. *CPR*, 1452–1461, p. 470.
3. *CPR*, 1452–1461, p. 631.
4. W. & E.L.C.P. Hardy, eds, Waurin, *Recueil des Chroniques et Anchiennes Istories de La Grant Bretaigne, à present nommé Engleterre*, vol. 5, Cambridge 2012, p. 335: '*quant le comte de La Marche se vey auz champz arme de toutes armes, il appela le mayeur et tous les notables de Londres, si prinst congie deulz et leur recommanda la ducesse sa mere*'.
5. Gairdner, *Paston Letters*, vol, 3, pp. 266–67.
6. *Penultimo die mensis Maii die sabbati viz. in vigilia sancte Trinitatis venerunt Cantuarium de partibus transmarinis dominus Georgius et dominus Ricardus filii ducis Eboraci et fratres regis Edwardi iiij*[ti]. Searle, ed., *The Chronicle of John Stone*, p. 83.
7. *CPR*, 1461–1467, pp. 131–32.
8. TNA, C 81/782.
9. TNA, C 81/782; TNA, C 81/783.
10. TNA, C 81/783.
11. TNA, C 81/783.
12. R.S. Sylvester, ed., St Thomas More, *The History of King Richard III and Selections from the English and Latin Poems*, London 1976, p. 65.
13. 26 June 1483: Petition to Richard, Duke of Gloucester, as quoted in the subsequent Act of Parliament of January 1483/4 (*titulus regius*). J. Ashdown-Hill, *The Secret Queen*, Stroud 2016, p. 273.
14. See J. Ashdown-Hill, *The Private Life of Edward IV*, Stroud 2016, chapter 10.
15. TNA, C 81/783.
16. TNA, C 81/783.
17. For a full description, see Wilkinson, *Richard, the young King to be*, pp. 88–89.
18. Searle, ed., *The Chronicle of John Stone*, p. 83.
19. M. Hicks, *False Fleeting Perjur'd Clarence*, 2nd edition, Bangor 1992, p. 7.
20. *CPR*, 1461–1467, p. 17.
21. 19 November 1461 & 8 February 1461/2; *CPR*, 1461–1467, pp. 115 & 149.
22. *CPR*, 1461–1467, p. 48.
23. Chamberlayne, 'A Paper Crown', p. 431, citing *Royal Commission on Historical Manuscripts: Third Report*, London 1872, p. 313.

24. *CPR*, 1461–1467, p. 110.
25. Record of the city of Canterbury, published in *Royal Commission on Historical Manuscripts: Ninth Report*, 2 vols., London 1883, vol. 1, p. 140. Chamberlayne, 'The Paper Crown', p. 430, refers to this, but mistakenly cites the publication date as 1872. I am grateful to the Norwich Library service for helping me check this.
26. *Royal Commission on Historical Manuscripts: Fifth Report*, 2 vols., London 1876, vol. 1, p. 590. Sadly, the letter itself now appears to have been lost.
27. *Royal Commission on Historical Manuscripts: Fifth Report*, 2 vols., London 1876, vol. 1, p. 590.
28. 'the Kynge made fulle moche of hym; in soo moche that he loggyd whythe the kynge in hys owne bedde many nyghtys, and sum tyme rode a huntynge be hynde the kynge, the kynge havynge a boute hym not passynge vj hors at the moste, and yet iij were of the Dukys men of Somersett. The kyng lovyd hym welle, but the duke thought treson undyr fayre chere and wordys, as hyt apperyd'. J. Gairdner, ed., *The historical collections of a citizen of London in the fifteenth century*, London (Camden Society, new ser., 17) 1876 [Gregory's Chronicle], p. 219.
29. IRO, HA 246/B2/498.
30. *CPR 1461–1467*, p. 131. For the full list, see below, Appendix 1.
31. BL, Add. MS 46349, f. 101r; A. Crawford, ed., *Howard Household Books*, Stroud 1992 (hereinafter *HHB*), part 1, p. 456.
32. He was knighted on 28 June 1461, at Edward IV's coronation.
33. BL, Add. MS 46349, f. 12v; *HHB*, part 1, pp. 170–71.The intended recipient of this letter is unknown.
34. A writ in the name of Edward IV was issued in favour of Cecily's servant, Richard Mannyng of Halstead, Essex, dated '*apud Clare octavo die mensis octubris anno regni Regis Edwardi quarti post conquestum Anglie tercio*': J. Ashdown-Hill, 'Suffolk Connections of the House of York', *Proceedings of the Suffolk Institute for Archaeology & History*, vol. 41 part 2 (2006), pp. 199–207, also W.G. Benham, ed., *The Red Paper Book of Colchester* (Colchester, 1902), p. 60. The original Red Paper Book is in the Essex Record Office. It has been subject to several systems of enumeration. Edward IV's writ is on the folio variously numbered 123v, C111v, or 84v. I previously thought that Edward IV himself was at Clare, Suffolk, on this date (see J. Ashdown-Hill, *Richard III's 'Beloved Cousyn', John Howard and the House of York*, Stroud 2009, pp. 26 & 147, note 8). But the document in question, while citing a writ issued by the king earlier in the year, was apparently issued by Cecily herself, and not by her son.

35. Cambridge University Library, Dept. of Manuscripts and University Archives, Rushford: Certificate, ref. 11/75.
36. BL, Add. MS 46349, f. 83r; *HHB*, part 1, p. 295.
37. BL, Add. MS 46349, f. 85r; *HHB*, part 1, p. 301.
38. Ashdown-Hill, *Richard III's 'Beloved Cousyn'*, chapter 4.
39. J. Ashdown-Hill, 'Suffolk Connections of the House of York', pp. 201–02. See also *Gothic*, no. 209 & plate 7.
40. BL, Add. Ms. 46349, ff. 59v-60r.; *HHB*, part 1, pp. 243–44.
41. Ashdown-Hill, *Richard III's 'Beloved Cousyn'*, chapter 6.
42. BL, Add. Ms. 46349, f. 47v; *HHB*, part 1, p. 220.
43. Soc. Ant., Ms. 76, f. 55v; *HHB*, part 2, p. 64.
44. Soc. Ant., Ms. 76, f. 115r; *HHB*, part 2, p. 160.
45. *CPR*, 1461–1467, p. 300.
46. Gairdner, *Paston Letters*, vol, 4, p. 83. For full details of the Cley / Clay family, see below, Appendix 4.
47. *CPR*, 1461–1467, p. 161.
48. *CPR*, 1461–1467, pp. 97–98; p. 163.
49. *CPR*, 1461–1467, p. 41.
50. *CPR*, 1461–1467, p. 57.
51. *CPR*, 1461–1467, p. 110, p. 145, p. 148.
52. *CPR*, 1461–1467, p. 74.
53. *CPR*, 1461–1467, p. 73.
54. *CPR*, 1461–1467, p. 216.
55. *CPR*, 1461–1467, p. 322.
56. *CPR*, 1461–1467, pp. 442, 444.
57. *CPR*, 1461–1467, p. 519.
58. See, for example, *CPR*, 1467–1477, p. 477–12 May 1474.
59. Ashdown-Hill, *The Private Life of Edward IV*, pp. 63 & 65.
60. This date is also cited in Warkworth's Chronicle, Gregory's Chronicle and Hearne's Fragment.
61. H. Ellis, ed., R. Fabyan, *The New Chronicles of England and France*, London 1811 (text of Fabyan's 1516 edition), p. 654.
62. See Ashdown-Hill, *The Private Life of Edward IV*, p. 110.
63. Ashdown-Hill, *The Secret Queen*, pp. 164-66
64. *CPR*, 1461–1467, p. 438.
65. Searle, ed., *The Chronicle of John Stone*, p. 92.
66. Bohn, ed., *The Chronicles of the White Rose of York*, pp. 5–30: Hearne's edition of 'The Chronicle of King Edward IV' (originally published 1719 'at the end of his Edition of Sprott's Chronicle') p. 18.

67. *CPR*, 1467–1477, p. 538.
68. *CPR*, 1467–1477, p. 89.
69. *CPR*, 1467–1477, p. 108.
70. *CCR*, 1468–1476, no. 286.
71. *CPR*, 1467–1477, p. 151.
72. *CPR*, 1467–1477, p. 89.
73. *CPR*, 1467–1477, p. 184.

Chapter 10: Cecily's Sons in Conflict

1. Scofield, *Ed.IV*, vol 1, p. 417; Hicks, *False, Fleeting, Perjur'd Clarence – George, Duke of Clarence 1449–78,* Bangor 1992, p. 30 & note 98.
2. *CCR*, 1461–1468, pp. 456–57.
3. Scofield, *Ed.IV*, vol 1, p. 416.
4. Hardy / Wavrin, vol. 5, p. 543.
5. Searle, ed., *The Chronicle of John Stone*, p. 99.
6. Hardy / Wavrin, vol. 5, p. 543.
7. *Quant le comte de Warewic vey le duc de Clarence il luy fist tres grant chiere car il desiroit de parler a luy. Lequel duc recheut les ambaxadeurs moult honnourablement comme bien le scavoit faire.* Hardy / Wavrin, vol. 5, pp. 544–45.
8. Hardy / Wavrin, vol. 5, pp. 458–59.
9. Hardy / Wavrin, vol. 5, pp. 546–47.
10. Mary of York, born 11 August 1467.
11. This phrase in parenthesis is an instruction to the clerk.
12. 'speak of', deleted.
13. 'and I', deleted.
14. 'not sorry', deleted.
15. A. Crawford, ed., *The Household Books of John Howard, Duke of Norfolk, 1462–1471, 1481-1483*, Stroud 1992, part 1, 580–81. Evidence in respect of the date of the letter can be found in J. Ashdown-Hill, ' "Yesterday my Lord of Gloucester came to Colchester …"', *Essex Archaeology & History* 36, 2005, pp. 212–17, and J. Ashdown-Hill, *Richard III's 'Beloved Cousyn', John Howard and the House of York*, Stroud 2009, pp. 35–37.
16. Searle, ed., *The Chronicle of John Stone*, p. 103.
17. 'Feria' in medieval Latin usage means a weekday. 'Feria ii' is Monday, 'feria iii' is Tuesday, 'feria iiii' is Wednesday, 'feria v' is Thursday and 'feria vi' is Friday. Saturday, and Sunday (the first day of the week), had their own names.
18. The hour of none was about 3 p.m.
19. John Oxne was the Prior of Canterbury Cathedral Priory from 1468 to 1471. Searle, ed., *The Chronicle of John Stone*, p. 162.

20. *Item hoc anno vij*^{o} *die mensis Junii, viz. feria iiij*^{a} *in vigilia translacionis sancti Aelphegi martiris, venit Cantuariam dominus Georgius dux Clarencie ac frater Edwardi iiij*^{ti} *regis Anglie et ffrancie inter horam iiij*^{tam} *et v*^{tam} *post nonam, et receptus fuit ad hostium ecclesie a priore Johanne Oxne et conuentu in capis viridibus decenter indutis cum responsorio: Summe Trinitati. Et hic permansit per duas noctes in camera domini prioris cum magna familia; et feria vj*^{a} *sequente recessit a Cantuaria versus Sandwycum.* Searle, ed., *The Chronicle of John Stone*, p. 109.
21. *Item eodem die [9 June] venit Cantuariam [Geo. Neville] dominus archiepiscopus Eboracensis.* Searle, ed., *The Chronicle of John Stone*, p. 109.
22. Searle, ed., *The Chronicle of John Stone*, pp. 109–10.
23. *Item feria iiij*^{a} *venit Cantuariam ducissa Eboraci ac mater illustrissimi regis Edwardi iiij*^{ti}*, et iacuit in camera domini prioris, et tenuit eius (sic) sicut dux Clarencie, tamen non cum tanta familia. Et die sequente recessit a Cantuaria versus Sandwicum ad filium illius, videlicet ad ducem Clarencie; et feria ij*^{a} *sequente iterum reuenit Cantuariam. Et die sequente fuit in vesperis, et dominico die in summa missa et in ij*^{is} *vesperis, et feria ij*^{a} *recessit a Cantuaria.* Searle, ed., *The Chronicle of John Stone*, p. 110.
24. *Et feria iiij*^{ta} *sequente reuenit Cantuariam a Sandwico dominus Georgius dux Clarencie, [et] dominus comes de Warwyk, et die sequente recessit versus castellum de Queneborow.* Searle, ed., *The Chronicle of John Stone*, p. 110.
25. Searle, ed., *The Chronicle of John Stone*, pp. 110–11.
26. Society of Antiquaries, *A Collection of Ordinances and Regulations for the Government of the Royal Household, made in Divers Reigns from King Edward III to King William and Queen Mary*, London 1790, 'Ordinances of the Household of George Duke of Clarence', p. 98.
27. M. Hicks, *Anne Neville*, Stroud 2007, p. 71.
28. J. Laynesmith, *The Last Medieval Queens*, Oxford 2004, p. 201, citing Warkworth's Chronicle.
29. *ou ilz atendirent leurs gens, et tantost eurent nouvelles que ceulz du North estoient bien avant en pays.* Hardy / Wavrin, p. 579.
30. The battle of Edgecote Moor. The site was at Danes Moor in Northamptonshire (six miles northeast of Banbury) and the battle was fought on 26 July 1469.
31. H. Ellis, ed., *Three Books of Polydore Vergil's English History comprising the reigns of Henry VI, Edward IV, and Richard III*, 1844, p. 123. Rivers and his second son John were taken prisoners at Chepstow, and beheaded at Kenilworth on 12 August 1469.
32. J. Strachey, ed., *Rotuli Parliamentorum; ut et Petitiones, et Placita in Parliamento*, vol. 6, (*ab Anno Duodecimo R. Edwardi IV. ad Finem eiusdem Regni*), London 1777, p. 232.

33. Hardy / Wavrin, p. 581.
34. Hardy / Wavrin, p. 585.
35. *le roy en eut les nouvelles dont il fut moult desplaisant, si dist quil estoit trahy, et fist habillier tous ses gens pour aller audevant de son frere le duc de Clarence et son cousin de Warewic lesquelz venoient audevant de luy et estoient desja entre Warewic et Coventry ou ilz furent advertis que le roy venoit a lencontre deulz.... si nestoit pas a croire que son frère de Clarence ne son cousin de Warewic voulissent penser trahison a lencontre de sa personne; pourquoy le roy se traist en ung village prez et se loga illec atout ses gens non gueres loingz du lieu ou estoit logie le comte de Warewic. Environ heure de myenuit vint devers le roy larchevesque dYorc, grandement adcompaignie de gens de guerre, si buscha tout hault au logis du roy, dissant a ceulz qui gardoient son corpz quil luy estoit necessaire de parler au roy, auquel ilz le nuncherent; mais le roy luy fist dire quil reposoit et quil venist au matin de lors il le orroit voullentiers. De laquele responce larchevesque ne fut pas content, si renvoia les messages de rechief dire au roy que force estoit quil parlast a luy, comme ilz le firent, et alors le roy leur commanda quilz le laissassent entrer pour oyr quil diroit, car de luy en riens ne se doubtoit. Quant larchevesque fut entre en la chambre, ou il trouva le roy couchie il luy dist prestement : 'Sire levez vous', de quoy le roy se voult excuser, disant que il navoit ancores comme riens repose ; mais larchevesque comme faulz et desloyal quil estoit, luy dist la seconde fois : 'Il vous fault lever et venir devers mon frere de Warewic, car a ce ne povez vous contrester' Et lors le roy doubtant que pis ne luy en advenist se vesty et larchevesque lemmena sans faire grand bruit au lieu ou estoient ledit comte et le duc de Clarence entre Warewic et Coventry*. Hardy / Wavrin, pp. 584–86.
36. Bohn, *The Chronicles of the White Rose of York*, p. 112.
37. Hicks, *Anne Neville*, p. 74; P. M. Kendall, *Warwick the Kingmaker*, London 1957, 1973, p. 256.
38. *El Re Adoardo fece bandire pubblice Georgio de Plantageneti alias dux Clarentie suo fratelo, Ricardo Nevil alias conte de Varuhic, cum alcuni altri soi sequaci*. Milan State Archives, J. Calmette & G. Périnelle, *Louis XI et l'Angleterre*, Paris 1930, p. 312.

Chapter 11: The Blaybourne Bastardy Myth

1. No authentic trace of this surname seems to have been found in fifteenth-century English records, though the surname 'Blak(e)bourne' is on record (*CPR*, 1452–1461; *CPR*, 1461–1467).
2. J. Stevenson, ed., *Letters and papers illustrative of the Wars of the English in France during the reign of King Henry the Sixth, King of England*, vol. 1, London 1861, p. 79.

3. See, for example, A. Crawford, *The Yorkists*, London 2007, p. 173.
4. Armstrong / Mancini, p. 110, (note 12). I am grateful to Olga Hughes for drawing my attention to this.
5. *Questo Christianissimo signor Re ha novamente havuto adviso de una gran novita sequita in Inghilterra. Pare ch'el conte de Verruich, quale e uno possente et gran signore in quello paese, havendo data una sua figliola per moglie al duca di Clarenza, fratello del Re de Inghilterra, ha facta una certa inventiva con dire che prefato Re de Inghilterra e bastardo, ne a lui legittimamente pertiene la corona et la signoria, ma che de direto et debitamente perviene al prefato duca di Clarenza.* Calmette & Périnelle, *Louis XI et L'Angleterre*, pp. 306–07.
6. *Tres chier et tres amé oncle. Nostre tres chiere et tres amée cousine la royne d'Angleterre est nagueres venue par devers nous pour nous dire et remontrer les tres grans injures, inhumanitez et autres enormes exces, delitz, qui on esté et sont chascun jour faiz et commis par Edouart de la Marche, ses aliez et complices, a l'encontre de nostre tres chier et tres amé cousin Henry, roy d'Angleterre, leur souverain et naturel seigneur.* Calmette & Périnelle, *Louis XI et L'Angleterre*, pp. 282–83.
7. Madden, 'Political Poems of the reign of Henry VI and Edward IV', *Archaeologia*, vol. 29, London 1842, pp. 318—47 (p. 330).
8. Madden, 'Political Poems', pp. 331–32.
9. MS Trinity College, Dublin, D.4, 18.
10. Madden, 'Political Poems', p. 333.
11. Madden, 'Political Poems', pp. 333.
12. M. Jones, ed., Philippe de Commynes, *Memoirs*, Harmondsworth 1972, p. 249.
13. *Ibid.*
14. *Rotuli Parliamentorum*, vol. 6, pp. 193–95.
15. Armstrong / Mancini, pp. 60–61.
16. '*conceptus est in camera proxima capellas palacii de Hatfelde*'. T. Hearne, *Liber Niger Scaccarii nec non Wilhelmi Worcestrii Annales Rerum Anglicarum*, vol. 2, London 1774, p. 462.
17. Jones / Commynes, p. 89.
18. Ellis / Vergil, p. 183.
19. Ellis / Vergil, p. 184. (Present writer's italics.)
20. A.H. Thomas and I.D. Thomley, eds., *The Great Chronicle of London*, London 1938, pp. 231–32 (present writer's emphasis).
21. 1442 *Natus est Edwardus, filius secundus Ricardi, Ducis Eboraci, & heres, Rex Angliae & Franciae, XXVIII° die Aprilis, hora II post mediam noctem in mane diei Lunae, apud Rothomagum, qui conceptus est in camera proxima capellas palacii de Hatfelde.* T. Hearne, *Liber Niger Scaccarii nec non Wilhelmi Worcestrii Annales Rerum Anglicarum*, vol. 2, London 1774, p. 462.

22. *Natus est Dominus Edwardus, secundus filius illustrissimi principis Ricardi, &c. in civitate Rothomagensi, XXVII°. die mensis Aprilis, post meridiem, hora. XIIII. minut. XLV*[to]*. anno Domini M°. CCCCXLII. incompleto*. Hearne / William Worcester, Annales, p. 525.
23. M. Jones, *Bosworth, Psychology of a Battle*, London 2014, p. 79.
24. Stratford, *Edward the Fourth*, pp. 11–12.

Chapter 12: The Second Reign of Edward IV

1. Jones / Commynes, pp. 184–85.
2. Hicks, *Anne Neville*, p. 92.
3. J. Bruce, ed., *Historie of the Arrivall of Edward IV in England and the Final Recouerye of his Kingdomes from Henry VI A.D. M.CCCC.LXXI*, London 1838, p. 10.
4. Bruce, *Arrivall*, pp. 11–12.
5. Bruce, *Arrivall*, p. 17.
6. *... se loga a lhostel madame dYorck sa mere, et la oy le divin service ce jour et la nuit ensievant, car cestoit le Vendredi Saint*. Hardy / Wavrin, vol. 5, p. 659.
7. Bruce, *Arrivall*, p. 21.
8. Gardiner, *Paston Letters*, vol. 5, pp. 135–36.
9. H.T. Riley, ed., *Ingulph's Chronicle of the Abbey of Croyland*, London 1908, pp. 469–70.
10. *CPR*, 1467—1477, p. 361.
11. '... to Circeter, co. Gloucester, and from thence to Warwick', *CPR*, 1476–1485, p. 72.
12. *CPR*, 1476–1485, p. 72.
13. *CCR, 1468–1476*, no. 947.
14. *CPR*, 1467–1477, p. 447.
15. *CPR*, 1467–1477, p. 563.
16. For a fuller examination of John Howard's relationship with his lawyers see 'L.J.F. Ashdown-Hill, THESIS, section 4.12'.
17. W.A. Copinger, *The Manors of Suffolk*, 7 volumes, vol. 3 (Manchester: Taylor, Garnett, Evans & Co., 1909), p. 192.
18. BL, Add. MS 46349, f. 65r; *hhb*, part 1, p. 257.
19. L.J.F. Ashdown-Hill, THESIS, sections 1:7 and 3:4
20. BL, Add. MS 46349, f. 9r; *hhb*, part 1, p. 165.
21. BL, Add. MS 46349, f. 81r; *hhb*, part 1, p. 290.
22. BL, Add. MS 46349, f. 12r; *hhb*, part 1, p. 170.
23. Arundel Castle MS, f. 122v (p. 129); *hhb*, part 1, p. 583.

24. Arundel Castle MS, f. 27r; *hhb*, part 1, p. 486.
25. ERO, D/ Dce L63r and L64r. See above, subsection 4.13.1.
26. Soc. Ant. MS 77, f. 110v; *hhb*, part 2, p. 481.
27. Soc. Ant. MS 77, f. 114v; *hhb*, part 2, p. 488.
28. Horrox & Hammond, ed., *BL Harleian Manuscript 433*, vol. 1 (London: Richard III Society, 1979), p. 143.
29. A. Crawford, *Letters of Medieval Women*, Stroud 2002, pp. 133–34, citing *Transactions of the Essex Archaeological Society, new series, 5 (1895).*
30. 'late of London, with other' crossed out.
31. The meaning of this slightly oddly worded negative phrase seems to be that they had no option other than to enforce the laws.
32. ERO, D/ Dce L63r.
33. In the bond (below) he is named as Guy Fowler. The modern version of his name is Guy Fairfax. He appears in the Howard accounts and there is a separate entry for him under FAIRFAX below.
34. As we know from the draft bond issued by Catesby and Townshend, Pigot did not serve in this instance. His name is found in other contexts, however, and he was one of the serjeants-at-law confirmed in post by Warwick upon the restoration of Henry VI in 1470: N. Neilson, ed., *Year Books of Edward IV, 10 Edward IV and 49 Henry VI, AD 1470* (London: Selden Society, vol. 47, 1930), p. xiv. See L.J.F. Ashdown-Hill, THESIS, subsection 4.14.2.
35. Tentatively dated by the ERO to March 1475/6, but in the light of the preceding letter a date in March 1474 seems more likely: ERO, D/ DCe L64r.
36. ERO, D/ DCe L76.
37. For a comparable situation, L.J.F. Ashdown-Hill, THESIS, subsection 4.1.3.
38. Inexplicably, the index to *HHB* treats John Sulyard's surname as identical to that of Thomas Suward or Syward. There is, in fact, no connection.
39. See J. Ashdown-Hill, 'Yesterday my Lord of Gloucester came to Colchester …', *Essex History*, vol. 36 (2005), pp. 212–17.
40. Arundel Castle MS, f. 25v; *hhb*, part 1, p. 481.
41. Arundel Castle MS, f. 27r; *hhb*, part 1, p. 485.
42. Arundel Castle MS, f. 42r; *hhb*, part 1, p. 500.
43. Arundel Castle MS, f. 27r; *hhb*, part 1, p. 486.
44. Arundel Castle MS, f. 42r; *hhb*, part 1, p. 500.
45. Arundel Castle MS, f. 42v; *hhb*, part 1, p. 502.
46. Arundel Castle MS, f. 44r; *hhb*, part 1, p. 508.
47. See L.J.F. Ashdown-Hill, THESIS, subsection 4.14.1.
48. Arundel Castle MS, f. 45r; *hhb*, part 1, p. 510.
49. BL, Add. MS 46349, f. 139r; *hhb*, part 1, p. 402.

50. The previous *legisperitus* was John Grene, who seems to have held the post from 1463–1471 (perhaps until 1472, but there are gaps in the record). Prior to 1463 no information on Colchester *legisperiti* is available, and the post may, in fact, have been newly created in 1463.
51. See above, subsection 4.13.3.
52. The final bay, together with the south porch, was not built until after Sulyard's death. The work was completed by his widow, Ann Andrew(s), and her second husband, Sir Thomas Bourchier (whom Ann married in 1490).
53. R. Horrox & P.W. Hammond, eds., *British Library Harleian Manuscript 433*, vol. 3, *second register of Edward V and miscellaneous material*, (London: Richard III Society, 1982), p. 238 (f. 332r).
54. E. Foss, *A Biographical Dictionary of the Judges of England, 1066-1870* (London, 1870).
55. Foss, *Judges*.
56. Ashdown-Hill, THESIS, subsection 4.10.1, citing R. Virgeo, 'The Murder of James Andrew: Suffolk Faction in the 1430s', *PSIAH*, vol. 34 part 4 (1980), pp. 263–68.
57. Foss, *Judges*.
58. *Lo ducha de Lenchastre* [*sic* = Gloucester] *quale per forza ha tolto per sua mogliere la figliula del quondam conte de Varviche, quale era maritata al principe de Ghales, stava in continua preparation de Guerra contra el duca de Clerens, el quale per haverli lo Re Odoardo suo fratello promesso lo contato de Vaviche, no voleva che l'altro l'havesse per casone del matrimonipo de decta figliuola de esso conte*. Calmette & Périnelle, *Louis XI et l'Angleterre*, p. 340.
59. Gairdner, *Paston Letters*, vol. 5, p. 199.
60. Hammond & Sutton, *Richard III, The Road to Bosworth* (hereinafter *Road*), p. 58, citing T. Hearne, ed., *A Remarkable Fragment of an Old English Chronicle*, Oxford 1715, p. 304.
61. *CPR*, 1467–1477, p. 439.
62. *CPR*, 1476–1485, p. 278.
63. Gairdner, *Paston Letters*, vol, 5, p. 236.
64. *CPR*, 1467–1477, p. 584.
65. *CPR*, 1467–1477, p. 599.
66. F. Sandford, *A Genealogical History of the Kings and Queens of England*, London 1707, pp. 391–92.
67. TNA, PSO 1/43; TNA, PSO 1/44; TNA, C 81/857; TNA, C 81/858; TNA, C 81/859.
68. C.L. Kingsford, ed., *The Stonor Letters and Papers 1290–1483*, 2 volumes, London 1919, vol. 2, p. 14.

69. Kingsford / Stonor, vol. 1, p. 117.
70. *CPR*, 1476–1485, p. 44.
71. A. & J. Nicoll, eds, *Holinshed's Chronicle as used in Shakespeare's Plays*, London 1927, p. 138.
72. *Et quia erat quaedam prophetia, quod post E. id est, post Edwardum quartum, G regnaret, sub hoc ambiguo Georgius dux Clarentiae, medus amborum fratrum Edwardi et Ricardi regum, dux ob hoc Georgius peremptus est.* T. Hearne, ed., *Joannis Rossi Antiquarii Warwicensis Historia Regum Angliae*, London 1716, p. 215.
73. Questioned under torture, Stacy reportedly confessed to having attempted to bring about the death of the king and his eldest son by the use of the black arts, and admitted casting their horoscopes to ascertain the likely dates of their deaths.
74. Mancini, pp. 62–63.
75. For a full account see Ashdown-Hill, *The Third Plantagenet*, chapter 12.
76. Thomas Blake was also initially condemned to death, but later pardoned.
77. *Harl. 433*, 3, 108; J. Gairdner, ed., *Letters and Papers illustrative of the Reigns of Richard III and Henry VII*, 2 vols., vol. 1, London 1861, p. 68; my emphasis.
78. See Ashdown-Hill & Carson, 'The Execution of the Earl of Desmond', *Ric.* 15 (2005), pp. 70–93.
79. In the following century something similar occurred in the case of Anne Boleyn. She was accused of witchcraft (among other things), and was therefore sentenced to be burned to death – albeit with the proviso that the king could commute her sentence to beheading.
80. *Oudit an LXXVII, advint ou royaume d'Angleterre que pour ce que le roy Edouard dudit royaume fut acertené que ung sien frère, qui estoit duc de Clairence, avoit intencion de passer la mer et aler descendre en Flandres pour donner aide et secours à sa seur duchesse en Bourgongne, vesve dudit defunct le derrenier duc, fist icellui roy Edouard prendre et constituer prisonnier sondit frère et mettre prisonnier en la tour de Londres, où il fut depuis détenu prisonnier par certaine longue espace de temps pendant lequel ledit roy Edouart assembla son conseil, et par la deliberacion d'icellui fut condempné à estre mené depuis ladicte tour de Londres traynant sur ses fesses jusques au gibet de ladicte ville de Londres, et ilec estre ouvert et ses entrailles gecter dedens ung feu, et puis lui copper le col et mettre le corps en quatre quartiers. Mais depuis, par la grant prière et requeste de la mere desdiz Edouard et de Clairence fut sa condampnacion changée et muée, tellement que, ou moys de Février oudit an, icellui de Clairance estant prisonnier en ladicte tour, fut prins et tiré de sadicte prison, et après qu'il ot esté confessé, fut mis et bouté tout vif dedens une queue de Malevoisye defonsée par l'un des boutz, la teste en bas, et y demoura jusques à ce qu'il eust rendu l'esperit, et puis fut tire dehors et lui fut le col coppé,*

et après ensevely et porté enterrer à .... avecques sa femme, jadis fille du conte de Waruik, qui mourut à la journée de Coventry avecques le prince de Galles, filz du saint roy Henry d'Angleterre, de Lancastre. B. de Mandrot, ed., *Journal de Jean de Roye 1460-1483, connu sous le non de Chronique Scandaleuse*, vol. 2, Paris 1846, pp. 63–64. Interestingly, de Roye's account, written from a Continental viewpoint, assumed that the prime cause of George's death was his desire to intervene in Burgundian politics on behalf of his sister, Margaret.

81. John Rous, using the English calendar then in use (according to which 1478 did not begin until 25 March) ascribed Clarence's death and burial to February 1477.
82. J. Ashdown-Hill, 'Norfolk Requiem: the Passing of the House of Mowbray', *Ricardian*, vol. XII (March 2001), pp. 198–217 (p. 205).
83. http://en.wikipedia.org/wiki/Henry_Holland,_3rd_Duke_of_Exeter (consulted March 2017).
84. http://en.wikipedia.org/wiki/Drowning-pit (consulted March 2017).
85. Gairdner, *Richard the Third*, Cambridge 1898, pp. 32–33, fn. 2.
86. '*Regina … estimavit nunquam prolem suam ex rege iam susceptam regnaturam, nisi dux Clarentie aufferretur: quod et ipsi regi facile persuasit. … Condemnatus fuit: et ultimo supplicio affectus. Supplicii autem genus illud placuit, ut in dolium mollissimi falerni mersus vitam cum morte commutaret*'. Mancini, pp. 62–63. Mancini states at the end of his text that he finished writing it on 1 December 1483.
87. J.B. Sheppard, ed., *Christ Church Letters*, London 1877, pp. 36–37, cited in *FFPC*, p. 128.
88. *CPR*, 1476–1485, p. 143.
89. But see other references to him as a servant of Cecily herself.
90. *CPR*, 1476–1485, p. 218.
91. Halsted, *Richard III*, Vol. 2, Appendix C (pp. 513-14), citing Cott. MS. Vitel. L. fol. 17.
92. 'Benedictine oblates do not take any vows. An oblate makes a promise, not a vow'. http://www.oblatespring.com/oblatespring0201oblatedetail.htm (consulted February 2017).
93. Soc. Ant. MS 76, f. 114r; *HHB*, part 2, p. 159.
94. Variant spellings of the surname include Hobard, Hobert, Hubbard, Hubberd, and Hubert. Unless otherwise attributed, the source in respect of James Hobart is J.B. Weller, 'The Wives of Sir James Hobart (1440–1517), Attorney General 1486–1507', *Ric.*12, no. 152 (March 2001), pp. 218–248.
95. Soc. Ant. MS 76, f. 136v; *HHB*, part 2, p. 192.
96. Scofield, *Ed.IV*, vol. 2, pp. 299-300.
97. *CPR*, 1476–1485, p. 283.

98. *CPR*, 1476–1485, p. 227.
99. *CPR*, 1476–1485, p. 269.
100. *CCR*, *1476–1485*, no. 862.
101. *CPR*, 1476–1485, p. 292.
102. *CPR*, 1476–1485, p. 337.
103. R. Horrox, 'Financial Memoranda of the Reign of Edward V', *Camden Miscellany*, vol. 29, London 1987, pp. 197–244 (p. 233). Horrox's title of this publication is somewhat misleading. The earlier description assigned to the source manuscript by the Historical Manuscripts Commission in the nineteenth century, which described it as 'a book of the customs received at various ports in the reigns of Edward IV and Edward V' was more accurate.

Chapter 13: The Accession of Richard III

1. Sandford, *A Genealogical History of the Kings and Queens of England*, p. 387.
2. Armstrong / Mancini, p. 59.
3. J. Ashdown-Hill, *The Dublin King*, Stroud 2014, pp. 34–37.
4. Soc. Ant., MS 77, f. 52r; *HHB*, part 2, p. 378. The messenger who brought the letter received half a gold angel.
5. Soc. Ant., MS 77, f. 53r; *HHB*, part 2, p. 383.
6. Soc. Ant., MS 77, f. 53r; *HHB*, part 2, p. 383. Howard certainly seems to have been in a hurry. His journeys to the capital were usually slower, with more frequent stops.
7. N. Pronay & J. Cox, eds, *The Crowland Chronicle Continuations 1459–1486* (hereinafter *Cr. Chr.*), London 1986, p. 153.
8. J. Ashdown-Hill, *The Private Life of Edward IV*, Stroud 2016, pp. 166–67.
9. Pronay & Cox, *Cr. Chr.*, p. 151 (written 1486); Great Chronicle of London (as cited – but not QUOTED in respect of the DATE – in K. Dockray, *Edward IV, a source book*, Stroud 1999, p. 146); H. Ellis, ed., R. Fabyan, *The New Chronicles of England and France*, London 1811, p. 667 (Fabyan died circa 1512, however, his Chronicle, as published concludes with the year 1540 – so it appears not to be contemporary.); C.L. Kingsford, ed., *Chronicles of London*, Oxford 1905, pp. 189, 278 (Vitellius A XVI – not contemporary – the Chronicle continues to the end of the reign of Henry VII); E. Hall, *Chronicle*, London 1809, p. 341 (published 1548; 1550 – so not contemporary).
10. L. Lyell & F.D.Watney, eds, *Acts of Court of the Mercers' Company 1453–1527*, Cambridge 1936, p. 146.
11. R. Davies, *Extracts from the Municipal Records of the City of York during the Reigns of Edward IV, Edward V and Richard III*, London 1843, pp. 142, 143, and footnote.

12. Armstrong / Mancini, p. 59.
13. Hence its assertion that the reign of his son, Edward V, lasted two months and eight days: *Obitus Edwardi V^ti^ xxij^o^ mens [sic* for *mensis] Junij regnavit ij menses et viij^o^ dies set non coronatus fuit occisus et nemo s[c]it ubi sepultus.* [The death of Edward V: 22 of the month of June, he reigned 2 months and 8 days but was not crowned, he was killed, and no one knows where he was buried.] However, that (and other claims of the Anlaby Cartulary in respect of dates) is very dubious. Fitzwilliam Museum, Cambridge, Ms. 329, f. 7r.
14. Edward specified in his will that he should be buried at St George's Chapel, in the spot which he had identified to the Bishop of Salisbury: A.F. Sutton and L. Visser-Fuchs, with R.A. Griffiths, *The Royal Funerals of the House of York at Windsor*. London 2005, p. 96.
15. Sutton *et al.*, *Royal Funerals*, p. 11.
16. The sources are unclear, stating 'Wednesday 17 April', which is impossible: Sutton *et al.*, *Royal Funerals*, p. 35, n. 243. However, on p. 14 Sutton *et al.* nevertheless repeat the impossible date of 'Wednesday 17 April', and subsequent errors in their chronology ensue.
17. John de la Pole, the eldest son of Edward's sister, Elizabeth of York, Duchess of Suffolk.
18. 'as the nyght weyned': Sutton *et al.*, *Royal Funerals*, p. 37, citing College of Arms, MS I.7, ff. 7–8v.
19. Armstrong / Mancini, p. 120, n. 63.
20. Armstrong / Mancini, p. 71; Pronay & Cox, *Cr. Chr.*, pp. 154–55.
21. Pronay & Cox, *Cr. Chr.*, pp. 154–55.
22. Kendall, *R3*, p. 164.
23. R. Edwards, *The Itinerary of King Richard III*, London 1983, p. 1.
24. Pronay & Cox, *Cr. Chr.*, pp. 154–55.
25. Kendall, *R3*, pp. 164, 173; Edwards, *Itinerary R3*, p. 1.
26. According to the Crowland chronicler, Buckingham and Gloucester met at Northampton. Pronay & Cox, *Cr. Chr.*, pp. 154–55.
27. Ashdown-Hill, *Richard III's 'Beloved Cousyn'*, p.86.
28. J. Ashdown-Hill, 'The Go-Between', *Ricardian*, vol. 15, 2005, pp. 119–21.
29. Kendall, *R3*, p. 178. The French threat accounts for Edward Woodville's sailing, but the fact that he took with him a significant part of the contents of the royal treasury is more dubious.
30. Kendall, *R3*, p. 179. The Crowland chronicler says 'the following night', which could conceivably mean the night of 1–2 May.
31. Hammond & Sutton, *Road*, p. 99; Pronay & Cox, *Cr. Chr.*, pp. 156–57.
32. J. Ashdown-Hill, *The Third Plantagenet*, Stroud 2014, plate 2.

33. Armstrong / Mancini, p. 121, citing *Registrum Thome Bourgchier*, pp. 52–3.
34. For details of the council meeting, see Ashdown-Hill, *Richard III's 'Beloved Cousyn'*, p. 93.
35. Hammond & Sutton, *Road*, pp. 102-03, citing *Facsimiles of National Manuscripts*, part 1, Southampton 1865, item 53.
36. There is no evidence for the claim which was put forward later (for example, by Vergil), to the effect that the sermons focussed on the bastardy myth in respect of Edward IV.
37. Armstrong / Mancini, p. 97.
38. *CCR*, 1476–1485, no. 1170.
39. Edwards, *Itinerary R3*, p. 4. Carson states (*R3MK*, p. 99) that Richard was actually residing at his rented accommodation: Crosby's Place, but using his mother's home as his headquarters.
40. See chapter 14 of *Beloved Cousyn*.
41. A.F. Sutton & P.W. Hammond, *The Coronation of Richard III – the Extant Documents*, Gloucester 1983, p. 92, citing Great Warbrobe Accounts, f.12b.
42. Sutton & Hammond, *The Coronation of Richard III*, p. 404, citing Great Warbrobe Accounts, ff.109 & 111.
43. Sutton & Hammond, *The Coronation of Richard III*, pp. 167; 169, citing Great Warbrobe Accounts, ff.109 & 111.
44. For a full exploration of the relevant evidence, see Ashdown-Hill, *Richard III's 'Beloved Cousyn'*, chapter 12, and / or Ashdown-Hill, *The Dublin King*, chapter 3. Also see Ashdown-Hill's forthcoming study of the mythology of the so-called 'Princes in the Tower'.
45. In 1484 Frenchman, Thomas Basin, reported a plot by a number of Londoners in favour of the sons of Edward IV. The sixteenth-century chronicler, John Stow, also speaks of a plot to abduct Edward V and his brother by setting off incendiary diversions in the neighbourhood of the Tower of London.
46. *CPR*, 1476–1485, p. 464.
47. *CPR*, 1476–1485, p. 374.
48. *CPR*, 1476–1485, p. 459.
49. *CPR*, 1476–1485, p. 441.
50. Horrox & Hammond, eds., *Harl. MS 433*, vol. 1, p. 3 (punctuation modernised). There is no year date given in the letter itself, but the only occasion when Richard III was at Pontefract in June was in 1484: Edwards, *Itinerary R3*, p. 20.
51. Horrox & Hammond, eds., *Harl. MS 433*, vol. 3, p. 194 (figures modernised).
52. *CPR*, 1476–1485, p. 522.
53. Edwards, *Itinerary R3*, p. 36.

Chapter 14: The Reign of Henry VII

1. Society of Antiquaries (hereinafter SoA), *A Collection of Ordinances and Regulations for the Government of the Royal Household, made in Divers Reigns from King Edward III to King William and Queen Mary*, London 1790, 'Orders and Rules of the House of the Princess Cecill, Mother of King Edward IV', p. 37. ('From a Collection of Papers, which formerly belonged to Sir Julius Caesar; now at the Board of GreenCloth, St. James's'.)
2. For example, the anonymous author of *The Cloud of Unknowing*.
3. https://en.wikisource.org/wiki/Caxton,_William_(DNB00) (consulted February 2017).
4. W. Hone, ed., *The Apocryphal New Testament*, London 1820, pp. 17–37 (full text, translated); M.R James, ed., *The Apocryphal New Testament*, Oxford 1924, pp. 70–79 (summary).
5. Fr. Gilbert, O.F.M.Cap., *What to see in Walsingham*, Walsingham 1948, p. 32.
6. http://www.sacred-texts.com/chr/lots/lots089.htm (consulted February 2017).
7. The Catholic Encyclopedia notes that 'Thalhofer (Liturgik, I, 633) inclines to the opinion that in the passages of Belethus (xxxix), Sicardus (III, iv), Innocent III (De myst. Alt., II, xlvi), and Durandus (V, ii, 13), which are usually appealed to in proof of this, these authors have in mind the small cross made upon the forehead or external objects, in which the hand moves naturally from right to left, and not the big cross made from shoulder to shoulder. Still, a rubric in a manuscript copy of the York Missal clearly requires the priest when signing himself with the paten to touch the left shoulder after the right'. http://www.newadvent.org/cathen/13785a.htm (consulted May 2017). I am grateful to Valerie Quinlivan for drawing this reference to my attention.
8. J.H. Blunt, ed., *The Myroure of Oure Ladye*, London 1873, p. 80.
9. SoA, 'Orders and Rules of the House of the Princess Cecill, Mother of King Edward IV', pp. 38–39.
10. On Saturday 1 February 1465/6, for example, they ate beef, mutton and rabbit: BL, Add. MS 46349, f. 156r; *HHB*, part 1, p. 435.
11. M.K. Dale & V.B. Redstone, eds., *The Household Book of Dame Alice de Bryene of Acton Hall, Suffolk, September 1412–September 1413*, Ipswich 1931, pp. 1–3.
12. Bohn, *The Chronicles of the White Rose of York*, p. 3. Hearne's edition had been published in 1719.
13. Bohn, *The Chronicles of the White Rose of York*, pp. 3–4.
14. *Rotuli Parliamentorum*, vol. 6, p. 289.
15. 'One is left with the impression that the duchess of Norfolk, in addition to wishing to extend Eleanor's endowment in order to create a second scholarship,

and to include prayers for herself and other members of the family, also had a desire to leave some record, however obliquely worded, of facts about her sister which could not easily be voiced in 1495 and which she knew were being deliberately confused and concealed elsewhere.' J. Ashdown-Hill, 'The Endowments of Lady Eleanor Talbot and of Elizabeth Talbot, Duchess of Norfolk, at Corpus Christi College Cambridge', *The Ricardian* vol. 14, 2004, pp. 82–94 (p. 92).

16. *CPR*, 1485–1494, p. 62.
17. *CPR*, 1485–1494, p. 127.
18. *CPR*, 1485–1494, pp. 142 & 160.
19. N.H. Nicolas, *Privy Purse Expenses of Elizabeth of York*, London 1830, p. lxxi.
20. Nicolas, *Privy Purse Expenses of Elizabeth of York*, p. lxxiii.
21. *CPR*, 1485–1494, p. 189.
22. *CPR*, 1485–1494, p. 236.
23. *CPR*, 1485–1494, p. 256.
24. *CPR*, 1485–1494, p. 270.
25. *CPR*, 1485–1494, p. 291.
26. *CPR*, 1485–1494, p. 369.
27. *CPR*, 1485–1494, pp. 369–70.
28. Kingsford, ed., *Chronicles of London*, p. 204.
29. Kingsford, ed., *Chronicles of London*, p. 204.
30. Kingsford, ed., *Chronicles of London*, p. 205.

Chapter 15: Cecily's Bequests, and what they Reveal

1. J. Nicholls and J. Bruce, eds., *Wills from Doctors' Commons. A selection of Wills of eminent persons proved in the PCC 1495–1695*, Camden old series, vol. 83, London 1863, pp. 1–8. Notes inserted in that earlier published version are included here in inverted commas (see below, notes 2-14).
2. 'The body of Richard Duke of York, (slain at the battle of Wakefield Dec. 31, 1460,) having been first buried at Pontefract, was solemnly removed to Fotheringay in July 1466'.
3. 'Margaret Countess of Richmond and Derby'.
4. 'Afterwards Henry VIII'.
5. ' = albs'.
6. 'Bridget, Cecil, Anne, and Katharine were her granddaughters, the daughters of King Edward IV.
7. 'Her daughter Elizabeth, widow of John de la Pole Duke of Suffolk, who died in 1491; or else the wife of the Duke mentioned in the next note, Margaret, daughter of Richard Lord Scrope'. [*sic – Elizabeth of York Duchess of Suffolk died in 1503 – this must be her.*]

8. 'Her grandson Edmund de la Pole, Duke of Suffolk'. [*Presumably correct, because John de la Pole, Duke of Suffolk, had died in about 1491.*]
9. 'Her grandson Humphrey de la Pole, who was a priest'.
10. 'There was no William de la Pole. Can William Stourton the husband of her grand-daughter Katharine de la Pole be intended? From the order in which the name occurs it seems not improbable'.
11. 'Anne de la Pole, mentioned by Dugdale as a nun of Syon. *The Revelations of St Bridget* was a gift peculiarly suitable to a member of that community'.
12. ' "Cloth of doth" in the register'.
13. 'Dutch?'
14. 'Margaret daughter of Sir Robert Whitingham was the wife of Sir John Verney. Her will dated 1505 is printed in the Verney Papers, 1853, p. 39'.
15. J & E Brown, 'The de la Poles, Earls and Dukes of Suffolk', Wingfield 2000, p. 7.
16. http://quod.lib.umich.edu/cgi/m/mec/med-idx?type=medhb&q1=portuos&rgn1=quote&operator1=And&q2=&rgn2=quote&operator2=And&q3=&rgn3=quote&qsort=alpha&size=First+100 (consulted September 2016).
17. Laynesmith, *The Last Medieval Queens*, p. 213.
18. A.F. Sutton and L. Visser-Fuchs, *The Hours of Richard III*, Stroud 1990, p. 39.
19. Sutton and L. Visser-Fuchs, *The Hours of Richard III*, p. 4.
20. Sutton and L. Visser-Fuchs, *The Hours of Richard III*, p. 39.
21. Edwards, *Itinerary R3.*
22. TNA, prob 11/11/458 f. 200r. I am grateful to Marie Barnfield for drawing my attention to Lessy's will, throughout which 'my Lady' refers to the Duchess of York.
23. Ashdown-Hill, THESIS, section 4.5.
24. H. Kleineke, 'Gerard von Wesel's newsletter from England, 17 April 1471', *Ric.*16 (2006), pp. 66–83 (p. 80).
25. N. Davis, *Paston Letters and Papers of the Fifteenth Century*, vol. 2, p. 406.
26. Gloucester probably came to Colchester in 1467, and he was probably accommodated at the abbey: J. Ashdown-Hill, 'Yesterday my Lord of Gloucester came to Colchester', *Essex History*, 2005.
27. See D. Baldwin, *The Lost Prince*, Stroud 2007
28. It was probably at the time of Henry VII's visit to Colchester that the official record for the year 1483 in the Colchester Oath Book was edited, to remove a reference to Edward V as a bastard. See Ashdown-Hill, *The Dublin King*, Stroud 2014, pp. 48–50.
29. R.F. Hunnisett, *The Medieval Coroner* (Cambridge: CUP, 1961, reprinted Florida 1986), p. 37.

30. J.C. Cox, *The Sanctuaries and Sanctuary Seekers of Mediaeval England* (London: Allen, 1911), p. 197.
31. *CPR 1452–1461*, p. 80.

Chapter 16: Cecily's DNA and her Dental Record

1. Ashdown-Hill, *The Last Days of Richard III*, chapter 11.
2. *Ibid.*
3. TNA, prob 11/11/458, f. 200v.
4. Sandford, *A Genealogical History of the Kings and Queens of England*, p. 392.
5. Joy Ibsen, 2 July 2004.
6. B. Sykes, *The Seven Daughters of Eve*, London 2001, pp. 260; 272.
7. M.A. Rushton, 'The Teeth of Anne Mowbray'. *British Dental Journal*, no. 119, 1965, pp. 335–39.
8. Rushton, 'The Teeth of Anne Mowbray', pp. 355–36.
9. Rushton, 'The Teeth of Anne Mowbray', p. 358.
10. Rushton, 'The Teeth of Anne Mowbray', p. 358.
11. E.g. by Dr Jean Ross; see R. Drewett and M. Redhead, *The Trial of Richard III*, Gloucester 1984, p. 66.
12. From Sixtus IV, St Peter's, Rome, 12 May 1477, 'To Edward King of England. Dispensation at the petition of the king, and also of his son, Richard, Duke of York, of the diocese of Coventry and Lichfield, and Anne de Mowbray of the diocese of Norwich, infants, for the said Richard and Anne, who have completed their fifth and fourth years of age, respectively (*sic*) to contract espousals forthwith, and as soon as they reach the lawful age, to contract marriage, notwithstanding that they are related in the third and fourth degree of kindred': *Calendar of Papal Registers – Papal Letters 1471–1484*, vol. 13, part 1, London 1955, p. 236.
13. A. Rai, 'Richard III – the final act', *British Dental Journal,* no. **214, 2013**, pp. 415–417.
14. Rai states (p. 415) that 'in 1483 Richard III succeeded his nephew, Edward V to the throne', whereas in reality the Three Estates of the Realm decreed that Edward V had never been king, so that in terms of regnal chronology Richard III actually succeeded Edward IV. Rai also suggests that the loss of Richard's upper left central incisor might have been due to a battle injury, a suggestion which was later denied by the University of Leicester.

Appendix 1: Alphabetical List of the Manors granted by Edward IV to his mother in 1461

1. In the *CPR* the place name is listed as 'Criche'.
2. In the *CPR* the place name is listed as 'Gussecho Bowne'.

3. In the *CPR* the place name is listed as 'Berdesfeld'.
4. In the *CPR* the place name is listed as 'Latcheley'.
5. Listed in the *CPR* as Worthy-mortymer.
6. Listed in the *CPR* as Mawardyn.
7. Moved to Cambridgeshire in 1965.
8. Listed in the *CPR* as Grandysdon.
9. The original text of 1461 reads 'Finner'. The historical name was 'Mere-Fina' meaning 'Pool frequented by Woodpeckers'. http://www.shelswellparishes.info/finmere/finmerehistory/history/books/millennium/CHPT03.pdf (consulted August 2016).
10. Possibly this refers to Drayton House, Guildford. Alternatively, maybe it means West Drayton, Middlesex.
11. Possibly Wootton Rivers?

Appendix 2: Members of the Entourage of Cecily Neville

1. *CPR*, 1467–1477, pp. 113, 271, 290, 619, 627; *CCR*, 1468–1476, pp. 417–18, no. 1496.
2. *CPR*, 1476–1485, p. 217.
3. *CCR*, 1476–1485, p. 373, no. 1272; Horrox & Hammond, eds., *Harl. MS 433*, vol. 1, p. 164.
4. Horrox & Hammond, eds., *Harl. MS 433*, vol. 1, p. 108.
5. Horrox & Hammond, eds., *Harl. MS 433*, vol. 1, p. 241.
6. *CCR*, 1476–1485, p. 314, no. 1061; *CPR*, 1476–1485, p. 372; Horrox & Hammond, eds., *Harl. MS 433*, vol. 1, p. 101, vol. 3, p. 198.
7. *CPR*, 1476–1485, p. 274.
8. Horrox & Hammond, eds., *Harl. MS 433*, vol. 4, p. 38.
9. *CCR*, 1476–1485, pp. 291; 341, nos. 981;1152.
10. Horrox & Hammond, eds., *Harl. MS 433*, vol. 1, p. 194.
11. Horrox & Hammond, eds., *Harl. MS 433*, vol. 1, p. 219.
12. Sutton & Hammond, *The Coronation of Richard III*, p. 320, citing PCC.1 Milles
13. C. Ross, *Edward IV*, London 1974, p. 7, and citing *CPR*, 1467–77, p. 439.
14. *CPR*, 1476–85, p. 411.
15. Sutton & Hammond, *The Coronation of Richard III*, p. 322.
16. *CPR*, 1452–1461, p. 572; also Gairdner, *Paston Letters*, vol. 3, p. 199. However, in the Paston records John's name is mistakenly listed as 'Thomas Clay'.
17. *CPR*, 1452–1461, p. 537.
18. *CPR*, 1461–1467, p. 92.
19. Gairdner, *Paston Letters*, vol, 4, p. 83.

20. *CPR*, 1461–1467, p. 294.
21. *CPR*, 1461–1467, p. 436.
22. https://en.wikipedia.org/wiki/Sir_John_Clay (consulted September 2016).
23. https://en.wikipedia.org/wiki/Sir_John_Clay (consulted August 2016).
24. *CCR*, 1476–1485, pp. 330, no. 1116.
25. *CCR*, 1476–1485, pp. 412, no. 1391.
26. *CCR*, 1476–1485, pp. 303, no. 1027.
27. Horrox & Hammond, eds., *Harl. MS 433*, vol. 3, p. 11.
28. *CCR*, 1476–1485, p. 313, no. 1055.
29. *CCR*, 1476–1485, p. 334, no. 1137.
30. *CPR*, 1461–1467, p. 6.
31. *CPR*, 1467–1477, p. 398.
32. *CPR*, 1467–1477, p. 524.
33. *CPR*, 1467–1477, p. 533.
34. *CPR*, 1467–1477, p. 629.
35. *CPR*, 1467–1477, pp. 109, 110.
36. *CPR*, 1467–1477, p. 177.
37. *CPR*, 1467–1477, p. 337.
38. *CPR*, 1476–1485, pp. 353, 395.
39. *CPR*, 1476–1485, pp. 424, 427, 478, 527.
40. *CPR*, 1476–1485, pp. 387, 498.
41. *CCR*, 1476–1485, p. 12, no. 38.
42. *CCR*, 1476–1485, pp. 172, no. 606.
43. *CPR*, 1476–1485, p. 30.
44. *CPR*, 1476–1485, p. 374.
45. *CCR*, 1476–1485, pp. 137–39, no. 479.
46. Horrox & Hammond, eds., *Harl. MS 433*, vol. 1, p. 259.
47. *CCR*, 1476–1485, pp. 27, no. 92.
48. *CPR*, 1485–1494, p. 220.
49. https://en.wikipedia.org/wiki/Henry_Heydon (consulted September 2016).
50. *CCR*, 1476–1485, p. 13, no. 42.
51. *CCR*, 1476–1485, p. 157, no. 545; p. 172, no. 606.
52. *CPR*, 1476–1485, pp. 110, 112.
53. *CPR*, 1476–1485, p. 223.
54. *CPR*, 1476–1485, p. 343.
55. *CPR*, 1476–1485, p. 353.
56. *CPR*, 1476–1485, p. 393.
57. *CPR*, 1476–1485, p. 397.

58. *CPR*, 1476–1485, p. 490.
59. *CPR*, 1476–1485, p. 416; Horrox & Hammond, eds., *Harl. MS 433*, vol. 1, p. 160.
60. For more on John Howard see Ashdown-Hill, THESIS, and *Richard III's 'Beloved Cousyn'*.
61. *CCR*, 1476–1485, p. 67, no. 217.
62. *CPR*, 1476–1485, p. 175.
63. *CPR*, 1476–1485, p. 196.
64. *CPR*, 1476–1485, p. 228.
65. Sutton & Hammond, *The Coronation of Richard III*, pp. 20, 23 (citing *Stonor Letters* vol. 2, 161).
66. *CPR*, 1476–1485, p. 218.
67. *CPR*, 1476–1485, p. 278.
68. *CPR*, 1476–1485, p. 303; *CCR*, 1476–1485, p. 256, no. 862.
69. *CCR*, 1476–1485, p. 256, no. 862.
70. NCC, will register, Caston, 125. www.girders.net/Les/Lessy,%20Henry,%20of%20Baketon,%20(fl.1482).docx (consulted February 2017).
71. *CPR*, 1476–1485, p. 369.
72. *Ibid.*
73. I. Arthurson, *The Perkin Warbeck Conspiracy*, Stroud 1997, p. 87.
74. Arthurson, *The Perkin Warbeck Conspiracy*, p. 75 (citing Armstrong, *England, France and Burgundy*, pp. 154, 156) & p. 87..
75. http://www.merriam-webster.com/dictionary/misprision (consulted September 2016).
76. Arthurson, *The Perkin Warbeck Conspiracy*, p. 85.
77. *CPR*, 1485–1494, p. 291.
78. *CCR*, 1476–1485, p. 149, no. 508.
79. *CPR*, 1476–1485, p. 168.
80. *CPR*, 1476–1485, p. 577.
81. Horrox & Hammond, eds., *Harl. MS 433*, vol. 1, p. 122.
82. Horrox & Hammond, eds., *Harl. MS 433*, vol. 3, pp. 161, 163, 164.
83. *CPR*, 1461–1467, p. 51.
84. *CPR*, 1476–1485, p. 374; Horrox & Hammond, eds., *Harl. MS 433*, vol. 1, pp. 97–98.
85. Horrox & Hammond, eds., *Harl. MS 433*, vol. 2, p. 196.
86. *CPR*, 1476–1485, p. 369.
87. *CPR*, 1476–1485, p. 105.
88. *CPR*, 1476–1485, p. 218.
89. *CPR*, 1476–1485, p. 515.
90. CCR, 1476-1485, pp. 138, 143, 303, nos. 479, 492, 1027.

91. *CPR*, 1476–1485, p. 186.
92. Sutton & Hammond, *The Coronation of Richard III*, p. 65.
93. Sutton & Hammond, *The Coronation of Richard III*, p. 393, citing G.W., f. 60.
94. *CPR*, 1476–1485, p. 223.
95. *CPR*, 1476–1485, p. 313.
96. *CPR*, 1476–1485, p. 263.
97. Horrox & Hammond, eds., *Harl. MS 433*, vol. 4, p. 195.
98. Horrox & Hammond, eds., *Harl. MS 433*, vol. 2, p. 185.
99. *CCR*, 1476–1485, p. 56, no. 177.
100. *CCR*, 1476–1485, pp. 291; 341, nos. 981;1152.
101. H. Verney, *Letters and Papers of the Verney Family*, London 1853, p. 5.
102. *Op. cit.*
103. *CPR*, 1476–1485, p. 182.
104. *CCR*, 1476–1485, p. 285, no. 963.
105. *CPR*, 1476–1485, p. 463.
106. *CPR*, 1476–1485, p. 395.
107. *CCR*, 1476–1485, p. 353, no. 1195.
108. *CCR*, 1476–1485, pp. 390–91, no. 1326.
109. *CPR*, 1476–1485, pp. 399, 488.
110. *CPR*, 1476–1485, p. 527.
111. *CPR*, 1476–1485, p. 525.
112. *CPR*, 1476–1485, p. 136.

Appendix 3: The Fifteenth-century Abbots of Colchester

1. VCH, *Essex*, vol. 2.
2. *CPR 1461–1467*, p. 33 names the abbot of Colchester as JOHN in 1461. This appears to be an error, since the same source notes both the death of Abbot William, and the subsequent election of John Canon in 1464 (pp. 332, 334, 338).
3. Sir John Howard supported his election.

Appendix 4: Lucy Fraser, 'Synopsis of Cicely; or the Rose of Raby. An Historical Novel (1795)'

1. http://extra.shu.ac.uk/corvey/corinne/1%20Musgrave/cicely.html (consulted December 2016).
2. *Ibid.*
3. Musgrave, *Cicely; the Rose of Raby*, vol. 4, p. 178.
4. Musgrave, *Cicely; the Rose of Raby*, vol. 4, p. 189.
5. Musgrave, *Cicely; the Rose of Raby*, vol. 4, p. 136.

Appendix 6: Where Cecily appears to have been living or staying on specific dates

1. St Benet's Abbey was Benedictine, and in this year Cecily became a Benedictine tertiary.

Bibliography

Original Documents

Anlaby Cartulary, Fitzwilliam Museum, Cambridge, Ms. 329

Arundel Castle MS

BL Add. MS 46349

College of Arms, Arundel MS 48

Essex Record Office, D/ Dce L63r

Essex Record Office, D/ DCe L64r

MS Trinity College, Dublin, D.4, 18

Society of Antiquaries of London, MS 76

Society of Antiquaries of London, MS 77

TNA, prob 11/11/458

Books

Armstrong C A J, ed., Mancini D, *The Usurpation [sic] of Richard III*, Gloucester 1989

Arthurson I, *The Perkin Warbeck Conspiracy*, Stroud 1997

Ashdown-Hill J, *Richard III's 'Beloved Cousyn', John Howard and the House of York*, Stroud 2009

Ashdown-Hill J, *The Last Days of Richard III*, Stroud 2010; 2013

Ashdown-Hill J, *The Third Plantagenet* , Stroud 2014

Ashdown-Hill J, *The Secret Queen*, Stroud 2016

Ashdown-Hill J, *The Private Life of Edward IV*, Stroud 2016

Barnardiston K W, *Clare Priory*, Cambridge 1962

Bates D & Curry A, eds, *England and Normandy in the Middle Ages*, London 1994

Blunt J H, ed., *The Myroure of Oure Ladye*, London 1873

Bohn J, *The Chronicles of the White Rose of York*, London 1843 (1845)

Bruce J, ed., *Historie of the Arrivall of Edward IV in England and the Final Recouerye of his Kingdomes from Henry VI A.D. M.CCCC.LXXI*, London 1838

Calendar of Close Rolls, 1461–1468, London 1949
Calendar of Inquisitions Post Mortem – see Internet – British History – Kirby
Calendar of Papal Registers – see Internet – British History; also Internet – British History – Twemlow
Calendar of Patent Rolls, 1374–1377, London 1916
Calendar of Patent Rolls, 1385–1389, London 1900
Calendar of Patent Rolls, 1422–1429, London 1901
Calendar of Patent Rolls, 1429–1436, London 1907
Calendar of Patent Rolls, 1446–1452, London 1909
Calendar of Patent Rolls, 1452–1461, London 1910
Calendar of Patent Rolls, 1461–1467, London 1897
Calendar of Patent Rolls, 1467–1477, London 1900
Calendar of Patent Rolls, 1476–1485, London 1901
Calendar of Patent Rolls, 1485–1494, London 1914
Calmette J & Périnelle G, *Louis XI et l'Angleterre*, Paris 1930
Clive M, *This Sun of York*, London 1973
Commynes P de – see Jones
Cox J C, *The Sanctuaries and Sanctuary Seekers of Mediaeval England*, London 1911
Crawford A, ed., *The Household Books of John Howard, Duke of Norfolk, 1462–1471, 1481–1483*, Stroud 1992
Crawford A, *The Yorkists*, London 2007
Crowland (Croyland) Chronicles – see Pronay; Riley

Dale M K & Redstone V B, eds., *The Household Book of Dame Alice de Bryene of Acton Hall, Suffolk, September 1412 – September 1413*, Ipswich 1931
Davies J S, ed., *An English chronicle of the reigns of Richard II, Henry IV, Henry V, and Henry VI*, London 1856
R. Davies, *Extracts from the Municipal Records of the City of York during the Reigns of Edward IV, Edward V and Richard III*, London 1843
Davis N, ed., *Paston Letters and Papers of the Fifteenth Century*, 2 vols., Oxford 1971 & 1976
Dockray K, *Edward IV, a source book*, Stroud 1999
Drewett R and Redhead M, *The Trial of Richard III*, Gloucester 1984

Ellis H, ed., Fabyan R., *The New Chronicles of England and France*, London 1811
Ellis H, ed., *Three Books of Polydore Vergil's English History comprising the reigns of Henry VI, Edward IV, and Richard III*, 1844

Fabyan R – see Ellis H

Foss E, *A Biographical Dictionary of the Judges of England, 1066–1870*, London 1870

Gairdner J, ed., *Letters and Papers illustrative of the Reigns of Richard III and Henry VII*, 2 vols., vol. 1, London 1861

Gairdner J, *The Historical Collections of a Citizen of London in the Fifteenth Century*, London 1876 (Gregory's Chronicle)

Gairdner J, *Paston Letters*, Gloucester 1986

Gilbert Fr., O.F.M. Cap., *What to see in Walsingham*, Walsingham 1948

Giles J A, ed., *Incerti scriptoris chronicon Angliae de regnis trium regum Lancastriensium Henrici IV, Henrici V et Henrici VI*, London, 1848

Gregory's Chronicle – see Gairdner

Hall E, *Chronicle*, London 1809

Halsted C, *Richard III*, London 1844, 2 volumes, vol. 1

Hardy W & E L C P, eds., J. de Wavrin, *Recueil des Chroniques et Anchienne Istories de la Grant Bretaigne, à Present Nommé Engleterre,* Vol. 5, 1891, reprinted Cambridge 2012

Harris B J, *English Aristocratic Women, 1450–1550*, Oxford 2002

Hearne T, ed., *Joannis Rossi Antiquarii Warwicensis Historia Regum Angliae*, London 1716

Hearne T, *Liber Niger Scaccarii nec non Wilhelmi Worcestrii Annales Rerum Anglicarum*, vol. 2, London 1774

Hicks M, *False, Fleeting, Perjur'd Clarence – George, Duke of Clarence 1449–78,* Bangor 1992

Hicks M, *Anne Neville*, Stroud 2007

Hicks M, *Anne Neville*, Stroud 2006

Holinshed R, *Chronicle* – see Nicoll

Hone W, ed., *The Apocryphal New Testament*, London 1820

Horne J M, ed., *Fasti Ecclesiae Anglicanae 1300–1541*, vol. 5, *St Paul's, London*, London 1963 – see Internet – British History – Horne

Horrox R & Hammond P, eds., *British Library Harleian Manuscript 433*, vol. 1, London 1979

Horrox R & Hammond P, eds., *British Library Harleian Manuscript 433*, vol. 2, London 1980

Horrox R & Hammond P, eds., *British Library Harleian Manuscript 433*, vol. 3, *second register of Edward V and miscellaneous material*, London 1982

Horrox R, ed., *British Library Harleian Manuscript 433*, vol. 4, *Index*, London 1983

James M R, ed., *The Apocryphal New Testament*, Oxford 1924
Johnson P A, *Duke Richard of York 1411–1460*, Oxford 1988
Jones M, ed., *Philippe de Commynes Memoires*, Harmondsworth 1972
Jones M, *Bosworth 1485 Psychology of a Battle*, London 2014

Kendall P M, *Richard the Third*, London 1955
Kendall P M, *Warwick the Kingmaker*, London 1957, 1973
Kingsford C L, ed., *Chronicles of London*, Oxford 1905
Kingsford C L, ed., *The Stonor Letters and Papers 1290–1483*, 2 volumes, London 1919

Laynesmith J, *The Last Medieval Queens*, Oxford 2004
Licence A, *Cecily Neville Mother of Kings*, Stroud 2014; 2015
Lincoln's Inn, *The Records of the Honourable Society of Lincoln's Inn: The Black Books*, vol. 1, 1422–1586, London, 1897
Lyell L & Watney F D, eds, *Acts of Court of the Mercers' Company 1453–1527*, Cambridge 1936

Mancini D – see Armstrong
Mandrot B de, ed., *Journal de Jean de Roye 1460–1483, connu sous le nom de Chronique Scandaleuse*, vol. 2 Paris 1846
Morley H, ed., John Stow, *A Survay of London*, London 1893

Nicoll A & J, eds, *Holinshed's Chronicle as used in Shakespeare's Plays*, London 1927
Nicolas N H, *Privy Purse Expenses of Elizabeth of York*, London 1830

Paston Letters – see Davis; Gairdner
Pronay N & Cox J, eds, *The Crowland Chronicle Continuations 1459–1486*, London 1986

Riley H T, ed., *Ingulph's Chronicle of the Abbey of Croyland*, London 1908
Ross C, *Edward IV*, London 1974
Rotuli Parliamentorum – see Strachey
Rous J – see Hearne
Royal Commission on Historical Manuscripts: Fifth Report, 2 vols., London 1876, vol. 1

Sandford F, *A Genealogical History of the Kings and Queens of England*, London 1707

Scofield C *The Life and Reign of Edward the Fourth*, 2 vols, London 1923, 1967

Searle W G, ed., *The Chronicle of John Stone Monk of Christ Church 1415–1471*, Cambridge 1902

Sheppard J B, ed., *Christ Church Letters*, London 1877

Society of Antiquaries, *A Collection of Ordinances and Regulations for the Government of the Royal Household, made in Divers Reigns from King Edward III to King William and Queen Mary*, London 1790

Stevenson J, ed., *Letters and Papers Illustrative of the Wars of the English in France during the Reign of Henry the Sixth, vol, 2, part 2*, London 1864

Stone J – see Searle

Stow J, *A Survay of London*, 1598 – see Morley

Strachey J, ed., *Rotuli Parliamentorum; ut et Petitiones, et Placita in Parliamento*, vol. 6, (*ab Anno Duodecimo R. Edwardi IV. ad Finem eiusdem Regni*), London 1777

Stratford L, *Edward the Fourth*, London 1910

Sutton A & Hammond P, *The Coronation of Richard III: the extant documents*, London 1984

Sutton A F and Visser-Fuchs L, with Griffiths R A, *The Royal Funerals of the House of York at Windsor*, London 2005

Sykes B, *The Seven Daughters of Eve*, London 2001

Thomas A H and Thomley I D, eds., *The Great Chronicle of London*, London 1938

Vaughan R, *Charles the Bold*, second edition, Woodbridge 2002, p. 159.

Vergil – see Ellis

Verney H, *Letters and Papers of the Verney Family*, London 1853

Victoria County History, *Essex*, vol. 2, London 1907

Wavrin – see Hardy

Weever J, *Antient Funeral Monuments*, London 1767

Weightman C, *Margaret of York Duchess of Burgundy 1446–1503*, Gloucester 1989

Willett C & Cunnington P, *The History of Underclothes*, London 1951, republished New York 1992

Wolffe B, *Henry VI*, London 1981

Worcester W, *Annales* – see Hearne; Stevenson

Novels

Musgrave A, *Cicely, or the Rose of Raby*, 4 volumes, London 1795

Scott W, *Anne of Geierstein*, Edinburgh 1829

Papers & Booklets

Ashdown-Hill J, 'The Red Rose of Lancaster?', *Ricardian*, vol. 10, no. 133, June 1996, pp. 406–420

Ashdown-Hill J, 'The Endowments of Lady Eleanor Talbot and of Elizabeth Talbot, Duchess of Norfolk, at Corpus Christi College Cambridge', *Ricardian* vol. 14, 2004, pp. 82–94

Ashdown-Hill J & Carson A, 'The Execution of the Earl of Desmond', *Ricardian* vol.15 (2005), pp. 70–93

Ashdown-Hill J, ' "Yesterday my Lord of Gloucester came to Colchester …" ', *Essex Archaeology & History* vol. 36 (2005), pp. 212–17

Ashdown-Hill J, 'Suffolk Connections of the House of York', *Proceedings of the Suffolk Institute for Archaeology & History*, vol. 41 part 2 (2006), pp. 199–207

Barnfield M, 'Diriment Impediments, Dispensations and Divorce: Richard III and Matrimony', *Ricardian* 17 (2007), pp. 84–98

Brown J & E, 'The de la Poles, Earls and Dukes of Suffolk', Wingfield 2000.

Curtis E, 'Richard Duke of York as Viceroy of Ireland, 1447–1460; with unpublished materials for his relations with native chiefs', *The Journal of the Royal Society of Antiquaries of Ireland*, Seventh Series, Vol. 2, No.2 (Dec. 31, 1932), pp. 158–186

Green C & Whittingham A B, 'Excavations at Walsingham Priory, Norfolk, 1961', *The Archaeological Journal*, vol. 125 (1968), pp. 255–290

Griffiths R A, 'Queen Katherine de Valois and a missing statute of the realm', *Law Quarterly Review*, 93 (1977), pp. 257–8

Horrox R, 'Financial Memoranda of the Reign of Edward V', *Camden Miscellany*, 4th series, vol. 29, London 1987, pp. 197–244

Laynesmith J, 'Yorkist children – lost bones "rediscovered"', *The Ricardian Bulletin*, March 2017, pp. 34–35

Madden F, 'Political Poems of the Reigns of Henry VI and Edward IV', *Archaeologia* vol. 29, 1842, pp. 318–347

Rai A, 'Richard III – the final act', *British Dental Journal,* no. 214, 2013, pp. 415 – 417

Rosenthal J T, 'The Estates and Finances of Richard, Duke of York (1411–1460)', *Studies in Medieval and Renaissance History*, vol. 2, 1965

Rushton M A, 'The Teeth of Anne Mowbray'. *British Dental Journal*, no. 119, 1965, pp. 335–39

Internet

https://historicengland.org.uk/listing/the-list/list-entry/1017519 (consulted April 2017)

British History

http://www.british-history.ac.uk/cal-papal-registers/brit-ie/vol6/pp128-147 (consulted December 2016)

http://www.british-history.ac.uk/cal-papal-registers/brit-ie/vol8/pp122-136 (consulted September 2016)

http://www.british-history.ac.uk/cal-papal-registers/brit-ie/vol8/pp212-237 (consulted September 2016)

http://www.british-history.ac.uk/cal-papal-registers/brit-ie/vol8/pp263-271 (consulted September 2016)

http://www.british-history.ac.uk/rymer-foedera/vol10/pp349-368 (consulted September 2016)

Horne J M, ed., Fasti Ecclesiae Anglicanae 1300–1541, vol. 5, St Paul's, London, London 1963, http://www.british-history.ac.uk/fasti-ecclesiae/1300-1541/vol5 (consulted December 2016)

Kirby J L, *Calendar of Inquisitions Post Mortem ... volume 20. 1–5 Henry V [1413–1418]*, British History Online 1995 http://www.history.ac.uk/cipm-20-part-iv (consulted December 2016)

'Milan: 1461', Calendar of State Papers and Manuscripts in the Archives and Collections of Milan: 1385–1618 (1912), pp. 37-106. http://www.british-history.ac.uk/report.aspx?compid=92248 (consulted January 2017).

Twemlow J A, ed., *Calendar of Papal Registers Relating To Great Britain and Ireland: vol. 7, 1417–1431*, London, 1906, http://www.british-history.ac.uk/cal-papal-registers/brit-ie/vol7 (consulted December 2017)

https://www.houseofnames.com/mauley-family-crest (consulted January 2017)

F. & C. Rol. Hudleston, ART. IX. 'Medieval glass in Penrith Church'. Read at Penrith, September 4th, 1951 http://archaeologydataservice.ac.uk/archiveDS/archiveDownload?t=arch-2055-1/dissemination/

pdf/Article_Level_Pdf/tcwaas/002/1951/vol51/tcwaas_002_1951_vol51_0012.pdf (consulted November 2017).

http://menopausesupplement.com/menopause-in-the-ancient-world/ (consulted January 2017)
http://www.merriam-webster.com/dictionary/misprision (consulted September 2016)

http://www.newadvent.org/cathen/13785a.htm (consulted May 2017)

Kowaleski M, review of a Museum of London Archaeological Report, 2011, https://scholarworks.iu.edu/dspace/bitstream/handle/2022/13031/11.02.26.html?sequence=1 (consulted Jan. 2017)

NCC, will register, Caston, 125. www.girders.net/Les/Lessy,%20Henry,%20of%20Baketon,%20(fl.1482).docx (consulted February 2017)

ODNB (consulted October 2016 – January 2017)
Dunn D E S, 'Margaret of Anjou'
Harper-Bill C, 'Beaufort, Joan'
Harper-Bill C, 'Cecily, duchess of York'
Harriss G L, 'Beaufort, Henry'
Harriss G L, 'Eleanor, duchess of Gloucester'
Harriss G L, 'Humphrey, duke of Gloucester'
Harvey I M W, 'Cade, John'
Hicks M, 'Holland, Henry, second duke of Exeter'
Pollard A J, 'Neville, William earl of Kent'
Pollard A J, 'Talbot, John, first earl of Shrewsbury'
Richmond C, 'Beaufort, Edmund'.
Tuck A, 'Neville, Ralph first earl of Westmorland'
Watts J, 'Pole, William de la, first duke of Suffolk'
Watts J, 'Richard, third duke of York'

University of Leicester
http://www.le.ac.uk/richardiii/science/genealogy.html (consulted October 2016)

Wikipedia
http://en.wikipedia.org/wiki/Drowning-pit (consulted March 2017) https://en.wikipedia.org/wiki/Henry_de_Grey (consulted January 2017)

https://en.wikipedia.org/wiki/Henry_Heydon (consulted September 2016)

http://en.wikipedia.org/wiki/Henry_Holland,_3rd_Duke_of_Exeter (consulted March 2017)

https://en.wikipedia.org/wiki/Ralph_Neville,_1st_Earl_of_Westmorland (consulted October 2016)

https://en.wikipedia.org/wiki/Sir_John_Clay (consulted September 2016)

https://en.wikipedia.org/wiki/Thomas_Grey_(of_Heaton) (consulted January 2017) https://en.wikisource.org/wiki/Caxton,_William_(DNB00) (consulted February 2017)

http://www.sacred-texts.com/chr/lots/lots089.htm (consulted February 2017)

http://www.theanneboleynfiles.com/guest-article-giveaway-jasper-tudor-debra-bayani/#ixzz4U7PRfSLq (consulted January 2017).

Unpublished material

Ashdown-Hill L J F, 'The client network, connections and patronage of Sir John Howard (Lord Howard, first Duke of Norfolk) in north-east Essex and south Suffolk', PhD Thesis, University of Essex 2008

Index